RELIGION DEFINED AND EXPLAINED

Also by Peter B. Clarke

THE WORLD'S RELIGIONS (*co-editor*)
ISLAM (*editor*)
ISLAM IN MODERN NIGERIA
THE STUDY OF RELIGION, TRADITIONAL AND
NEW RELIGIONS (*co-editor*)
WEST AFRICA AND ISLAM
WEST AFRICA AND CHRISTIANITY
THE NEW EVANGELISTS (*editor*)
BLACK PARADISE

Also by Peter Byrne

ETHICS AND LAW IN HEALTH CARE
AND RESEARCH (*editor*)
HEALTH, RIGHTS AND RESOURCES (*editor*)
MEDICINE IN CONTEMPORARY SOCIETY (*editor*)
MEDICINE, MEDICAL ETHICS AND THE VALUE OF LIFE
(*editor*)
NATURAL RELIGION AND THE NATURE OF RELIGION
RIGHTS AND WRONGS IN MEDICINE (*editor*)
THE PHILOSOPHICAL AND THEOLOGICAL
FOUNDATIONS OF ETHICS

Religion Defined and Explained

Peter B. Clarke

Senior Lecturer in the History and Sociology of Religion
King's College, University of London

and

Peter Byrne

Lecturer in the Philosophy of Religion
King's College, University of London

St. Martin's Press

27066321
DLC

1-7-94

First published in Great Britain 1993 by
THE MACMILLAN PRESS LTD
Houndmills, Basingstoke, Hampshire RG21 2XS
and London
Companies and representatives
throughout the world

A catalogue record for this book is available
from the British Library.

ISBN 0–333–53841–2

Printed in Great Britain by
Ipswich Book Co Ltd
Ipswich, Suffolk

First published in the United States of America 1993 by
Scholarly and Reference Division,
ST. MARTIN'S PRESS, INC.,
175 Fifth Avenue,
New York, N.Y. 10010

ISBN 0–312–09472–8

Library of Congress Cataloging-in-Publication Data
Clarke, Peter B. (Peter Bernard)
Religion defined and explained / Peter B. Clarke and Peter Byrne.
p.   cm.
Includes bibliographical references and index.
ISBN 0–312–09472–8
1. Religion.   I. Byrne, Peter, 1950–   . II. Title.
BL48.C5535   1993
200—dc20

92–42691
CIP

Contents

Acknowledgements

The authors gratefully acknowledge permission to use material from the following sources in Chapters 1 and 4: Byrne, P. (1988) 'Religion and the Religions', in *The World's Religions* edited by S.R. Sutherland et al. (by kind permission of Routledge, Chapman & Hall); Byrne, P. (1991) 'A Religious Theory of Religion', in *Religious Studies*, Vol. 27, no. 1 (by kind permission of Cambridge University Press).

Introduction

It is characteristic of nineteenth- and twentieth-century approaches to the study of religion that they gave rise to large-scale theories of religion. The aim of this study is to survey and appraise a selection of these theories and the intellectual enterprise that lies behind them. Five major forms of theory are covered: religious, philosophical, socio-economic, sociological and psychological. In the course of discussing these theories we consider two aims in drawing up a definition of religion, either to produce an operational definition or an essentialist one. Among the major forms of definition of religion examined are: substantive, functionalist, experiential, and family resemblance.

What is characteristic of large-scale theories of religion (leaving aside religious theories considered in Chapter 4) is their comprehensive and radical nature. They tend to be comprehensive in endeavouring to explain religion as a whole. They do not seek to add to our explanatory understanding of religion merely by making more of the facts about particular religions known, nor by interpreting specific religious phenomena. They tend to seek in contrast an explanation of religion as such. They provide answers to the question of why the very phenomenon or institution of human religion exists at all. They wish to offer an interpretation and explanation of this entire facet of human life. Why should they seek these ends? The relevant assumption which justifies such large-scale theorising appears to be that there is something problematic about the very existence and meaning of the facet of life we know as human religion. Something about the typical pattern of beliefs and behaviour we call 'religion' makes the thinkers we consider question why it should exist at all and question its overall meaning and purpose.

In having these large-scale aims, and these kinds of background assumptions, such theories tend to be radical in their thrust. The radicalness of large-scale theories of religion is something that we define in detail in Chapter 3. Granted the assumption that there is something problematic about why religion exists at all, it is tempting to explain religion by showing how it is caused by something external to itself. 'Explaining religion' tends to become synonymous with outlining a psychological or social mechanism which causally generates religious belief and behaviour. The assumptions that lie behind the search for such a mechanism, and the endeavour to show that religion is sufficiently explained by an external cause, of their very nature undermine the fundamental beliefs of the various religions. The inner logic of these explanations is to debunk and dismiss the assumptions that religious beliefs have a real reference to non-mundane states and entities, and that religious life is in part the outcome of human commerce with such transcendent, sacred realities.

Radical and comprehensive theories generate in addition special demands on the business of defining religion. Piecemeal and tentative attempts to give the word 'religion' a useable sense by summing up in a definition some of the salient and characteristic features of members of the class of religions are not enough. A grand theory of religion seeks some core, essential unifying feature or features of religion. It must do so, on pain of otherwise admitting that there is no uniform class of things called 'religions' which all require explanation, and the same explanation at that.

In exploring the intellectual underpinnings of these approaches to the definition and explanation of religion we are anxious to get away from the simplistic diagnosis that they are based on bringing naturalistic assumptions to the study of religion. We try to find common methodological assumptions behind grand theories of religion in Part One. Assumptions specific to individual thinkers are pointed to in our selective illustrations of theories of religion in Part Two of the study. For reasons which emerge in Chapters 2, 3 and 4, the choice in the definition and explanation of religion is never simply between naturalism, entailing radical, unifying theories of religion, and anti-naturalism, entailing some kind of confessionally based interpretation of religion. We endeavour in these chapters to identify middle ground between these extremes. We acknowledge problems in how to characterise it and defend its viability, but we contend that it exists. It enables us to suggest that the study of religions may be consistently all of the following: a human study (like history and sociology); uncommitted to any confessional assumptions; not atheistic or sceptical in its very methods or aims; and based on the working assumption that the interpretations and explanations of religion that matter are ones that start from the beliefs and concepts which directly inform the life of the religious believers themselves.

In what sense does this book itself define and explain religion? It contributes to these tasks in only a modest way by defending a general approach to the enterprises of defining and explaining religion. This approach calls for tentative and cumulative explanatory knowledge of religion. This will be knowledge built up in the course of detailed study of particular religious phenomena. It will consist in knowledge of: the salient, characteristic features of religion; the detailed course of religious history; conceptual connections within the web of religious beliefs and meanings; general patterns in religious change and development; and interconnections, causal and interpretive, between religious phenomena and non-religious social and historical facts.

The grand theories of religion which illustrate our methodological discussion in Part One have a lasting importance. In many respects they have contributed to the explanatory knowledge mentioned in the previous paragraph. If we finally reject them, and the assumptions on which they rest, it is partly because we doubt whether, in this area, explanatory knowledge can ever be summed up in a theory of religion.

Note
'He' and 'his' are used in this book to represent the common gender, so in appropriate contexts import the feminine and the masculine.

Part One

1
The Definition and Essence of Religion

THE DEFINITION OF RELIGION

The task of defining 'religion' appears to be a necessary underpinning of the explanation and theory of religion for three reasons.

The theorist of religion must know in the first place what things are to be included within the scope of his explanatory account. He must delimit the area of his enquiry in some fashion, and to do so appears to require some definition of 'religion', some statement which will indicate what is to be included under the heading 'religion' and what is not. In the second place, a definition of 'religion' appears to be required if the theorist is to offer some initial interpretation of religion, an interpretation which will indicate why religion needs to be explained, and what its significant features are. It does not seem as if the task of explaining religion can begin at all unless some interpretation of religion is offered. This interpretation is initially indicated, implicitly or explicitly, in the theorist's definition of religion. The final reason behind the apparent necessity of defining 'religion' relates to the need for a theory of religion to show religion's unity. If an explanation of religion as a whole is offered its proponent must be convinced that religion is the kind of thing which can be explained uniformly. The kind of radical theories of religion we focus on do not offer explanations of this or that religious phenomenon, allowing that other religious phenomena might have a quite different explanation or need no explanation at all. What is explained is religion as such or in itself. Through definition a radical theory of religion needs to show that religious phenomena can be treated as a unity and in what their unity consists. The final reason for offering a definition of religion then connects with the second – that of offering some interpretation of religion. This final reason for linking theories of religion with the quest for definitions of 'religion' can be summed up as follows: the explanation of religion requires the theorist of religion to show that religion has an essence and what this essence might be.

The explanation of religion, then, needs the support of a definition of religion: to delineate the initial object of theorising, to establish the initial character of that object, and to convince us that religion is a unity. These purposes of definitions of 'religion' are connected with different stages of enquiry into the nature of religion. The initial demarcation of the class of religions is related to the beginning of the theoretical study of religion. It is frequently argued that without an initial definition at this stage of enquiry the student of religion will not know which things are to be studied. Definitions offered at this stage of the study of religion and for this purpose we shall call 'operational' definitions of religion. Operational definitions may offer a preliminary interpretation of religion, but the task of producing an interpretation can only be fully accomplished after the survey of religions is complete. It will be at the end of this survey of religion also that an account of religion's essence can be given. This summing up of the essential unity a theory postulates in religion will also encapsulate its final interpretation of religion. A definition of 'religion' offered at this stage of enquiry and for these purposes we style an 'essentialist' or 'theoretical' definition.

It follows from the points made so far that if there are difficulties in, or objections to, providing an acceptable definition of 'religion' at any of the key stages in the study of religion, these will be difficulties in, and objections to, seeking a grand theory of religion. One of the most important areas of criticism we shall explore in relation to the theorists of religion considered in the second half of this work will focus on the adequacy of their treatment of the definition of 'religion'. Many of the difficulties in the definition of 'religion' can, however, be considered in advance of examining the detailed theories of religion we shall describe and criticise. In the remainder of the first section of this chapter we shall examine difficulties in giving a satisfactory operational definition of 'religion'; in the second section problems in the search for essentialist definitions will be set out.

There are three initial sources of doubt about the possibility of producing a satisfactory operational definition of 'religion'. They relate to conflicts and unclarities in the ordinary use of 'religion'; the confused meaning left to the word from its history; and the obvious divergence in scholarly purposes and approaches to the definition of 'religion'.

No one who defines 'religion' for the purposes of the study of religion believes himself to be producing a stipulative definition of an entirely new coinage. He is making more precise and clear a word with an established sense. So ordinary usage must provide some guidance in constructing a definition. But ordinary use is in this case vague. A standard definition of 'religion' from a general dictionary is 'prevalent system of faith and worship' (*Concise Oxford Dictionary*). Nothing could be more vague or less calculated to give the scholar guidance. Moreover, ordinary use tolerates conflicts in the meaning of 'religion' quite happily: it would be correct in ordinary English to say both that China of the 1970s had no religion and, in another context, that Maoism had become the religion of the Chinese Republic in that period.

The difficulties in pinning down a customary sense to the word 'religion' are increased by the obvious fact that it is Western in origin and has gone through radical shifts in meaning during the course of centuries. This creates doubts about its applicability to non-Western institutions and about whether it has acquired any stability of meaning. Its original classical sense of 'rendering due service to the gods' underwent a transformation in Christian hands to refer to a special virtue, in the family of justice, of giving God his due (in the way of rites, obedience, etc.). This theological meaning has been whittled away in modern thought in the direction of producing a neutral means of picking out systems of belief and action which have beliefs analogous in important respects to those of the theistic outlooks we are familiar with in the West, and/or have ritual structures similar to those of systems directed toward service of a personal God. Much of the resultant unclarity and conflict surrounding the task of defining 'religion' reflects the problems in producing, from this unpromising beginning, an agreed and clear definition which will pick out a more or less universal aspect of human belief and behaviour. (For a fuller discussion of this problem see Byrne, 1989: 210–11).

Added to the above difficulties is the fact that resolution of the vagaries of ordinary usage and the rather chaotic history of the category 'religion' depends in practice on the particular purposes and prejudices of individual scholars. Compare F. Max Mueller's definition of 'religion' as 'a disposition which enables men to apprehend the Infinite under different names and disguises' (Mueller, 1893: 13) with that offered by a contemporary sociologist:

> A religion is (1) a system which acts (2) to establish powerful, pervasive and long-lasting moods and motivations in men by (3) formulating concepts of a general order of existence (4) and clothing these conceptions with such an aura of facticity that (5) the moods and motivations seem uniquely realistic.
>
> (Geertz, 1966: 4)

Mueller has a concern to show how all religions, no matter how unpromising, put men in the presence of what Christians call 'God'. Geertz does not share this theological aim. On the contrary, he requires a definition which will suit a study of tribal, 'primitive' religions, where it is taken for granted by the scientist of religion that these systems are wholly human constructs.

It is not surprising in the light of the above facts that there should be different approaches to the definition of 'religion' in the contemporary study of religions and a seemingly endless debate between proponents of these approaches. Four styles of definition are particularly important for contemporary scholarship: experiential, substantive, functionalist, and family resemblance.

Experiential definitions of 'religion' attempt to find some general form of experience that is characteristically religious and use this as the fundamental identifying feature of religions. Mueller's talk of the ability to apprehend the Infinite is a clear illustration of this approach. In contemporary literature W.L. King's attempt to identify the religious via the 'depth dimension in cultural experiences at all levels' shows the experiential approach in action (King, 1987: 286).

A substantive definition of 'religion' identifies religion through the content of the typical beliefs associated with it (usually through pointing to a theistic content to those beliefs). E.B. Tylor's definition of religion as belief in spiritual beings is a classic example of this approach (Tylor, 1903: 424). Having beliefs of a theistic sort is then a necessary condition at least of something's counting as a religion. M.E. Spiro's definition of 'religion' as 'an institution consisting of culturally postulated interaction with culturally postulated super-human beings' is a contemporary example (Spiro, 1966: 96). A notable fact about such definitions is their attempt to preserve connections with the historic meaning of 'religion' as referring to worship and service of the gods (or God).

Functionalists prefer to define 'religion' not in terms of *what* is believed by the religious but in terms of *how* they believe it (that is in terms of the role belief plays in people's lives). Certain individual or social needs are specified and religion is identified as any system whose beliefs, practices or symbols serve to meet those needs. Thus Eric Fromm defines 'religion' as: 'any system of thought and action shared by a group which gives the individual a frame of orientation and an object of devotion' (Fromm, 1950: 21). A fuller definition along these lines is provided by Yinger:

> Religion, then, can be defined as a system of beliefs and practices by means of which a group of people struggles with these ultimate problems of human life. It expresses their refusal to capitulate to death, to give up in the face of frustration, to allow hostility to tear apart their human aspirations.
>
> (Yinger, 1970: 7)

The three approaches listed so far all share one common assumption: that we ought to seek to lay down necessary and sufficient conditions for the use of the word 'religion'. Family-resemblance approaches to the definition of 'religion', following an insight from Wittgenstein's later philosophy, deny this common assumption. They assert that there is no single feature, or set of features, such that all religions must have it if they are to be religions or which guarantees that a system must be a religion if it possesses this feature or set. Alston (1966) and Southwold (1978) are typical of family resemblance theorists in stating that we can list characteristic features of the typical members of the class 'religions', but that to be a member of this class entails only that an example of religion have a sufficient selection of relevant characteristics. Southwold lists ten such characteristic features, including: a central concern with god-like beings, ritual practices, an ethical code, an association with an ethnic group, a mythology, a priesthood or similar elite, and a body of scripture or similarly exalted oral tradition. It is part of the family resemblance approach to assert: that religions are bound together in a family by a network of overlapping similarities and not by any strict identity; and that our conception of what counts as relevant similarities and a sufficient selection of religion-making characteristics can and must be extended in the actual survey and study of religions.

The difficulty of choosing between such rival accounts may be illustrated briefly by attending to the debate in contemporary anthropology and sociology of religion between substantive and functionalist approaches to the definition of 'religion'. Functionalists assert that a certain social and/or personal function of ideas and rituals is sufficient for something's counting as a religion; substantive theorists deny this, contending that having beliefs which relate to god-like or superhuman beings is at least a necessary condition for the presence of religion.

A leading point of contention in this debate is whether there can be non-theistic religions. A famous criticism of nineteenth-century substantive definitions was launched by Durkheim in *The Elementary Forms of the Religious Life* (1967: 29ff) based on the apparent conclusive counter-example of recognised forms of religion in Buddhism, Taoism and Jainism which had no central concern with gods or superhuman beings. Since there are real, living examples of non-theistic religions, theistic belief cannot be a necessary condition of something's counting as a religion. Spiro has a three-fold response to this classic objection (Spiro, 1966: 91ff). He contends that there is no reason at the outset to suppose that religion must be a universal phenomenon in human society. It is no defeat of a definition of 'religion' if it yields the conclusion that an important world-view and ritual system in a given culture is not a religion. He also claims that our readiness to class Buddhism as a religion may reflect the fact that Buddhism in its popular manifestations in fact tends to treat the Buddha as a god and is in any case bound up with devotion to and supplication of local spirits. Spiro finally claims that the consequences of wanting to count non-theistic systems as religions will be catastrophic. Refusal to accept that some important world-views and social systems are not religions will produce vagueness in the meaning of 'religion'. Without a reference to the clear criterion of belief content, universalists will be forced to identify religion by its role in providing a focus for personal or social life (an object of 'ultimate concern'). But on this criterion baseball or playing the stock market could count as religions in modern America.

Functionalists can respond to this type of criticism by arguing that it is possible to specify a precise type of role that religion plays in society, one that clearly unites Buddhism and Christianity in the class of religions, but excludes baseball. The function allotted to religion in Yinger's definition is not merely that of ministering to what a group regards as most important. It is rather that religion concerns types of needs and satisfactions which can be said to be ultimate and transcendent because they concern those basic features of life and the world which threaten the human condition. Religion aims to achieve states of being in which such basic facts as death, suffering, conflict can be overcome. Religions have, in other words, a similar and characteristic goal: salvation.

Functionalists will also claim that it is wrong to give up at the outset the notion that religion is a universal phenomenon in society. Tying religion to a type of belief content automatically does that, because it will limit the presence of religion to those societies where beliefs of this sort can be found, whereas if religion is distinguished by its concern with ultimate and inescapable human needs then there is a presumption that it will be present in all societies.

This last issue is worth pausing over. The predisposition to universalism in the definition of 'religion' comes in part from the way in which religion is viewed in relation to human nature. If religion is a universal phenomenon in human history and society, then it is possible to see it as representing some primary instinct in or facet of human nature. The explanation of religion assumes in consequence a greater importance. Something fundamental to human life in society is being tackled by the theory of religion and not merely an institution important in some localities and epochs. This predisposition to universalism in the understanding of religion also shows itself in the way in which the word 'religion' is used not merely as a means of referring to a class of things (equivalent to 'the world's religions'), but also as the name for a human disposition which the religions express or exemplify. This produces a further nuance in the definition of 'religion'. Sometimes a definition intends merely to state the criteria which enables us to identify something as a religion. Sometimes it may only do this indirectly: it picks out directly the human trait 'religion' which any genuine member of the class of religions embodies.

Brief examination of the functionalist and substantive approaches reveals why it is hard to establish an agreed meaning for 'religion'. The identification of religion is seen to rest on the presence of a number of independent variables; which of these is given priority is open to dispute; and the precise interpretation of the variables is also seen to pose problems.

All these points can be illustrated by a matrix (adapted from Yinger, 1970: 14):

A

	Theistic	Non-theistic
Ultimate goals	1	2

B ———————————————————————————————— B

	Theistic	Non-theistic
Non-ultimate goals	3	4

A

In square 1 in the above diagram would go a theistic religion such as Christianity; in square 2 a non-theistic 'religion' such as Jainism. Those who describe the occupants of 2 as religions do not consider line A–A to be an important boundary in classification. In square 3 would go a magical system of belief. Those who treat magic and religion as fundamentally alike will regard boundary A–A as important. But those more impressed by the similarities between the inhabitants of squares 1 and 2 will see B–B as the important boundary line. All will agree that what occupies square 1 is a religion and that what occupies square 4 (such as Western technological thought) is not. In advance, however, of considering specific purposes in studying religion and its neighbours there appears to be no clear reason for deciding in favour of one of the two important boundaries in the matrix. Matters are even worse than this suggests, for a little reflection will indicate that neither of these alleged crucial boundaries is crystal clear. The distinction between theistic and non-theistic world-views might appear to be uncontroversial and to establish a real likeness between all systems that fall into either squares 1 and 3. But it is notoriously difficult to establish a core meaning for 'God' or 'gods' and Spiro's favoured core of 'super-human agent' will not do. There are many theological systems in Christianity (and other theisms) which stress the impersonality of God and distance him (it) from any thought of a superhuman agent. Max Mueller's 'Infinite' does not appear to be a superhuman being. Some thinkers, such as Sir James Frazer (Frazer 1922: 57), contend in any case that, even if magic and religion are alike in focusing on superhuman agents, they are to be contrasted at root because they take up different attitudes to the gods. It matters more to Frazer that religious systems seek to supplicate the gods, while magic in contrast seeks to manipulate them. The boundary represented by B–B may also be difficult to interpret in many cases, even if it is not as elastic as suggested by Spiro. While we may be inclined to place a secular system such as Marxism in category 4 because it offers only a political, worldly remedy for contingent ills, the classless society of communist mythology may take on the character of a religious goal or end. It can look like a never-to-be-attained cure for inescapable facts of social life (such as conflict and self-interest).

The great variety of competing definitions of 'religion' and the difficulties in proving anyone to be correct point in our view not to the futility of the enterprise, but to the need to accept a looser, more informal mode of definition. A family resemblance definition appears to be indicated. Among the merits of a family resemblance approach to the meaning of 'religion' are the fact that it can preserve elements of other definitions while explaining the conflict between them. Each correctly captures an important religion-making characteristic, yet falsely seeks to erect it into a necessary (or necessary and sufficient) condition for the existence of religion. Moreover a family resemblance account will cope with the obvious facet of the meaning of the word 'religion' revealed by its history: that meaning has been extended in different directions from a common root or core. The concept of religion has proved valuable in the study of action and belief systems precisely because it is an open-textured one: a concept without fixed, clear-cut boundaries and whose instances are united by overlapping analogies.

The family resemblance idea of word meaning and concept formation was developed by Wittgenstein in his *Philosophical Investigations*. If it applies to 'religion' then we should expect to find the following facts in our use of the word: (a) There will be a characteristic set of features to be seen in the examples of religion (such as those listed by Southwold – see above). (b) Over and above the fact that they are religions, there will be no single feature or set of features to be found in each and every example of religion. (c) There will be no limits to be set in advance to the kind of combinations of characteristic features newly discovered or developing religions might be found to exemplify, nor will there be absolute limits to the additional features such new examples could add to the set. (d) The various examples of religion will then be related by a network of relationships rather than shared possession of necessary and sufficient conditions for membership of the class. (e) The meaning of the word 'religion' will nonetheless be projectible: that is, having rehearsed the characteristic features of religion in an inclusive family resemblance definition or having become acquainted with some central examples of religion, one will be able to say of newly found examples whether they are religions or not.

Features (c) to (e) point implicitly to the unsoundness of an argument relied upon by many proponents of strict definitions of religion, an argument which tells us that if we cannot define 'religion' through necessary and sufficient conditions, then we cannot know what are to count as examples of religions. On the contrary it is only because we possess an ability to master and apply the concept of religion that precedes the search for any strict definition of it that we can judge whether proposed definitions are adequate or not. We do so by seeing whether they allow us to class as religions things we would ordinarily count as such and whether they take account of the characteristic features we normally associate with religion. It is perhaps nearer the truth to see the ability to define 'religion' as following on from an acquaintance with and understanding of the phenomena of religion, rather than to see such an understanding as being created by a definition. The family resemblance approach best captures this fact.

A useful exemplification of the family resemblance definition of 'religion' is provided by those approaches which place religion in the broad category of a human institution, then list its characteristic dimensions as an institution and the typical specific differentiating features of those dimensions (see Kitigawa, 1967: 41; Smart 1971: 15ff; Byrne, 1988: 7ff).

The characteristic dimensions of religion include: theoretical (for example, beliefs, myths and doctrines), practical (for example, rites and moral codes), social (for example, churches, priests, monks), experiential (for example, emotions, visions, attitudes). The typical differentiating features of these dimensions to religion as a human institution include its objects, goals and functions. The typical object of religion as an institution is given in describing the content of its theoretical dimension and the focus of its practical and experiential ones. Its belief will concern god-like beings or more generally sacred, non-empirical realities. Its characteristic practices and modes of experience will be devoted to and focus on supernatural beings or transcendent aspects of reality. The goal of this type of institution will be shown in its practical and sociological dimensions and be in part defined by its theoretical. This goal will be salvation or liberation from limiting factors of mundane existence: generally the achievement of some ultimate good or well-being. The function of this entire system of dimensions will typically be to provide some sense of meaning or unity to an individual's or a group's life. In summary religions are human institutions which typically have theoretical, practical, experiential and social dimensions. They are distinguished by characteristic kinds of objects (gods or transcendent things), goals (salvation or liberation) and functions (the provision of meaning and unity to group or individual life).

This definition can fit the family resemblance picture because, in the first place, it need not insist that all the dimensions of religion be present in every example of religion. According to W. Robertson Smith many ancient classical and semitic religions were largely systems of rites ('series of acts and observances') in which the element of doctrine and belief was unimportant and undeveloped (Smith, 1923: 20–1). And we can surely accept the possibility of other religions in which, by contrast, ritual and the social structures necessary to organise and conduct it had not developed or were unimportant. Moreover, we can accept that the specific distinguishing features of religion (object, goal and function) are exemplified in different degrees, and manifested in quite different ways in different religions. If we say that all religions have as their object 'the sacred' this does not point to a determinate property which all religions share. 'Sacred' is an umbrella term which hides differences rather than reveals obvious unity. A general contrast between the sacred and the profane is implied in it but how this contrast is drawn will differ from case to case, as different religions will be seen to have particular ways of distinguishing the special type of object or state which is their focus.

The family resemblance approach to the meaning of 'religion' sets boundaries to the application to the word, not by checking off putative examples of religion against an agreed list of determinate properties, but by judging that systems of belief and/or action do or do not contain sufficient of the dimensions and specific distinguishing features of religion. The inclusion or exclusion of something from the class is achieved not by deduction from a precise rule of class membership but by analogical modes of thought. The members of the class 'religions' are bound together by analogies and it is the strength and usefulness of connecting analogies that we judge in deciding how far to extend the class.

This will allow us to give the concept of religion boundaries. A distinction between a religion and a mere philosophy, for example, may be drawn and be found useful even though a philosophical system may have an object, goal and at least personal function that parallel those of religion proper. The lack of both the characteristic shape of the experiential dimension we find in religion and the social dimension will usually be sufficient to draw the boundary in this kind of case, though if a set of philosophical beliefs acquired either one of these other dimensions the argument for excluding it from the class of religions would be weaker. We might, on the other hand, come across institutions in human life which displayed the four dimensions of religion but without its specific distinguishing characteristics. A system of politics may display dimensions of theory, practice (even ritual), experience and sociological structures. But if it has no concern with sacred objects, makes no attempt to rise above utilitarian goals and displays no desire to function as the ultimate source of meaning in human life, then it is not a religion.

The family resemblance approach can fulfil its promise of explaining the merit of other definitions by arguing that they usually fasten upon one of religion's dimensions and specific distinguishing features and erect these into necessary and/or sufficient conditions of the existence of religion. Thus Mueller's definition of 'religion' in terms of the ability to perceive the Infinite through the finite picks out the experiential dimension of religion and uses his own interpretation of the sacred object (that which is unlimited, infinite) as that dimension's distinguishing feature. Thereby the presence of a certain type of spirituality becomes necessary and sufficient for the applicability of the label 'religion'. There will be both truth and error in this and other 'single property' definitions of 'religion' from the family resemblance point of view. Truth will be present in the successful picking out and characterisation of *one* of the important analogies binding members of the class. Error will flow from failure to perceive the nature of analogical thought, specifically in the refusal both to acknowledge that a *range* of analogies might bind together members of an analogically determined class and to see the appropriateness of being open to the discovery of further analogies that might link and extend the membership of the class of religions.

The possibility of constructing a family resemblance definition of 'religion' demonstrates that the word has some meaning, but the attractiveness of this approach also raises some initial doubts about the aims of radical theories of religion. These doubts centre on two linked questions: (a) Does the phenomenon of religion in history have the kind of unity that theories of religion require? (b) Would it be right to give a uniform interpretation of religion or assume that it uniformly requires an explanation?

We have seen that large-scale theories of religion must assume some uniformity in religion if they are built on the assumption that religion as such needs and can be given an explanation. If someone offered an explanatory theory of religion, it would be right to infer that he proposed that the mere fact that something was an instance of religion meant that it required an explanation. He would seem to be committed in turn to supposing that all the members of the class were of the same general type and called for a broadly similar explanation. We have seen, however, that a case can be made for the analogical character of the basis of our classification of things as religions.

A theory of religion may start from some determinate feature associated with religion, such as belief in superhuman beings, and assume that all institutions built around this feature need explanation and that this feature imposes a uniform interpretation and explanation upon them. Yet we have seen that there are grave doubts about taking any such determinate feature as a common, necessary mark of all religions. A theorist of religion may have little ground to assume that in this feature he has the ground for explaining *religion*. We must find vaguer distinguishing traits such as 'having a sacred object' that appear to be genuinely universal, but just because of their vagueness there is no reason to suppose that the possession of such a feature makes all religions alike in meaning, general character, origin and need for explanation. One of the implications of the family resemblance picture that appeals is the idea that apparent common features to all examples of a family of instances turn out to be determinable properties that take on different characteristics in their many realisations.

Belief in the unity of religious phenomena is connected with belief that the class of such phenomena has precise limits. Understanding a class noun in terms of family resemblance brings with it the opposing notion of the open-endedness of a class. If the class of religions has the open-endedness that the family resemblance picture suggests, then, *even if* we had found a single interpretation and explanation of religion that fitted all the members we had encountered so far, we would have to concede the possibility of there being new examples of religion which manifested the nature of religion in a different way and to which the favoured explanation did not fit.

THE ESSENCE OF RELIGION

We noted at the beginning of this chapter that a complete picture of the definition of 'religion' could not be revealed simply by considering what was possible in the way of an operational definition. It is open to the radical theorist of religion to argue that a true picture of the uniformity and limits of religion cannot be gained at the stage of initially defining 'religion'. He may accept that at this stage religion appears to be a family of members without any essential unity. But a true picture of the uniformity of and limits of religion will emerge when we move to the search for a theoretical definition which will give the essence of religion lying behind the shifting sets of features visible on the surface. The family resemblance understanding of religion's nature will then prove to be only provisional. If there was a successful explanatory theory of religion, one of its achievements would be to show how, despite their outward appearance of diversity, religions and their many features are all linked, their multiplicity of outward features being derivative from some central, underlying property or set of properties.

Theorists of religion who adopt this search for a theoretical/essentialist definition are committed to a strong version of the belief that all religions share a common core. Belief in a common core to religions can be motivated by a number of concerns, including the important apologetic one of seeking to demonstrate harmony in doctrine, ethics or experience between major faiths. Theorists of religion, however, are particularly interested in seeking underlying unity as a means to explanation. They will therefore tend to understand the relation between the underlying core of religion and the outward characteristics of religions on the model of 'essence and manifestation'. Behind all religions lies a shared essence. There are different religions because this essence is manifested in different historical and social circumstances. The unique features of a particular religion can be explained by showing how the core features of religion would produce the outward features of the religion in question given the particular setting surrounding this manifestation of religion. The essence of religion is thus its true nature, in that the features of this essence are unvarying in all religions, underlie all other features and are capable of explaining all else in religion.

A definition of 'religion' that arose from a search for religion's essence would have two distinctive advantages over an operational definition. It could, in the first place, be said to be a *true* account of the nature of religion. An operational definition would at best be a true account of ordinary usage, but its adequacy would largely be a matter of its suitablity to the purposes behind it. By contrast, if we discovered an essence to religion, we would be able to describe the true source of religion's unity and the true explanation of its manifold characteristics. Such a definition would produce a second valuable consequence in so far as it would be the means of settling boundary disputes over the demarcation of religion in a sure and objective fashion. The religions shown to possess the essence would be linked together in fundamental respects. Those things our operational definition had previously allowed to be marginal examples of religious phenomena but which did not possess the essence of religion would be shown to be radically unlike the central cases of religion. They might be religion's mimics but would not be representative of religion itself.

Because of their connections with truth and falsehood essentialist definitions are styled 'real' definitions (as opposed to 'nominal' definitions). They are not merely true accounts of the use of words but true descriptions of the nature of things. Many reject such real definitions on the ground that the postulation of essences is hopelessly metaphysical and a priori. Postulation of essences in things is not empirically testable and therefore has no place in scientific enquiry. It cannot for this reason be allowed in the scientific study of religion (see Spiro, 1966: 85–6, 89). This is, however, much too short-sighted. There is in fact an established role in the empirical sciences for belief in essences, even though this belief may have been associated all too often in the past with the obscurities of metaphysics. The radical theories of religion can be seen to be drawing tacitly on two features of natural science in their offer of essentialist definitions of religion. Once these connections with science are understood the acceptability of the search for essence in general should be clear and we should be able to understand why most grand theories of religion offer essentialist definitions of 'religion'.

The two features of scientific thought that can be drawn on in the search for an essence to religion are its concern with theoretical definition and its tacit understanding of the logic of natural kind terms. One of the purposes of definition that a textbook on logic will list is 'to explain theoretically'. If we found in a work on chemistry a definition of 'acid' as 'any substance containing hydrogen as a positive radical', or of 'water' as 'that substance with the molecular structure H_2O', we would be wrong to see the purpose of the definition as being to summarise ordinary usage or help the non-chemist pick out samples of the substance defined. The object of the definition is to summarise the theoretically best explanation we have of how the substance defined behaves. The definition pursues this object by selecting that feature or features of the substance which causally account for the presence and display of all its other characteristic features. This causal account is part of a theory which lies behind the definition and which describes the relationship between what is mentioned in the definition and the rest of the attributes of the substance. The definition offered can be said to be true of the thing defined in so far as the causal account and theory behind it can be said to be true. Moreover, the attribute mentioned in the scientist's theoretical definition of a substance may be said to be the thing's essence in a clear, intelligible sense. For they represent that which is always present in examples of the substance, that which underlies and is causally responsible for all its other attributes and powers.

If the theorist of religion is to use this non-metaphysical notion of an essence in his search for an explanatory unity in the phenomena of religion, he needs also to suppose that some of the logic of natural kind terms applies to 'religion'. It is part of our notion of a natural kind that its various instances exhibit a real unity despite their apparent differences. We should expect the properties of such instances to mutually illuminate one another and for there to be no end to the range of similarities discoverable amongst instances of the kind. If a chemist is investigating the properties of water or gold he knows that, since he is dealing with a natural substance, it is no mere matter of linguistic custom that things are or are not examples of water or gold. We may feel inclined to call substances which look and behave like water or gold by these terms, but it is a question of truth whether they are properly described as such. All true examples of the substance will possess its common nature. A sample will either have this nature or it will not. It is this which enables us to say that no matter how much 'fool's gold' looks like gold, it is not in reality real gold. The real, as opposed to merely conventional, unity of the objects he investigates enables the scientist to delimit the scope of his enquiries in a precise way and to seek genuinely true laws to explain the attributes and behaviour of that which he investigates. There are laws descriptive of the behaviour and properties of water, because all examples of the substance share a common inward constitution which determines their behaviour and properties (see Harré and Madden, 1975: *passim*).

Scientific definition of natural kind terms takes on four special characteristics as a consequence of these general facts (see Byrne, 1980: 62–7). (a) We can see from the above why scientific definition frequently re-defines ordinary words in terms of very unfamiliar characteristics. The scientist's focus is not on the manifest, normally recognised qualities of substances but on properties which may be hidden to customary knowledge. (b) Classifications under such definitions are then dependent on expert understanding of the true nature of things. (c) Expert knowledge of things' fundamental properties may overturn familiar classifications, which may be revealed as superficial in the light of a knowledge of essences. (d) Whether something really is an example of a natural kind such as gold remains a matter of strict truth or falsity to be settled by the knowledge of essence that science can provide.

The attractiveness of the belief that religion has an essence to those committed to offering an explanatory theory of religion lies in the thought that something akin to scientific understanding can be brought to bear on religion. Like a natural science, the science of religion will be able to delimit precisely the object of its study and will be able to discover true laws to explain religion's attributes and behaviour. With an essence to religion there would be a real, non-conventional way of picking out true examples of religion and hope of being able to explain the many facets of religion by reference to generalisations from its essence.

One of the major difficulties in assessing the search for an essence to religion is that each essentialist definition can only be judged in the light of the theory in which it is embedded. An essentialist definition is a theoretical one, fully intelligible only in the context of the theory it trails behind it. To decide on the adequacy of the definition inevitably involves commenting on the worth of the theory of which it is a part. One mark of whether something is put forward as an operational or an essentialist definition is whether the definition is meant to be intelligible independently of a theory of religion or not. Thus, a simple definition of 'religion' such as Tylor's 'religion is belief in spiritual beings' may begin life as an operational definition and be transformed in the course of argument into an essentialist one as its key terms become more and more embedded in a theory of religion. This is indeed what happens to Tylor's definition in thè course of the argument of *Primitive Culture*. The apparently straightforward feature 'belief in spiritual beings' becomes deeper and more elaborate as part of an account of the first philosophy of mankind – animism – and its sources and effects. To comment on Tylor's definition in its full weight of meaning is to adjudicate on the strength of his account of animism's sources and effects. Tylor's definition will also illustrate the important point that whether a definition of 'religion' is an operational or an essentialist one is not dependent on its content, but on the intention behind it and the context of thought in which that intention is embodied. For we see that one and the same definition, at least in the form of words, can serve both as an operational definition and as a statement of religion's essence, depending on the relation between the features of religion it picks out and a theoretical account of religion's workings.

We see that no final verdict on the search for religion's essence can be given without considering the entire enterprise of constructing theoretical explanations for religion. However, some preliminary comments on essentialist definitions of 'religion' will be offered. The difficulties these suggest in construing 'religion' as a fit object for essentialist definition will in turn be prima facie problems in regarding religion as a proper object for explanatory theorising. The prima facie problems in seeing the class of religions as united by an underlying essence lie in two areas: (a) disanalogies between 'religion' and scientifically definable natural kind terms; (b) difficulties in finding candidate essential properties for religions which can be present throughout the class despite many outward differences between its members.

The disanalogies between 'religion' and scientifically definable natural kind terms come out when we consider whether we might accept that the main features of these scientific definitions outlined above apply to 'religion'. Even a brief survey of them can indicate why they apply only problematically at best to the case of religion (see Byrne, 1980, for a fuller discussion).

It is true that many theorists of religion seek to define 'religion' in terms of the unfamiliar. A clear example is provided in the opening pages of Feuerbach's *The Essence of Christianity*. Instead of a standard definition of 'religion' we find it defined as a form of human self-consciousness: 'Religion being identical with the distinctive characteristic of man, is then identical with self-consciousness – with the consciousness man has of his own nature' (Feuerbach, 1957: 2) If we accept Feuerbach's theory of religion, something not normally associated with the nature of religion turns out to be fundamental to its essence, since the theory purports to show how such obvious features as belief in God arise from man's self-consciousness. As with the case of natural kind terms the nature of religion in its essence is unknown and unguessed prior to the 'discoveries' of the theorist.

Why should this procedure seem acceptable in the case of natural kind terms but decidedly suspicious in the case of 'religion'? If it were acceptable, then it would bring in its train the other features of scientific, theoretical definition. We should expect that what counts as a religion is finally a matter for expert judgement, that our ordinary classifications of things as religions were quite capable of being overturned: all because there was a 'true nature' of religion which members of the class either lacked or possessed and which was only discernible by someone armed with a true theory of religion. We submit that these are implausible consequences for the meaning of 'religion'. The fact, for example, that we feel sure that such a central example of religion as Islam could never be excluded from the class, no matter what someone claimed to discover about the true underlying essence of religion, points to radical differences between the logic of 'religion' and scientifically definable terms. There is such a thing as expertise in the knowledge of religions, and the study of religions can add to our ability to classify things as religions, but we would be reluctant to accept that our ordinary classifications could be upset by the deductions of a theory of religion. When we approach the question of whether a marginal system of belief such as Marxism is to be counted a religion, we may well feel that this is not an absolute matter of truth or falsity, such as would be the case if the class of religions were bound together by the hidden possession of a common essence. It appears rather a matter of the utility for explanatory and interpretative purposes of pressing such analogies as exist between this marginal case and central examples of the class.

The discovery of apparent disanalogies between 'religion' and the paradigm cases of words capable of essentialist definition should lead us to press very hard two vital questions concerning any account of religion's alleged essence. We must first ask if any suggested essence really does show a genuine inner unity in the central examples of religion. If no account does this, but all force us to dismiss from the denotation of 'religion' some central cases (on our preliminary classification) then the scientific analogy behind belief in religion's essence is indeed weak. We must further ask if the suggested accounts of religion's essence really do seem to explain the many characteristics of the various central examples of religion our operational definition gives us. If no account of an essence to religion does this, then, again, the analogy between defining the subject matter of religious study and the subject matter of a natural science is shown to be weak.

The second major prima facie problem in giving an essentialist definition of 'religion' (the apparent lack of plausible candidates for universal, core features of religion) deserves some preliminary consideration, which might illuminate the later examination of particular theories of religion. We can press any belief in the existence of a common core or essence to religion with the question of how much real unity there is among the religions of history. We have already seen in the examination of proposed operational definitions of 'religion' how difficult it is to maintain that a single feature or set of features is held in common by all the religions. We saw in fact that this could be maintained only at the cost of making these features very vague or of excluding from the category of religion some important cases of putative religious systems. It is not obvious on preliminary enquiry, and without deciding in advance on important boundary disputes between religion and its near relatives, that there is a clear set of features that constitute a common core to religion.

The particular prima facie difficulty in common core and hence essence theories of religion revealed by our discussion of the definition of 'religion' relates to the beliefs that distinguish the world's religions. The examples of non-theistic religions discussed show how problematic it is to locate a common core to religions in the specific content of their theoretical dimensions. Consideration of these examples in relation to an alleged essential feature such as 'belief in gods or superhuman beings' seems to indicate that the religions are not united by any common doctrines or a philosophic outlook. To show that some doctrines or philosophical outlook really did provide a common essence to religions it would not be enough to demonstrate that these were shared by all the faiths. It would also have to be shown that such doctrines were central and vital in the religions which allegedly shared them as a common core. What is precisely maintained by some writers on Buddhism and other 'non-theistic religions' is that in important forms of these religions, while belief in gods may be present, it does not occupy a fundamental role in the theoretical, practical, social and experiential dimensions of the religion. Gods are not connected with the chief object and goals of the religion (see von Glasenapp, 1970: 30). The sharing of a common doctrinal element may not unite two religions in a common core or essence, for in one it may be central and in another peripheral.

Given what we have seen about pursuing the search for a common essence through the theoretical dimension to religion, it is not surprising that some important theorists of religion base their accounts of religion's inner unity on some unobvious, hidden feature(s) which all genuine religions share, a feature which can accompany a wide variety of mythical and doctrinal contents. This is one reason why some version of functionalism is frequently found as the basis of theories of religion. A unifying single function to religion can be asserted despite surface divergences among faiths. Common function is unlikely to be revealed except through the close examination of religion in the light of theory. A psychological function (as hinted at in Feuerbach's account of religion's essence) or a social function (as specified by Durkheim's account to be considered in Part Two) could be served by religions with differing content to their theoretical dimensions and thus be the source of genuine unity in diversity.

The adequacy of essentialism through functionalism is something that can only be considered by looking at some specific theories that display this feature. One further means of seeking an essence to religion that undercuts philosophical and doctrinal differences will be considered before concluding the argument of this chapter.

It is one of the attractions of experiential definitions of 'religion' for some that they offer the prospect of uncovering a common essence – an essence that can be present despite doctrinal differences. The experiential approach is worth considering because it shows brief discussion of a further important idea: that since religion's essence lies in a mode of experience 'beneath' outward doctrines, religion cannot be given any adequate public definition at all. If we fasten upon the experiential dimension to religion and detach this from the other dimensions it is open to us to see it as unifying all faiths and also as unconnected with anything that is part of the public profile of religion. Thus we reach the conclusion that the true essence of religion lies in something beyond public analysis and description.

The possibility of this approach is implicit in Mueller's definition of religion cited above (the ability to sense the Infinite within the finite). This points to the notion that religion's essence consists in a general form of spirituality or religious experience, which underlies all faiths. Different doctrinal accounts of the object of religion may then be seen as so many varied conceptualisations of the one core experience. The non-experiential dimensions of religion can be seen as secondary to this core experience, being ways of evoking or manifesting it. Rudolph Otto's comments on his own candidate for an experiential essence to religion (the 'numinous' experience) are typical of this approach to religion's essence: 'There is no religion in which it does not live as the real innermost core, and without it no religion would be worthy of the name' (Otto, 1950: 6). Though Otto tries to describe the phenomenological content of this experience (in terms of mystery, power and love) he illustrates the inclination to say that an experiential essence to religion is inexpressible and knowable only from the 'inside'.

> This mental state is perfectly *sui generis* and irreducible to any other, and therefore like every other absolutely primary datum, while it admits of being discussed, it cannot be strictly defined. There is only one way to help another to an understanding of it. He must be guided and lead . . . through the ways of his own mind, until he reaches the point at which 'the Numinous' in him perforce begins to stir, to start into life and consciousness.
>
> (Otto, 1950: 7)

The importance of the experiential dimension in religion should not be underestimated, nor should the power of this particular picture of its importance in the understanding of religion. However, the thesis that religion's essence is hidden because it is located in a core experience or spirituality largely independent of doctrinal differences has major difficulties in it. It is, in the first place, paradoxical in character. The numerous accounts of religion's inner core resting on the notion that this is irredeemably esoteric contain definitions and explanations of religion (after a fashion), while insisting that the theory of religion is a hopeless enterprise from the beginning. If the common core to religion were truly beyond public definition how could we argue for and claim to know the fact that this core genuinely did unite all faiths? The generalisation of the claim that an experiential core is at the heart of all religions depends on the experience not being esoteric after all. There must be fruitful, reliable connections between the experiential core and the exoteric marks of belief, behaviour and social structure for the general presence of the experience to be noted. If there are no such connections then the thesis does indeed produce a paradox: if the thesis were true it is hard to see how it could be known to be true.

The ability to generalise about the experiential dimension of the world's religions depends on close interconnections between it and other dimensions of religion. It can be argued on other grounds that such connections exist and ensure a continuity rather than a radical break between experience in religions and their observable credal, behavioural and sociological structures. The fact that we can find generically similar experiences in many religions (such as Otto's numinous experience of mystery, power and love) is compatible with there being major differences between specific examples of these general types in different faiths. These important specific differences exist because the experienced character of the object of such experiences is affected by the different doctrinal accounts of that object and the differently ordered routes through which spirituality is cultivated and directed in the religions (see Katz, 1968, for a well-argued case for this conclusion in relation to mystical experience). Religious experience occurs in a context: of specific beliefs and devotional paths. It contributes to, but is also shaped by, its context. An obvious objection to the attempt to produce a general religious experience or spirituality which is common to all religions is that the end result is irredeemably vague and thin. They thus, once more, buy unity between religions only at the cost of ignoring real differences.

To stress the interconnections between experience in religions and credal, behavioural and sociological structures is to emphasise how, though religious experience may be deeply personal, it is part of a publicly shareable and shared institution. The question before the theory of religion is whether the unique features of religious experience mean that it – and religion as a whole – cannot be treated as a human, public, cultural phenomenon. We support the arguments of those who deny this implication (see Byrne, 1988: 23–6; Wiebe, 1981: 9–10).

CONCLUSION

In this chapter we hope to have shown how the enterprise of defining religion is important for the theory of religion, and particularly for the construction of radical theories of religion. At the same time we have seen how this enterprise is the source of initial problems and difficulties for the theory of religion.

Seeking a definition of 'religion' entails seeking some unity amongst the many things that this word denotes. The radical theorist of religion must suppose some prior unity in the class of religions to make this class the plausible subject of theoretical investigation. In the course of that investigation he must hope to demonstrate a more profound unity in religion by showing how it can be given a unitary explanation. At two stages, therefore, he has to face and overcome what we may call 'the differences' of religion, that is all those idiosyncratic features of particular religious systems which *seem* to indicate that the class of religions is not bound together by any strict unity. It is the importance of the differences of religion which made us suggest that a family resemblance definition was the most reasonable operational definition of 'religion' to adopt. The importance of the differences of religion was stressed again in discussing whether there was any common essence that bound religions together.

All definition, in any field of enquiry, is an attempt to seek unity in diversity. The theorist of religion need not be embarrassed by the mere fact that there are differences among the members of the class he wishes to unify by theoretical explanation. This problem does not spell the end of grand theories in other fields and is successfully overcome in many branches of scientific enquiry. The questions we must pose about the definition of 'religion' are specific to this subject matter and the various theories that are offered in an attempt to unify it and explain it, though they do reflect, of course, wider issues concerning the possibility of fruitful theorising about human institutions, and the differences between the subject matter of the human and the natural sciences. Of the various theories of religion to be considered we must ask how much unity in religion do they presuppose, whether this unity is compatible with the evident differences of religion and whether the theory provides grounds for dismissing these differences or for thinking they can be overcome.

Some prima facie and general doubts have been aired on the likelihood of theories of religion being able to answer these questions satisfactorily. If they are found to fail on this score, we would have to conclude at the end of our survey of the theory of religion that none had demonstrated that religion *as such* needed a theoretical explanation nor that the explanation of religion was in all cases to be the same. The radical theorist might, on this assumption, have been able to demonstrate that some central cases of religion required a radical explanation and that the explanation was thus and so. But the fact that they did need explanation and that the explanation took the form it did would rest on facts about them and not on facts that pertained to religion as a whole or as such. We would be leaving open the possibility that other forms of religion escaped both the necessity of explanation and the applicability of the explanation offered. This possibility will be found to be of particular significance when forms of explanation are considered (those of Freud and Marx) which treat religion as a form of disease for which the theorist must provide a pathology.

2
The Dynamics of Explanation

In the Introduction to this volume we tried to point to the distinctive features of the explanatory theories of religion that emerged in the nineteenth and twentieth centuries. Comprehensiveness and radicalness were picked out as characteristic of the grand enterprise of constructing and advancing theories of religion in authors such as Marx, Freud and Durkheim. Unlike the more limited attempts to describe and explain religious phenomena in disciplines such as the history of religions, the focus of such theories of religion is not upon specific facts and developments in religion. Rather, the type of theory we are interested in seeks an explanation of religion as a whole – hence comprehensiveness. An explanatory theory of religion which has this aim cannot take the existence and character of religion for granted. The very existence of religion is something that in some way requires explanation. The theorist cannot then be finally content with the small-scale explanations of specific facts in the history of religion, explanations which account for one religious fact in terms of other facts and features of religion. He must suppose that even the most apparently fundamental features of man's religious life themselves require explanation in terms of things outside religion altogether. His explanatory theory of religion will in consequence show the radicalism we mentioned in our Introduction. It will seek to explain the existence and fundamental character of religion in terms of facts which are outside the surface life of religion and which religious believers are unaware of and would have difficulty in acknowledging. As we pointed out this radicalism in modern explanatory theories of religion is strengthened through their association with scepticism about religion and the inheritance of the Enlightenment.

The possibility of critical questioning of the aims of explanatory theories of religion has already emerged in our discussion of the definition and essence of religion. For if we have cast at least some doubt on the degree of unity to be found in the class of religions, we have thereby questioned the possibility of seeking a comprehensive explanatory theory of religion. In this chapter we shall examine the general nature of explanation, and of the explanation of human institutions in particular, to see again if some initial comment can be offered on the enterprise of explaining religion.

The philosophical literature on the nature of explanation is enormous and the issues raised within it manifold. A full survey will not be offered here. Enough will be done to present a thesis and antithesis on the possibility of radical explanation of a human institution such as religion, enabling a synthesis to be offered of opposing views in Chapter 3, which will in turn provide a perspective for finally appraising the pretensions of radical, comprehensive theories of religion.

One particular model of the nature of explanation will be seen to license radicalism in the explanation of human behaviour and to be centrally connected with the analogy between the theory of religion and scientific theory we have already seen to be important in discussing religion's essence. To this model we shall oppose one developed especially for the explanation of human action. This second model has the contrasting implication that religion cannot be explained by facts outside itself.

EXPLAINING AND ACCOUNTING FOR

The concept of explanation is a difficult one to pin down. Very generally, what links the many types of explanation together is the fact that explanations are attempts to meet requests for understanding. Complexities and diversity among types of explanation exist because of the wide range of things concerning which we seek understanding and the manifold ways in which understanding of these things may be lacking.

If successful explanations provide understanding of the thing explained, then it is possible in *some* contexts to distinguish explanation from describing and interpreting.

An explanation of something may also be a fuller description of it; but not all descriptions are explanations. We may say of a narrative 'It describes what took place when Britain declared war on Germany in 1939 but it does not explain why it took place.' We may conclude of an empty explanation of an event that it merely re-describes it in other terms – as when someone answers the question 'Why do these pills put people to sleep?' with 'Because they have soporific power'. The answer to the why-question does not really explain the event for it merely describes the tendency of the pills to put people to sleep in a new way (see Hospers, 1967: 243). In some contexts, then, the idea of an explanation that has real content implies that it is more than a mere description of the event or fact to be explained.

To explain is sometimes to do one and the same thing as interpret, as when one explains (that is, interprets) a proverb for someone. Yet in other contexts to interpret an event by answering the question 'What is happening?' may still leave open the explanatory question 'Why is it happening?' Successfully interpreting a piece of political activity may leave the explanation of the activity unclear. (Compare: 'What exactly is the policy behind this government's treatment of higher education?' with 'Why on earth does it have this policy?)

It is a matter of controversy how far these distinctions between explaining, on the one hand, and describing and interpreting, on the other, can be applied in the case of religion. Is it really one thing to describe and interpret religion successfully and another to explain it? If we properly described and interpreted the features of a particular religion to someone, what more could be required and offered by way of explaining it?

The answers to these questions depend on the type of explanation appropriate to religion. Only explanations of a certain sort can be contrasted with descriptions and interpretations.

There are at least three uses of 'to explain' in English, which give us three corresponding types of explanation: to make known in detail, to make intelligible and to account for (Atkinson, 1978: 98). We might explain a machine's workings by making its component parts known in detail. We might explain someone's words by making them intelligible, perhaps through paraphrasing them in familiar terms. We might explain an event by accounting for it, such as through citing its cause.

All three types of explanation can be present in the study of religion. Consider how we might explain the doctrine of the Trinity. We might make it known in detail by describing the complex of beliefs that makes it up. Further description of the structure of the doctrine may be perfectly satisfactory as an explanation in the right context. We might attempt to make it intelligible by giving familiar analogues for the symbols it employs (persons, substance, etc.). We might seek to account for it by describing its origins in early Christian thought and seeking the causes of its development into the status of dogma. To account for here would be to give an explanatory narrative.

That there are various types of explanation that might be provoked by different requests for understanding directed at the same phenomena illustrates the truth that there is no such thing as *the* explanation of a thing. What explanation we give of something will depend on the question we ask about it. Explanations are relative to a context of enquiry and the nature of that context will determine the nature of the explanation sought and offered.

It should be apparent from the brief survey of explanation offered so far that no sharp distinction can be sought between describing and interpreting, on the one hand, and explaining, on the other, unless we have accounting-for explanations in mind, and perhaps only certain subtypes of them. An explanation which makes known in detail is no more than a fuller description of the thing to be explained. Explanations which make intelligible could equally be said to be interpretations. The real differences between explaining and describing/interpreting come with forms of accounting-for explanations. In many contexts to account for something is to cite its cause and doing this may be fundamentally different from describing or interpreting it. It is in contexts, such as scientific ones, where we seek causal explanations of things and events that to explain is to account for and is more than describing or interpreting.

To understand the impulse behind the major explanatory theories of religion we must appreciate the grounds for thinking that a true accounting-for, causal explanation of the phenomena of religion must be a radical one, an explanation that sets aside the categories of religion itself and subsumes them under those provided by a general account of the workings of the psyche or society. One set of grounds for this leading assumption of many theories of religion is derived from the desire to produce a truly scientific explanation of the facts of human history and culture.

The requirements of scientific explanation seem to point to radicalism in the explanation of religion because they involve either or both of two things: a) the search for laws as the basis of adequate explanation; b) the uncovering of hidden causal mechanisms behind events. These requirements have appeared to many thinkers to lead to radicalism in the explanation of a whole range of human institutions, and not just religion. They have led many to suppose that our understanding of human culture as a whole is provisional and to efforts to construct a science of man or society which would replace our ordinary ways of accounting for events in the human world. To put alongside this type of ground for seeking a radical (and, of course, comprehensive) explanation of religion there are reasons peculiar to the nature of religion itself which will appear forceful to anyone influenced by the Enlightenment's critique of religion. One source of nineteenth-century theories of religion is the influence of eighteenth-century rationalist attacks on religion. Many of the leading exponents of grand theories of religion were atheists who wished to foster the cause of unbelief by producing radical explanations of religion (Evans Pritchard 1965: 14–15). In addition the least degree of scepticism about the existence of the objects of religion has appeared to demand that we cannot rest with concepts internal to religion in explaining it. Crudely: if we are doubtful about the existence of the gods, concepts that refer to them cannot figure in any explanations we might offer of how institutions built on beliefs in the gods develop and maintain themselves. The two sets of grounds for radicalism in the explanation of religion will now be explored in greater detail.

If we consider the kind of explanation of the Christian doctrine of the Trinity referred to above, we can see how someone who thinks that science provides the paradigm of accounting for explanations should regard it as at best provisional. If we combine the three sorts of explanation of the doctrine cited (describing its content and structure in detail; interpreting it through making its component terms intelligible; accounting for it by giving a narrative of its development), we have an explanation that seems to be both typical of the historiography of religions and also hopelessly unscientific. The explanation uses the categories of the Christian religion itself and consists largely of a fuller description, in its context, of the phenomenon to be explained. Particular facts from the religion concerned are cited. Interpretive analogies are offered from both religious and non-religious contexts. Connections are made between one religious fact and another through the setting out of a narrative. The terms of the narrative will in turn make connections between events in the life of the religion and its host culture. The narrative might even draw upon some rough generalisations about the motives of religious people or about the development of religious concepts. While this kind of explanation may be the stuff of historical writing about religion, it is easy to appreciate the charge that it is not truly scientific and does not meet the standards set for an adequate accounting-for explanation by scientific explanation.

The last point can be clearly seen if we consider the covering law model of scientific explanation. According to this model, which is held by many to be the paradigm of accounting-for explanations, one explains an event or phenomenon by showing it to be the outcome of the event's surrounding circumstances and a law or laws. A covering law explanation has the following form:

(a) Law(s)
(b) Set of initial conditions
(c) Event to be explained.

(a) and (b) constitute the 'explanans', (c) the 'explanandum'; and there is a deductive relation between explanans and explanandum. Covering law explanations are also called 'deductive nomological explanations'. One of the main proponents of the claims for this model of explanation describes how it functions thus:

> A D–N explanation answers the question 'Why did the explanandum-phenomenon occur?' by showing that the phenomenon resulted from certain peculiar circumstances . . . in accordance with . . . laws. By pointing this out, the argument shows that, given the particular circumstances and laws in question, the occurrence of the phenomenon *was to be expected*; and it is in this sense that the explanation enables us to understand why the phenomenon occurred.
>
> (Hempel, 1970: 336)

There are two important conditions of adequacy in a covering law explanation. One is that the statements of law and initial conditions should jointly entail the explanandum, so that *given* the conjunction of the laws governing the thing to be explained and its surrounding circumstances it had to occur. The second is that the generalisation which links initial conditions and explanandum should have true law-like form (or 'nomological force'). By this is meant that it should not be tied in its statement to particulars of time and place – it should therefore be expected to hold universally. Moreover, it should be distinguishable from any merely accidental generalisation that happens to have held up till now, but cannot be expected to hold in the future.

These two conditions of adequacy yield a third and most important mark of a valid explanation according to the proponents of the covering law model. It is that any such explanation could have been used to predict the event it explains if its terms had been known in a different order. If prior to an event's occurrence we had known of the relevant initial conditions and law, then, given the fact that the truth of the statement describing the event follows with certainty from that describing the initial conditions and law, the event could have been predicted with confidence. What makes a covering law explanation a valid explanation once an event occurs also makes it a means of predicting an event before it occurs.

Part of the power of the covering law model resides in the manner in which it enables those who accept it to make connected distinctions between levels of observation and theory in the structure of a branch of enquiry, and between what is merely descriptive in a body of knowledge and what is truly explanatory. Observational knowledge in a discipline is encapsulated in those propositions it contains which refer directly to particular facts and events, or, as in the case of accidental generalisations, merely summarise knowledge of particular phenomena. Theoretical knowledge will consist of those true propositions in the discipline which contain no essential reference to particulars and which have the true universality of propositions with nomological force. Ideally a theory is a set of universal propositions of this sort. They will be of increasing generality, capable of deductive systematisation, so that the least general of them can be seen to be entailed by the most. With the addition of propositions vouched for by observation and descriptive of particular phenomena, the set of deductively related statements which is the theory can be used to deduce, and thus to explain/predict, further descriptions of particular facts. The distinction between the descriptive and explanatory parts of a body of knowledge follows neatly from this: descriptive knowledge belongs to observation, but explanatory knowledge belongs to the realm of theory and statements of universal law. If we accept the covering law model as *the* correct picture of an accounting-for explanation, we will therefore have to accept the consequence that no account of an event or phenomenon which remains at the level of particular facts can be explanatory of that event or phenomenon. A description which relates a fact to other particular facts associated with it remains a description, not an explanation. At best such a description could count as an elliptical explanation, with the relevant law left unstated, but understood (Hempel, 1970: 415–17).

Why should anyone suppose that the covering law model does give *the* correct picture of an accounting-for explanation? One reason could be this: at the level of explaining specific events to account for is to give the cause of the thing to be explained and to cite the cause of an event is always to presuppose that there is some covering law linking the cause to the event. If to account for developments in the history of religion is to give the causes of those developments, then some laws must be assumed to link the causes cited and the facts in religion they are alleged to explain. Hempel's argument for this conclusion runs as follows:

> In the context of explanation, a 'cause' must be allowed to be a more or less complex set of circumstances and events . . . And as is suggested by the principle 'same cause, same effect' the assertion that those circumstances jointly caused a given event implies that whenever and wherever circumstances of the kind in question occur, an event of the kind to be explained takes place. Thus the causal explanation implicitly claims that there are general laws . . . in virtue of which the occurrence of the causal antecedents . . . is a sufficient condition for the occurrence of the explanandum event.
>
> (Hempel, 1970: 348–9)

Hempel's point is the straightforward one that what makes the antecedents of an event its cause, and not merely an accidentally associated phenomenon, is that these types of antecedents can be expected to lead to this type of event regularly. Thus a causal link has to be an instance of a law-like regularity and something which provides the grounds for a covering law explanation.

Not everyone accepts that the covering law model does give the essence of scientific explanation, but if we accept for the sake of argument that it does and that scientific explanations are the paradigm of accounting-for explanation, then we can see that the consequences for the non-comprehensive, non-radical explanations to be found in the historiography of religions will be severe indeed. All areas of enquiry which rely on historical explanations would in fact be under suspicion. For it is characteristic of the discipline of history that it explains events through their connections with other particular events. The way in which one event is connected with another so that the latter can be an explanation of the former is through an appropriate narrative that links them together. Narratives, as Atkinson points out (Atkinson, 1978: 112), may have a measure of universal force attaching to them, but this is not to say that they succeed in being explanatory only because of the tacit presence of universal laws linking their component elements. If the historian explains an event through narrative, he may be committed to supposing that a similar sort of narrative should explain a similar sort of event on another occasion, but he would find it difficult to draw up anything like a universal law to give expression to this simple requirement of consistency in reasoning. And if he did direct his efforts to discovering the laws allegedly behind his explanations we should probably judge him a bad historian, for his first and main interest should be the specifics of the particular historical occurrences he is trying to explain. Historians do of course make and employ generalisations in their work, but no proponent of the covering law model would be satisfied either with the limited role these play in historical narratives or with their rough and ready character. Moreover, there is an entire class of explanations in the study of history and which seem to defy any recasting in covering law terms, namely all those explanations which account for events by showing them to be the outcome of human purposes and intentions.

A historian in the course of explaining the outbreak of the First World War might tell us how on 23 July 1914 the Austro-Hungarian government sent an ultimatum to Serbia 'with intent to humiliate her'. This is an accounting-for explanation but it relies on no general laws about the circumstances in which one person or nation will send ultimata to others or about how the desire to humiliate others will be manifested in action. No such laws exist. We know, truistically, that human agents will take appropriate steps to enact their desires and motives, but the almost infinite variety that is possible in the expression of motive appears to defy summary in terms of laws. There is no precise law or basis for prediction in the statement that agents will take appropriate steps to enact their purposes. Historians and ordinary folk do rely on some rough generalisations about human behaviour in understanding others. But these are not treated as ready candidates for expansion into covering laws. We are as much interested in the exceptions to them as in their confirming instances.

All in all, historiography would appear to be a discipline ripe for reform or rejection if the covering law model for scientific explanation is accepted as universally normative. At best it seems to await completion by the addition of the precise laws of human politics, society and psychology that the covering law exponent thinks it requires. Completing historical explanations by uncovering these laws entails corresponding changes in the nature of historical description as well. How an event is to be explained and whether it can be subsumed under a law depends on how it is described. To take a simple illustration: if a description of an event ties it too closely to a unique context or stresses its unique features too much, it may foreclose the possibility of it being linked to other events by laws *under that description* (Danto, 1968: 219–20). For any law that successfully links events together will have to abstract to some degree from their specific features in order to do so. It is an interesting feature of ordinary historical writing about the doings of people and nations that, to a large extent, it employs the everyday descriptions of political and social events and human behaviour that abound in normal, non-technical, intelligent conversation. The covering law explanation exponent may well argue that the reason historiography does not throw up any true laws to explain historical events is precisely because ordinary vocabulary is not adapted to the end of a true scientific explanation of the human scene. The completion of historiography with true laws will entail the re-description of the event which it records. It will involve in particular the re-description of human behaviour to enable law-like generalisations to be formulated which will replace our ordinary ways of explaining human action.

It is thus hard to avoid the conclusion that the attempt to model explanation in disciplines employing historical modes of understanding on scientific explanation will lead to radicalism in those disciplines. It will have the consequence of overturning customary explanations and descriptions used in these disciplines. It will in turn lead us to be sceptical of the ordinary ways in which we describe ourselves and our doings that historical understanding tends to draw on. What will be threatened in the end is what has been described as 'the priority of appearances' in our understanding of ourselves (Scruton, 1980: 36–7). It appears to us that the motives and considerations we normally appeal to as interpretive and explanatory of human behaviour really do account for why we do what we do. The historian will generally draw on this customary understanding of what moves events in the human world. An attempt to replace normal, purposive accounting-for explanations with truly 'scientific' ones will tell us that how we appear to ourselves is not how we are in reality. Our picture of the human world and what accounts for the behaviour that constitutes it is at best highly limited, at worst largely mistaken. Our ordinary ways of describing it mask what really moves events in it.

Radicalism derived from the covering law model applies equally to the study of religion in so far as this uses the methods of narrative history. In the historiography of religions we will find the same combination of narrative structures, descriptions of human purposes and motives, and rough and ready generalisations about the subject matter (in this case about characteristic patterns in religious thought and action) that is exhibited in general history. For exactly the reasons noted already, we will be unable to fit these modes of explanation into the covering law pattern. The radical reconstruction of religious explanations that would follow if the pattern of scientific explanation were applied would also bring into question 'the priority of appearances' in this area. For run-of-the-mill histories of religion employ the vocabulary that is used by those who participate in that behaviour. It is thus locked into the modes of understanding implied in that vocabulary. Once more, the ordinary ways human agents have of understanding themselves and their world appear to be under threat from the manner in which the demands of explanation are interpreted in the study of the human world.

The inherent power of scientific analogies in explanation to lead to demands for radicalism in the explanation of religion can be seen yet more clearly if we now turn to the second model of scientific explanation we need to discuss. This may be termed the mechanistic model of explanation. 'A scientific explanation of happenings, whether individual happenings or sequences of events, consists in describing the mechanism which produces them' (Harré, 1972: 170). This model of scientific explanation agrees with one of the leading assumptions of the covering law account, namely that a phenomenon is not explained merely through describing its association with other particular phenomena. In a genuine explanation there must be an explanatory link between the phenomena in the explanans and the explanandum: in the case of this model the link is an account of a causal mechanism. This will be something that, when triggered by the phenomenon in the explanans, generates the phenomenon in the explanandum. Accounting-for, causal explanations will be ones that uncover the causal mechanisms that link sets of happenings to one another. On this model there is also a distinction to be drawn between the descriptive and explanatory/theoretical parts of genuine

science. To the descriptive part of a discipline will belong its record-
ing of specific events and happenings; to its explanatory/theoretical
part will belong the models it offers of the mechanisms in nature
which link the reports to be found in the descriptive part (Harré,
1972: 24). Laws are also to be found in the theoretical part of a science
and play a useful role in bringing coherence to the science's description of observed happenings and events, but the real explanatory
power of a theory lies not in the laws it includes. Rather it lies in the
models it contains of the mechanisms which underlie the general
connections recorded in the laws. A theory is a complex of statements and pictures (models). Thus the kinetic theory of gases does
not merely contain the various laws which summarise the relationships between temperature, pressure and volume in a gas: it also
contains a model of the nature of gases which points to the mechanism which might account for these relationships.

   This model of accounting-for explanation provides one way of
understanding what a theory of religion is. The theories to be considered in the second half of this volume can be seen as attempts to
describe social or psychological mechanisms, which, given certain
antecedents, will explain why religion is generated in human life.
There is a natural link between the desire to seek a science of man or
society and the postulation of such mechanisms to explain aspects of
human belief and behaviour. This desire leads to radicalism in the
explanation of religion and other human institutions because ordinary or historical explanations of these things deal much more in the
association between particular phenomena, and the everyday vocabulary of human motives and purposes they employ makes no
attempt to explain human behaviour in terms of causal mechanisms.
Indeed, it actually seems to inhibit this. Once more, an extension of
a model of scientific explanation into human affairs will take us
down the road of rejecting ordinary descriptions and explanations
and encourage us to penetrate or unmask the surface of how the
human world (or religious life) appears to us.

The search for explanatory mechanisms in the fashion of the natural
sciences leads us onto the second major reason for seeking radical,
comprehensive theories of religion: scepticism concerning the truth
of religious claims. Scepticism about the existence of the sacred is
connected with the question of what mechanisms could possibly
generate the existence and character of religion. Some argue that if

we are doubtful about the real existence of the objects of religion, then their existence and activity cannot figure in any account we give of the source of religion. Rather, we shall have to assume that human causes alone explain the existence of religion and the belief in the gods is but an illusion. Thus if we are initially sceptical about religion our account of the mechanisms that are responsible for its existence must be subversive of its basic beliefs and concepts. Scepticism will then fuel a radical theory of religion. Furthermore, we might argue that as scientists of religion our account of the causes of religion can refer only to human, mundane realities. This might appear to be a condition of the possibility of a scientific study of religion. Religion would be beyond scientific study and explanation if the real existence of sacred things were required in its explanation, for such things would by definition be beyond the reach of empirically based enquiry.

A scientific explanation of religion must assume that we need no actual commerce between human beings and the sacred objects referred to in religion to explain religion's character and existence. But this is to say that a scientific description of the mechanisms of religion is committed to the falsity of religion's belief in the reality of the sacred and must be based on the assumption of the illusory character of this belief. Scientific explanation of religion leads back to religious scepticism and will inevitably offer subversive, radical explanations of religion. Religious scepticism and scientific (that is, wholly human) explanation of the mechanisms of religion appear, therefore, mutually to imply one another. Out of this mutual implication comes the need to give a radical explanation of religion.

The underlying thought behind the argument just outlined is that one cannot have an explanation of religion, as opposed to a mere description, which is uncommitted as to the truth or falsity of religious beliefs. If we are committed to the existence of sacred things, then their existence and activity will have to figure in accounts of that which generates religion, whereas, if they do not exist, we shall have to refer to human causes only in explaining how religious beliefs arise. Our human explanation will have to account for the illusion that they do exist and the illusion that religion is generated through real commerce with them. An explanation of religion cannot be neutral about whether the sacred really exists, though a straightforward description of religion may. An explanatory account is either committed to the reality of the sacred and prepared to use its reality to explain facts in religion, or committed to its unreality and prepared to show how the false belief in its reality arises. The choice is between a religious, committed account of the mechanisms of religion, or a sceptical, radically subversive account of these mechanisms.

A contemporary account of the explanation of religion in terms of this contrast can be found in the argument of Wiebe's *Religion and Truth* (1981). This contrast will be illustrated in action in some of the writers discussed in Part Two. For the moment, however, we have said enough to show why some think that an explanation of religion must entail producing a radical theory of religion.

EXPLAINING HUMAN INSTITUTIONS

So far we have looked at the case for saying that the demands of explanation require radicalism in the theory of religion. If this requirement is to be questioned it must be done by showing how the explanation of religion might escape the interpretation of the general requirements of explanation that we outlined. The most promising way of making explanations in religion exceptions to covering law or mechanistic explanations is to contend that there is something in human actions and institutions in general that makes scientifically based models of explanation ill-suited to them. We shall summarise the case for this conclusion in what follows, beginning with points about the nature of human acts and moving on to the institutions in which they are commonly embedded. Out of this will emerge an argument for accepting religious concepts and beliefs as they stand in both the description *and* explanation of religion. This will be linked to a stance in the study of religion called 'methodological agnosticism'.

By the end of this chapter we will have presented a dialectic in the dynamics of explanation. A case for radicalism and comprehensiveness in the explanation of religion will have been matched by one for conservatism and neutrality. In the chapter which follows a synthesis of these conflicting perspectives will be offered, which enables us finally to specify when a radical, comprehensive explanation of an institution such as a religion might be in place and when not.

The two models of scientific explanation we described allowed a sharp distinction to be drawn between describing and interpreting on the one hand and explanation on the other. There are, however, strong arguments for saying that scientific explanations of this sort do not apply to the phenomena of the human world, and thus not to religion. The study of human nature must then be very different from that of non-human nature. We shall look at this thesis in the well-developed form it takes in such sources as Peter Winch's *The Idea of a Social Science* (1958). We begin by considering the explanation of human acts. Very important implications for the explanation of religion as a human institution will emerge from the arguments of Winch and others. From the beginning we shall see that whether description and interpretation can be sharply distinguished from explanation is deeply controversial when the study of human affairs is in question.

The case for saying that human acts cannot be explained according to the paradigms of scientific explanation can be set out under six heads (see Anscombe, 1957, and Davidson, 1968, for the source of this case): (a) Human acts are different in nature from the actions of inanimate things and mere bodily movements. (b) Reasons, purposes and intentions are vital in the constitution of human acts. (c) Beliefs are central in reasons and the like. (d) Beliefs plus intentions provide both the description and the explanation of human acts. (e) Explaining, describing and interpreting are equivalent in the explanation of human acts. (f) Scientific paradigms are thus inapplicable to the explanation of human acts. These six points will now be expounded in turn.

(a) To appreciate this point we need to think of the contrast between a fully voluntary human act and the behaviour of an inanimate object or the non-voluntary movements of the body. We could compare such examples as: advancing a pawn in chess; the movement back and forth of a pendulum; the beating of one's heart. In all three we can ask: 'Why is this happening?' But only in the first case do we have an *act*; only the first is the product of intention and thought; only the first is done for a reason; only of the first can we ask: 'Is it appropriate, right, advisable, etc.?' Human acts as illustrated by the first example have a special level of significance. They have, crudely, an inside as well as an outside. Only a description which takes account of this inside, the background of the act in reasons and the like, will be adequate.

(b) One of the key things which distinguishes a voluntary human act from a mere sequence of movements is that such an act is the product of intention. This is not to say that it must be preceded by a conscious act of intending, but that it must be done intentionally. An act is done intentionally when it is done for a reason. We can appropriately ask a certain why-question of an intentional act – namely: 'Why did the agent do it?' 'What was his reason in doing it?' Though we may speak of the reasons why a pendulum swings in a certain way or why the heart beats as it does, we are not in these cases speaking of the reasons the *pendulum* or the *heart* has for moving or behaving in its characteristic way. But in the case of intentional action we would be speaking of the reasons the agent has for doing as he does. The fact that acts are done for a reason that the agent has is linked to other things as well: for example, they can embody motives, purposes and desires. Such characterisations are linked but not synonymous. They stem from the root of inner significance that is to be found in human acts.

(c) From what has been said it should be clear that understanding a human act involves digging out the intention and thus the reasons encapsulated in it. The agent's own beliefs are crucial in this task. What intention or reason is embodied in an act depends on the agent's beliefs about the context of the act. If A points a pistol at B and pulls the trigger, what exactly he is trying to do depends very much on whether he believes the gun to be loaded. This points to a further respect in which acts of human agents have an inner significance: in embodying intentions, reasons and the like, they also embody the beliefs of human agents.

(d) To identify properly a human act we have to discover what intentions and beliefs are embodied in it. The example given above illustrates this point. We can reflect that two sequences of bodily movements can be alike in external respects even though, done for different reasons and moved by different beliefs, they amount to two different acts. Moreover, two sequences of movements which are different externally can amount to the same act if they are the means of enacting the same set of intentions and beliefs. Without the agent's intentions and beliefs we cannot establish what act is being performed, as distinct from the bodily movements he goes through. This in turn leads us to see the strong connections between fully describing a human act and explaining it (in the sense of accounting for it). To describe an act fully is to delineate the agent's intentions and beliefs within the act. But to set out these intentions and beliefs is to answer the question. 'Why was the act done?' To answer that question is to account for the act. So the following thesis appears to be true: when we discover the inner significance of an act we both discover exactly what the act is and account for it at the same time. In the case of human acts there is no sharp distinction between describing and explaining.

(e) The three types of explanation distinguished in this chapter run together in the case of explaining human acts through agents' reasons and beliefs. An explanation in terms of reasons accounts for the act, because it shows why it was done; but it also makes the act known in detail, because it gives a fuller description of it; and finally it makes the act intelligible because it sets out the meaning of what is done – in much the same way that we might set out the meaning of an utterance. It is because these three types of explanation become equivalent in the case of explaining acts through reasons, that explaining, describing and interpreting cannot be separated in this context. Explanation through reasons works by citing further particular circumstances (that is beliefs, reasons and intentions) which are contextually connected with the thing to be explained and make this explanandum intelligible. The explanation is thus a further description and interpretation of the explanandum. The explanation does not take us away from the thing we seek to explain and the further particulars that surround it, as it would if it cited general laws or some hidden causal mechanism. It is because explanation through reasons remains tied to a particular phenomenon and what is present in its immediate context that accounting for it remains equivalent to the other types of explanation and is not to be distinguished from describing and interpreting.

(f) Explanation in the case of human acts appears to work without the aid of explanatory theory. The citing of beliefs, reasons and intentions does not appear to require knowledge either of covering laws or causal mechanisms in order to succeed as an explanation. Thus the paradigms of scientific explanation do not apply to the explanation of human acts. One ground for pressing these paradigms upon all forms of explanation has been seen to reside in the notion that all genuine causal explanations must have a tacit body of theoretical knowledge behind them. If explanation through reasons does not invoke such a theoretical background it could be because there are fundamental differences between it and causal explanation. In a causal explanation there is a contingent relationship between the effect to be explained and the cause offered. But the relationship between an act and the reason that explains it is an internal one, for one function an act's reason performs is to identify the kind of act it is. Generally speaking, causes and reasons are just different kinds of things. A cause is an object, event or state of affairs; a reason is something expressed in a proposition or embodied in a belief.

The upshot of this sixfold case about the explanation of human behaviour is to assert that there is a fundamental distinction between human acts and events in the natural world. The presence of a level of meaning within human acts absent from any merely natural occurrences is the ground of this distinction. This level of meaning provides the source of explanation of human acts. Hence the search for explanations of human behaviour must be different in character from the search for explanations in natural science and must be governed by different criteria of adequacy. Given that the 'human sciences' must have as one of their chief objects the study of human behaviour, then they cannot be modelled on the natural sciences. They cannot be scientific in the sense of exhibiting the same structure of observations and theories found in natural science, but only in being critical, ordered attempts to gain understanding. In particular, they cannot stand in the same relationship to their subject matter as natural scientific disciplines do to theirs. The natural scientist uses his own beliefs about his subject matter to construct a theoretical comprehension of it. The concepts he employs belong, not to the things he studies, but to the discipline he brings to bear on those things. But the student of human affairs must, if he is explaining human acts, uncover the beliefs of the agents he is studying, for it is in their beliefs that the source of his understanding and explanation lies. This in turn means that the concepts his explanatory accounts employ will not simply belong to his discipline but will reflect as well the concepts of the agents he studies (Winch, 1958: 87).

The above argument seems to imply that the source of the explanation of human religious behaviour lies in the concepts and beliefs of the religious themselves and that these will limit the range of explanations that can be offered of this behaviour. There seems no room, then, for radical explanations of religion as we have defined them.

To press the case against seeking radical and comprehensive theories of religion further we need to consider whether larger aspects of human affairs beyond specific human acts can also be argued to escape scientific paradigms of explanation. This we shall do by briefly discussing the explanation of human institutions. These are indeed linked to human acts, for it is frequently the case that acts are only intelligible against the background of human institutions. Acts may belong to institutions in so far as the beliefs that inform acts are connected to the concepts provided by a human institution. In this way the sense of an act may be determined by the agent's membership of some institution. The full explanation of the act will accordingly consist in setting it in the context of the appropriate institution.

A strong version of this thesis about the relation between human acts and institutions can be found in Peter Winch's *The Idea of a Social Science* (Winch, 1958). For Winch, when we describe someone as performing an act, say, of 'voting for Labour at the last election', we are not just saying that he made some marks on a piece of paper. Doing that only counts as 'voting for Labour' if it is informed by appropriate beliefs. But the relevant beliefs are only available to those who live in a certain social context. Only a society with the relevant institutions of popular democracy and political parties could provide someone with the concepts that in turn make possible holding beliefs which enable an act to have the sense of 'casting a vote'. Explanation of an action which brings out its background in beliefs, reasons and intentions will therefore bring out its background in institutions. A full explanation of a series of acts will accordingly go on to delineate the institutions in which it is set. Through the connecting link of concepts and beliefs, institutions provide the range of reasons for action open to an agent and thus the range of actions he can perform.

An individual's participation in social institutions provides him with an array of concepts, beliefs, reasons and actions because such institutions are systems of rules, norms and expectations. Norms and the like are contained within the concepts the institution furnishes. They must be grasped by those who hold the beliefs the institution makes possible and they provide the framework against which reasons for action in the institution can exist. They must be at least tacitly understood in the performance of the acts available to participants because they are constitutive of those acts. Thus what lies behind saying of someone that they have the concept of 'casting a vote', have the belief that in doing such and such they are voting, can perform an act having this sense, and have reasons for voting one way rather than another, is a set of norms defining the institutions in which these concepts, beliefs and acts can be found (Winch, 1958: 49–50).

Social institutions are analogous in the above respects to other normative phenomena such as games. What enables someone to have the concept of 'advancing a pawn' and to perform the relevant action is that they understand the norms which define this concept and its corresponding action. To be able to participate in the game is to be able to grasp the norms which define it and which constitute the concepts and actions associated with it. The fact that many social institutions are traditional in character and therefore may lack a system of explicit, codified rules should not blind us to the normative character of these institutions, for a tradition must have a normative aspect to it. A tradition is not to be equated with mere habit but is to be seen as something which provides standards against which actions can be judged as correctly or incorrectly continuing the tradition, standards which direct choices between actions (Winch, 1958: 49). To understand an institution will in some respects be like understanding a game. It will involve setting out and making intelligible the norms that define the institution. Like actions done for a reason, institutions have an 'inside' as well as an 'outside'. These may be visible as behaviour, social structures or sets of office holders. But unless one understands the rules that bind these things together and give them their meaning one does not understand the institution, just as someone who saw all that was going on at a tennis match but did not grasp the rules would completely fail to understand what he was witnessing.

Following MacIntyre, we can sum up Winch's case on the explanation of human behaviour in society as follows (MacIntyre, 1970: 115–16). First we make a piece of behaviour intelligible as the outcome of motives, reasons and decisions. This is not to give a covering law or causal explanation but to give the sense or meaning of the behaviour. Second the act is made further intelligible and its meaning fully brought out by setting the reasons behind it in the context of the norms of a given form of social life. These norms shape the meaning of behaviour by determining the range of reasons open to an agent and by being constitutive of those reasons and the behaviour they inform.

The importance of this scheme for the explanation of social behaviour for our theme is that it appears to rule out radical explanations of social behaviour (including religious behaviour.) Explanations of social behaviour are not causal, do not involve general laws, do not need to be reached via induction or experiment. They are based simply on asking the participants what they are doing and why, thereby uncovering the complex web of reasons, beliefs, concepts and norms that lie behind what they are doing. As Baker and Hacker note, an agent's specification of what rules he is following typically have an authoritative status. If an agent says he was making a promise, or kicking a goal in doing such and such we do not think he is offering a hypothesis which he has reached by inductive observation and which only further observation and theorising can confirm. 'They are rather explanations of the rules he was trying to follow' (Baker and Hacker, 1984: 258). So, far from radical explanations of human behaviour and institutions being required, we see that the picture of explanation in Winch places a premium on uncovering the agent's own understanding of what he is doing and why he is doing it. An explanation of a rule-governed form of social life which does not base itself on what its participants recognise as its meaning will simply fail to engage with the meaning it does have. The explanation offered by the social scientist will render in more explicit form the norms which the participants themselves acknowledge. The participants need not be supposed ever to have formulated these rules in any deliberative way, indeed they may escape precise formulation at all. They exist as norms which inform and guide the behaviour of participants through such things as the expectations they are seen to entertain of one another's actions, the way they criticise each other's behaviour and the reasons they offer to justify their conduct. Clearly a set of norms would not exist as the norms which shape an institution unless they did in actuality inform the behaviour of the participants in the institution and they would not do that unless they were manifestly present in the understanding the participants had of what they were doing. Winch draws an analogy with what is involved in explaining a foreign language (Winch, 1958: 115). An explanation of what is said in the language will not work if it consists in the formulation of laws about the frequency of utterances of a given type among speakers of the language. The explanation that works will have to bring out the meaning of what is said and that will involve reference to things that speakers of the language themselves acknowledge in using it and not to things which, like statistical laws of word use, they are totally unaware of.

Out of these reflections on Winch we see the case emerging for saying that the understanding participants of a social institution have of what they are doing, and why they are doing it, must be normative for the historian's or social scientist's account as well. His task will be to render that understanding clear and make it intelligible, perhaps through appropriate analogies and connections, to those who stand outside the institution. Social life turns out to be an improper target for theories which are based on an external observer's view of it and which leave the insider's behind.

The importance of these conclusions for religion lies in the possibility that we can see the world's religions as examples of rule-governed forms of social life (hence the significance of our placing them in the genus 'human institution' in Chapter 1). The dimensions of belief, practice, social structure and experience shown in the central examples of religion are knit together by norms which define the point of these institutions and are constitutive of the beliefs, acts, offices and experiences we find in these institutions. As with other forms of behaviour related to rule-governed forms of social life, religious behaviour will have an inside as well as an outside. The true description of what transpires in a religious rite like the Christian Eucharist cannot rest content with a description of the bodily movements that take place. It will have to uncover the beliefs and reasons of the agents which reveal the acts that are being performed. These will be informed by the key concepts of the religion which will in turn be normatively interrelated and have normative consequences for the behaviour of those who participate in the institution. So we have the familiar pattern of explaining and describing particular acts by uncovering the reasons behind them and of making those reasons intelligible by setting them in the context of the norms provided by the rule-governed forms of social life to which they belong. All this involves making clear what participating agents themselves acknowledge, or could be led to acknowledge, as governing and informing their behaviour. To this might be added the student's own interpretive analogies to render what he describes intelligible. There is no need for a radical and comprehensive theory of religious institutions. Explaining here has nothing to do with theorising, but with further description and interpretation instead.

We have attempted to deflect the demand for radical explanatory theories of religion by suggesting that the paradigms of scientific explanation on which these theories draw do not apply to human, social behaviour. But what of the other source of the desire for such theories? We have seen that they can also rest on the claim that scepticism about the reality of sacred things entails we cannot take account of religion's own explanations of its existence and character. The explanation of religion has to deal in factors the religious are unaware of, for the things they prefer to in giving the explanation of religious phenomena cannot be admitted to exist by the scientific student of religion. Now we seem to have ignored this argument and swung to the opposite extreme – that of endorsing the believer's own explanations of his beliefs and thus the objective reality of the sacred.

Apart from the influence of modern scepticism about the reality of sacred things, two important reasons may be advanced for concluding that the student of religion cannot tolerate any references to sacred realities in his explanation of religion. In the first place his explanatory accounts of religion would become hopelessly inconsistent with one another. For his explanation of one religion would contain references to one set of sacred objects, and his account of a second religion would contain references to a different and incompatible set. The pantheon of sacred things to be gleaned from the world's religions does not form a consistent whole. Given that the gods of one religion can only exist if the gods of another do not, the study of religions cannot rest content in its explanatory tasks with reporting the beliefs of the various religions and thus becoming committed to competing sacred objects. Furthermore, the study of religion, if it is to be possible at all, must have a basis in empirically discernible facts and relations. The student of religion, cannot therefore pretend to knowledge of the existence of a sacred realm of reality and how it operates to produce human religious belief and behaviour. To claim this is to claim *religious* knowledge, as opposed to knowledge about religion. Should the student of religion once pretend to have religious knowledge there is an end to the possibility of agreement and progress in the explanation of religion. Religious knowledge is notoriously something disputable and disputed. Commitment to the truth of claims about the sacred must be avoided at all costs, on pain of destroying the study of religion as an academic discipline.

We have put the case for methodological scepticism as strongly as possible but nonetheless we feel that it is misconceived. So is the complaint that, in relying on the beliefs of the participants in religion to explain it, we are thereby endorsing those beliefs or the references they make to sacred things. Neither scepticism nor commitment is in order. Relying on the beliefs and norms arising out of religious institutions brings with it instead a third stance, that of methodological agnosticism (see Smart, 1973: 158).

We have argued that to explain religious behaviour we must, if it is an instance of action which is done for a reason, describe its 'inner' meaning, entailing that we delve into its background in the beliefs and norms of the religion it belongs to. Consider again the example of explaining the behaviour that takes place in the Eucharist. No adequate explanation or description of this behaviour could confine itself to the externals of what goes on. Description and explanation will have to mention the point of what is happening. In characterising the point of this ritual behaviour many beliefs about the object of Christianity (that is God-in-Christ) must be mentioned and their relationship to the behaviour set out. The worshippers' beliefs about the object of their religion would thus be called upon by the student of religion to complete the description and explanation of the actions he observes. But this does not entail that the scholar himself shares these beliefs. They are used by the student of religion because they inform and therefore explain the behaviour of the religious. All the beliefs about Christ and the Eucharist mentioned in his account would be in reported speech, and thus be neither endorsed nor denied. Though the object of religion (in this instance God-in-Christ) would figure largely in the observer's account, it would, to use the technical expression, be 'bracketed' (Smart, 1973: 57). All the statements the scholar makes about God and Christ would be preceded by an implicit 'It seems to the participants as if . . .'. The existence and nature of the object of religion would figure in the account of the behaviour only in and through the participants' beliefs about that object. So the inside of the behaviour could be grasped in the student's explanation through reliance on the believers' descriptions of what they are doing and why, without any commitment to the existence or non-existence of a real sacred object having been made. This is what is meant by methodological agnosticism.

The possibility of methodological agnosticism depends on a number of related elements. First is the simple point that to describe a belief is not to endorse it. The second is that the normal force of referring expressions is cancelled when they occur in the context of reported beliefs and indirect quotation. If I use the phrase 'the Loch Ness Monster' in an affirmative, unconditional proposition then I will usually be taken to have committed myself to the existence of something corresponding to it. But if I use it to report the content of another's belief its normal referential force is cancelled. (This is why the student of religion is not committed to a fantastic pantheon if he reports the varied beliefs about the sacred from the world's religions.) Third is the fact that whether a belief does inform someone's acts and provides their meaning has little to do with its actual truth.

It is the relationship between the belief and the behaviour that one who explains the agent's actions needs to rely on, and not the relationship between the belief and reality. Fourth is the truth that the real existence and character of the sacred object appears to be irrelevant in the generation of human religion *except as the sacred is perceived through the medium of human belief.* If, for example, we explain the Trinity doctrine as in part a response to the experience of the Apostles at Pentecost it matters not whether we judge the divine reality to have actually displayed itself as it appeared to do in the phenomena of Pentecost. In the explanation the important thing is that it seemed to the early Christian community as if it did, that they had the belief that it did. If our chosen route into the explanation of religion is via the beliefs of the religious, then the character of the sacred need only concern us as something about which folk have beliefs. It is only their beliefs about the character of the sacred that matter in our explanation. What the sacred is like in itself (whether in fact it really exists) need not concern us *as students of religion.*

The outcome of neutrality in the explanation of beliefs and acts within human institutions can be illustrated in non-religious examples. Thus if we were to account for the prevalence of belief in a stationary Earth among medieval astronomers we would describe the reasons these folk had for this belief and make these reasons intelligible against the background of the norms of understanding and argument that constituted the tradition of thought from which the belief sprung. Naturally we would not be taken as committing ourself to the truth of the belief thus explained or the adequacy of the reasons that lay behind it. We commit ourselves merely to the thought that the modes of thought and experience behind the belief are intelligible as grounds for it, if seen in the light of the institutional setting to which they belonged.

The type of explanation of human belief and behaviour we have just sketched appeals to agents' reasons and the nature of institutions. Such explanations appear to be conservative ones, leaving no room for the radical theorist to impose his own theoretical explanation on the phenomena. The only hope for the possibility of such an imposition appears to lie in discovering some strategy which might enable the theorist of human behaviour to set aside agent-inspired sources of explanation. Now, we are ready in some contexts to argue that an agent's avowed reasons for an action delude us and him as to its true character. Sometimes we open up the possibility of distinguishing between the agent's reasons and the true sources of his acts by referring to the former as mere 'rationalisations' of his conduct. In cases such as these it might be quite wrong to base our explanation of what an agent is doing on his own beliefs about his conduct, and the point of his action might be quite other than his avowed reasons would suggest.

Here we point to the possibility that in some types of human behaviour there might be a case for the primacy of an observer's explanation of human conduct over the view that arises out of the participant's beliefs. It is a possibility that we must explore in the next chapter for it might indicate when and when not we are right to rely on the beliefs of participants in religion for an interpretation and explanation of religious behaviour. Of particular importance in our discussion will be the notion that it is in the case of irrational behaviour that the gap between an agent's understanding and the true source of conduct opens up. Exploring the nature of the distinction between rational and irrational behaviour in the following chapter will be found to provide a way out of the dialectic of explanation offered in the discussion so far. Both the demand for radical, comprehensive theories of human institutions like religion and the demand for conservative, participant-based accounts of these institutions may be reconciled if the first is found to be appropriate to irrational institutions and the latter to rational ones.

For the moment we wish to highlight one important fact about behaviour which is regarded as disguised by false, self-deceiving reasons (mere rationalisations). In some cases of this sort it may be no use in a defence of the primacy of the agent's own 'reasons' to show the behaviour is part of a human institution whose norms establish it as correct or justified. For the institution itself might come under suspicion; it might not in reality be as it appears to be to its participants. It might be the means by which participants are able to be deceived about the true point of their conduct. Its mistaken and misleading norms might be the very things which enable agents to confuse mere rationalisations for genuine reasons. One example will suffice. Consider the belief, with its attendant practices, that a person's character and destiny are determined by the position of the stars and planets at his birth. No doubt some people whose actions are informed by this belief could offer 'reasons' for their belief and conduct and these reasons might be given an appearance of intelligibility by the institution of astrology. A whole network of concepts connected with the practice of the casting of horoscopes could be cited as lying behind these 'reasons'. But to an external observer they could well appear as a set of conventions which hide the true sense of this area of human conduct, which enabled rationalisations to wear the mask of reasons and which were the very devices by which the true source and point of the institution of astrology are hidden from those who participate in it.

The relationships between beliefs, actions, reasons and institutions need further examination.

3

Forms of Explanation in Religion

RADICALISM AND RATIONALITY

In the preceding chapter we developed a contrast between radical, observer-based explanations of religion and conservative, participant-based explanations. This contrast is connected with the theme of the priority of appearances in our approach to human belief and behaviour. We are familiar with, and readily accept, the notion that the sense and meaning of an individual's acts may not be as they appear to him. The much used categories of rationalisation and wishful thinking provide ways in which we may penetrate behind the appearance of someone's conduct to its true meaning. A radical theory of religion must seek to extend the use of such ideas so as to make a convincing case for concluding that an entire human institution has one meaning to its participants and yet quite another one in reality.

It is right to greet this claim for large-scale illusion in human, social life with a measure of scepticism. What we need to do now is to establish a more precise idea of how any such theory could successfully make this claim. This will involve spelling out more clearly how the rationality of an institution such as a religion could be determined and how this is related to judging the meaning of this institution. In the idea of rationality lies a way of resolving the contrast between the two modes of explanation (radical, observer-based and conservative, participant-based). Most people, even those who participate in religion themselves, will easily accept the idea that some people's engagement in the life of religion is irrationally based and really moved by concerns that will not or cannot be acknowledged by the individuals concerned. Religion is no more immune to the perversities in human belief and volition than any other form of social life. It is less clear how irrationality could be predicated of religion as a whole.

We have suggested that radical theories of religion must move from the platitude that some people are irrational in their religion to the striking claim that religion is itself irrational. This claim will entail that religion is one of those human institutions which serves to mask from their participants the true source and meaning of their actions. The theorist needs to distinguish such masking institutions from those which may be taken at face value. A ground for making this distinction may perhaps be found in the notion of rationality, given that it is capable of playing a similar role in the case of individual action. If religion is a masking institution then the true nature of religion is not apparent from its outward, manifest features. The true meaning of religious behaviour will be hidden from those who participate in it. This kind of perspective on religion will inevitably take us back to the thought that religion has an essence – a core of explanatory features lying beneath the surface of religious life. This is another reason why radical theories of religion are committed to essentialist understandings of the nature of religion.

The notion of religion as a masking institution will be clearly illustrated in the discussion of sample, radical theories of religion in Part Two. We will see in a number of authors the familiar contrast between the surface concepts of religious belief and discourse, on the one hand, and the hidden, explanatory features of religion, on the other. On the surface we have notions of God, heaven, salvation and so on. These cloak the realities that are really referred to in religious discourse and which really move religious action. The nature of the hidden realities behind religion will differ from theory to theory. They may be the features of human species consciousness (Feuerbach), the forces of class interest and conflict (Marx), or the moral ties that bind society together (Durkheim). But each account is similar in being able to supply a re-definition of religion in terms of the true object, goal and function that is hidden behind the avowed concepts of religious believers.

RATIONALITY AND THE EXPLANATION OF ACTION

We have argued that the theorist of religion needs a strong justification for seeking a hidden meaning and explanation when confronted with what the believer says. This justification can only lie in pointing to some form of dislocation in the connections between belief, reasons and behaviour, which would in turn allow us to conclude that the meaning of religious action was not given by relying on the beliefs apparently informing it. We must now explain how the notion of rationality might enable such a dislocation to be postulated. This involves explaining what it means to say that a human institution is irrational.

These tasks will be tackled by summarising and commenting on an important article by Alisdair MacIntyre: 'Rationality and the Explanation of Action' (MacIntyre, 1971: 244–59). We have selected MacIntyre's contribution to the nature of social explanation from the many books and articles on the topic because of the clarity it brings to the discussion of the clash between conservatism and radicalism in approaches to the explanation of human action.

MacIntyre's general aim is to show that we must make a distinction between explaining rational and explaining irrational action, a distinction dependent partly on the further distinction between rational and irrational belief. As an example of accounting for a rational belief MacIntyre cites the case of the acceptance in the seventeenth century of the claims of Galilean astronomy. The explanation will deal in the observations and evidence that Galileo and others had made available and also to the canons of reason and argument which made the inferences from the evidence seem plausible. The explanation boils down to setting a process of rational reflection within the norms of a human institution (here a particular phase of scientific thought). The process of rational reflection and the institution in which it is embodied can be made more intelligible by making reference to the historical context surrounding them. But no sufficient account of the rise of these beliefs can be provided by pointing to social or economic factors alone, for if these beliefs really were produced by a process of reasoning set in the context of norms of argument, then this rational process must constitute at least a necessary condition for the occurrence of the belief in question. If evidence, deliberation and reasons within an institution are necessary conditions for the rise of beliefs, factors independent of them cannot be sufficient for this rise on their own. As MacIntyre points out, if people's beliefs are the genuine product of reason and deliberation, then they have made themselves in a measure independent of those 'social or psychological factors which on occasion lead men to act or believe regardless of where reason points' (1971: 246).

In summary, the argument for the distinctiveness of the explanation of rational beliefs goes as follows. If beliefs really are the outcome of reasons, then awareness of those reasons provides a

necessary condition for the existence of the beliefs. Factors independent of deliberation cannot then amount to sufficient conditions
for the beliefs' existence. So the explanation of the beliefs remains
tied to the reasons which moved the agents concerned and thus to
the concepts and notions they were aware of. Explanation of the
beliefs can move beyond these reasons only to take into account the
normative, institutional setting of the process of deliberation and the
surrounding necessary conditions provided by the historical context
of the institution.

So far this picture of explanation conforms to that which Winch
regards as appropriate for the human world. But it can be reversed
according to MacIntyre when we come to irrational beliefs. An irrational belief may purport to be the outcome of rational deliberation,
but it is not. It is one which the agent would have come to hold
regardless of any 'reasons' he was aware of. It is one caused by non-
rational factors. Reference to deliberation and the like does not provide a necessary condition in the explanation of this belief. It follows
that a description of the surrounding circumstances of the belief,
such as the psyche of the agent, his social and economic circumstances, may provide a sufficient causal explanation of his holding
the belief. If these circumstances *are* sufficient then the agent's avowed
reasons for the belief are irrelevant to its explanation. An account of
why that belief is held need not be tied to these reasons, nor to any
setting they may have in an institution. In accounting for such a
belief we can stand outside any justification the agent offers for his
belief. Our explanation of it will inevitably deal in factors which he
could not fully acknowledge, for if he did recognise that his belief
was sufficiently explained by non-rational factors, he could not continue to hold it as he does. So the force of asking whether a belief is
rationally held is that it brings out the extent to which that belief can
be sufficiently explained by causal circumstances such as the agent's
emotions or the influence of social factors upon him.

A historian can offer an explanation of belief in terms of antecedent circumstances external to the agent's own reflections where he
notes that the belief rises and falls with these circumstances alone
and without reference to any set of reasons or arguments. In such a
case it can be seen that reason-independent circumstances are sufficient to account for the belief. MacIntyre gives the example of a
historian's explanation of the prevalence of witchcraft beliefs in
seventeenth-century Europe as a scapegoat for social frustration
(1971: 244–5). The explanation works by describing circumstances of

social tension, which generate powerful emotions which in turn bring about beliefs. The beliefs provide an outlet for these emotions and satisfy them by creating a social stereotype (the witch) who can serve as an object for the emotions. The 'theology' of belief in witches is irrelevant to the explanation except as something which is itself in need of explanation. It matters not that this theology is embedded in an institution with its characteristic forms of action. This theoretical, normative structure is not really operative in the ultimate genesis of the beliefs, but can only serve as a mask behind which the true causes of the beliefs are hidden. If witchcraft beliefs are good examples of beliefs that do not arise out of reason, then the theology of witchcraft does not provide a reliable source of the meaning of the beliefs and actions characteristic of the institution.

It follows from MacIntyre's account that the terminus of explanation for rational beliefs is where Winch places the end point of social explanations. Such explanations will end in an account of the norms of that intellectual tradition or institution which make the agent's reasons and beliefs intelligible. By contrast the terminus in the explanation of irrational beliefs will be 'causal generalisations which connect antecedent conditions specified in terms of social structures or psychological states – or both – with the genesis of beliefs' (MacIntyre, 1971: 247). This difference highlights the need for historians and social scientists to exercise philosophical judgement in so far as they attempt to explain human beliefs. Their enquiries cannot be absolutely neutral if the presence or absence of rationality is such a crucial feature for explanation. Something akin to philosophical understanding is required to enable distinctions to be made between which mental processes are to be counted as embodying reason and deliberation and which not. It seems that only after such philosophical judgement on the genesis of belief can a radical theorist of religion go on to argue that religion must be a candidate for explanations which invoke scientific generalisations or mechanisms. We will seek to show in discussion of sample theories of religion in Part Two how they involve judgements on the rationality of religion which are of a philosophical sort.

Given the fact that acts gain their identity from the beliefs they embody, an assymetry in the explanation of rational and irrational beliefs will have consequences for them too. A rational act will be one which is in accord with the beliefs of the agent and where those informing beliefs are themselves rational. Its explanation will terminate in the setting of these beliefs in the context of the norms of the form of social life which makes them intelligible. An act can be irrational on either one of two scores. It may be expressive of irrational beliefs or it may not really be consistent with the agent's beliefs. In the former case, though some initial intelligibility is given to the act by showing its background in the agent's beliefs, those beliefs will not be counted as a self-contained set of reasons on the agent's part for performing the action. If irrational, we will need to seek causes outside of reason for why those beliefs are held by the agent and shape his acts. Where there is no match between the agent's avowed beliefs and his acts, then the agent has no reason to act as he does. What he does is intelligible in the light of intentions which in fact clash with what the agent is known to believe. The agent then has no reason to act as he does and whatever moves him to act is not the pressure of reason.

In sum: rational action is action in accordance with rational belief. Irrational action either fails to cohere with belief at all or coheres only with irrational belief (MacIntyre, 1971: 255–6). In both types of irrational action, when we take an agent's actions and beliefs back to the institutional setting which is supposed to make them fully intelligible, we find a gap which can only be filled by citing facts of which the agent is unaware, but which provide the theorist with the best explanation *he* can offer to the existence of this gap.

In the first type of irrational action the gap in question is between the agent's beliefs, on the one hand, and the facts and justified inferences from them that he might have been aware of. Since the agent's beliefs are not in reality the result of any rational inferences from the facts as he was aware of them some account other than a rational one has to be given of why he nonetheless acquires and continues to hold on to these beliefs. Something about the way these beliefs are acquired or held on to indicates that they cannot be taken as genuine reasons for action. They do not become intelligible as reasons by placing them in the context of the norms of any background institution for it remains the case that processes other than deliberation and the awareness of evidence are sufficient to explain them. Any institution which is really involved in the explanation of these beliefs will be one which is operating so as to help in the subversion of the understanding. How it does so will inevitably not be revealed in the agent's own perception of it and will thus call for external explanation.

In the second type of irrational action the need for external explanation will be even more marked. The agent is unaware of a lack of fit in his avowed beliefs and those implicated in the immediate intentions embodied in his acts. Hence, his understanding of what he is doing and why is problematic. Something outside that understanding must be discovered to account for this dislocation between belief and behaviour and the limitations in the agent's own understanding. The institutional setting of the agent's acts may be important in the explanation of this mode of irrational action, but not as in itself making it intelligible. If irrational behaviour is persistent and widespread among many agents, then it is tempting to seek enduring psychological and social mechanisms which may be responsible for dislocation between belief, reasons and conduct. An important social institution lying behind such dislocation will be one performing the task of helping to disguise to human agents the true character of their actions. Our account of it as observers will inevitably be in conflict with how participating agents see it. In irrational conduct on a large scale the observer will be on the lookout for mechanisms which blind people to the irrationality of their own thinking and acting and to 'the irrationalities of their own social order' (MacIntyre, 1971: 256).

MacIntyre's description of the assymetry in the explanation of rational and irrational conduct enables legitimate circumventions of the case for conservative, participant-based explanations of the social world outlined in the previous chapter. The circumvention is accomplished by noting how there can be gaps, in the form of irrationalities, between reasons, belief and conduct. In such cases a portion of the human world is shown to be incapable of providing from within itself the terms for its own understanding. It is revealed to be an elaborate rationalisation of behaviour whose true meaning is hidden from those who display it. The complex of belief and behaviour having ceased to be explanatory, some account external to the agents' own understanding of what they are doing is wanted. This will be in effect an account of how they are deceived by the institutions which provide an apparent meaning to their conduct. In facing up to radical and comprehensive theories of religion we are meeting the possibility that religion, as such, provides in all its various forms a deceiving institution of this type. We might then search for the mechanisms that produce it and the generalisations about society and the psyche that govern it, on the assumption that these will be hidden to the participants in religion.

Reliance on MacIntyre's case for the possibility of external explanation of religion entails a re-examination of the case made in the preceding chapter for saying that human acts cannot be explained in causal terms. We seem to have found room within the sphere of voluntary human acts for causal and covering law explanation after all.

We need to find a way of harmonising causal, covering law explanations of human action with rational, normative explanations if our preferred route out of the dialectic of explanation is to be viable. The first point to note in harmonising these two approaches to the explanation of action is that we have uncovered in irrational action a mean between acts in the full sense and mere bodily movements. Irrational actions of either sort distinguished above may embody intentions and beliefs in an immediate way sufficient for us to ascribe an apparent meaning to them. Yet they lack the full meaning possessed by rationally motivated acts. This lack of the full level of inner significance enables their explanation to be found in external causes. The continuity between rational and causal explanations of human action revealed by the nature of irrational action is further strengthened by the realisation that it is something in the *causal* background of action that allows us to judge it to be rational or irrational. A rational act is one which is moved (that is, caused) by an awareness of reasons. An irrational act is one that is caused by something other than awareness of reason. While a reason cannot of itself be a cause, being aware of a reason can and does serve as a causal background to action. Something counts as a genuine reason for an agent's action if awareness of it did play a part in the causation of it. Irrational acts are those which are not in any material respect caused by awareness of reasons. (If reasons are cited by the agent they are mere rationalisations which played no part in moving his act.) The level of significance which comes from associating acts with reasons only sticks to them because awareness of such reasons plays a part in causing them. (See Davidson, 1968: 85–92; MacIntyre, 1971: 255. But readers should note that their, and our, account of causes and reasons is controversial: compare Skorupski, 1990, and Bond, 1983: 21–6.)

Ordinary judgement about the rationality of conduct is in effect judgement about how far genuine awareness of reasons played a part in influencing people. The psychological or sociological theorist is merely taking such judgement further in seeking causal generalisations to account for patterns of social action. That our ordinary knowledge of how acts are caused – whether by the influence of reason or of other factors – is not expressed in terms of statable general laws about action is not proof that it is not causal knowledge. If I stand close to the mill race I can tell that the force of the water is what makes the mill wheel go round even though I do not know any of the relevant laws of mechanics. Much of our ordinary knowledge about the motivation of action may be causal in its implications without being based on causal generalisations (Davidson, 1968: 91–2).

A renewed look at the relation between reasons and causes thus suggests two important conclusions. First, knowledge of the inner significance of human action that we ordinarily possess is linked to causal knowledge. Second, the psychological or social theorist could be extending and exploring this causal knowledge in valid ways when he produces general laws and mechanisms giving external causes of classes of human action. On the assumption that religious behaviour is irrational, then there can be a role for such a theorist to produce generalisations and mechanisms that account for religion. These generalisations and mechanisms would amount to a body of theoretical knowledge about the true character and explanation of religion unknown to participants in religion.

RATIONALITY, TRUTH AND RELATIVISM

The arguments we have adapted from MacIntyre's 'Rationality and the Explanation of Action' raise many important issues. We have space to mention only two: the relation between truth and rationality, and the relativity of judgements of rationality. Our aim in taking up these particular issues is to explain more clearly what we mean by 'irrational' and examine how a whole system of belief could be said to be irrational. This will enable us to set out more clearly what a radical, comprehensive theory of religion has to establish to attain credibility.

In beginning with the relation between truth and rationality, we must note that MacIntyre's case is explicitly based on a sharp distinction between judging the truth and judging the rationality of a belief. For MacIntyre 'true' applies to the nature of what is believed, 'rational' applies to the manner in which it is believed (MacIntyre, 1971: 248, and cf. Hollis, 1987: 189). It is possible for someone to believe something in a manner which is rational, because his believing is guided by reasons and evidence, and yet that belief turn out to be false. On the other hand, someone may believe something irrationally and yet it turn out that it is true. 'Rational' is needed as a comment on the manner in which someone believes something, because it is *how* someone acquires and holds a belief that is relevant to the way in which the provenance of the belief is explained. In producing explanations of the origins of beliefs the nature of what is believed seems to be irrelevant. But if MacIntyre is right in this then the problem we face is that of seeing how anyone might even begin to show that an entire institution, such as a religion, or an entire class of institutions, such as religion, might be irrational. The most that could be shown appears to be that particular participants in religion are irrational in their believing. All that the theorist has to go on in judging the rationality of a religion or of religion is the character of what is believed. Somehow a link between judging the character of what is believed in religion and the manner in which it is believed has to be forged if an intelligible ground for a radical, comprehensive explanation of religion is to be found.

A minimal definition of 'rational belief' is provided by Richard Swinburne: 'A subject S . . . will have . . . a rational belief if and only if his belief that p is probable given his inductive standards and given his evidence' (Swinburne, 1981: 45). This makes the rationality of a subject's belief relative to his background knowledge and canons of argument. Swinburne's definition picks out a class of beliefs of a subject that are arrived at in a certain way. The underlying feature of rationally held belief is that the subject is moved to accept it by considerations which genuinely bear on its truth. It is an important defining feature of belief that belief necessarily aims at the truth, for when a human agent is deciding what he believes and whether he ought to believe it, he is also deciding on what is the case so far as he can judge. Irrational belief is possible because many factors may influence and invite someone's assent to a belief and only some may be marks of the truth of that belief. (For this account of rational belief in much greater detail see Edgely, 1969: 90ff.)

Beliefs that are rational in Swinburne's minimal sense tend to be true, for they are at least the product of a concern for truth on the agent's part, and backed by what the agent considered to be marks of the truth. Nonetheless they may be false, because the information on which they were based was limited or unreliable in some respects. 'Rational belief' often takes on the force of 'reliable, creditworthy belief' when we use it to pick out those beliefs arrived at through reflection on accurate, comprehensive information. 'Rational' then comes close in meaning to 'true' and 'probable'. It comments on the adequacy of what is believed. A similar range of meaning is to be found when 'rational' is used of actions. It may refer in a minimal sense to the manner of an agent's act, as when it refers to acts arising consistently out of beliefs acquired through some concern with the truth. It may also be used to comment on the propriety of an act, indicating what anyone acting on adequate beliefs would have done in the circumstances.

The manner in which someone acquires a belief and the adequacy of what they believe may be linked, if there are instances where what is believed is so remote from the truth or any available evidence that no one can come to believe it unless they believe irrationally in the minimal sense.

In fact there are cases where we recognise that what is believed must from its very nature be the kind of belief arrived at through the influence of non-rational factors. If a man in 1991 were to believe that he was Napoleon Bonaparte only a lapse from reason could explain how he came to this belief. A similar point applies to the holding of beliefs which are clearly contradictory. From the nature of contradiction, anyone who believes contradictory beliefs believes at least one thing that is false. Should falsehoods or contradictions be evident enough only a lapse from concern with the truth or similar failure to be guided by reasons will explain how the subject can come to hold them. MacIntyre himself makes the point that there are some beliefs that are so obviously true (he refers to commonsense beliefs about the environment) that no one with a concern for the truth and basic capacities for reflection could fail to hold them (MacIntyre, 1971: 253). But then the converse of this also holds: anyone who holds beliefs which contradict obvious truths or which are obviously false on some other ground is likely to be believing irrationally. It is not only obviously false or contradictory beliefs that are irrationally held by their very nature. Beliefs might, of their nature, be clearly in advance of any evidence that could support them. If someone told us that he knew which party would win the first general election after 2050, we would know from the nature of the case that he could have no grounds for his guess even if it turned out to be true.

Looking at the content of what is believed in religion offers the only hope a radical theorist might have for saying that religion as a whole or as such is to be treated as a masking institution ripe for external explanation. Argument has to be offered for concluding that *any* manifestation of religious belief is to be explained as the out-come of non-rational factors which are hidden to believers themselves. That some people are driven to engage in religion through the influence of non-rational factors is obviously insufficient to do this. If one individual embraces religion out of, say, wish-fulfilment driving fantasy, this is not yet to prove that no one could acquire faith except through these means. The content of belief may be true and faith be attainable through some other route even though non-rational factors are sufficient to explain some people's route into religion. To make religion as a whole or as such the subject for external explanation it would have to be contended that there was no route into religious belief and behaviour except through some set of non-rational causes. But only the content of what is believed in religion could tell us this. We would have to identify typical beliefs of the religious as so grossly false or absurd that no one could be presumed capable of reaching these beliefs except through factors operating independently of awareness of evidence and canons and traditions of rational argument.

All radical, comprehensive theories of religion rest on the presumption that religion is the work of unreason and they tend to rest this presumption, whether explicitly or not, on the perception of gross falsity or absurdity in religious belief. This is how a coherent reconstruction of them will have to represent their approach to the explanation of religion. It is not merely the assumption that religion is false or beyond the evidence that generates the demand to explain religion through mechanisms and laws external to itself. It is the assumption that religion has a kind of falsehood or absurdity that reflects back on how it is acquired and maintained. What is required is a judgement on the content of belief that will carry definite implications for the manner in which it is believed. Simple falsity of religious beliefs will not do this, nor again will it be enough to point to the scholar's personal or professional commitment to the non-existence of the gods to show why he must explain religion through hidden, external causes. Contemporary historians of science are committed to the non-existence of the ether, but their explanation of this characteristic belief of late nineteenth-century physics need point to nothing other than the good reasons that were then available, but since refuted, for accepting it. The existence of the gods has to be shown to be something that the operations of reason could never convince anyone of.

Two important presumptions appear to unite radical, comprehensive theories of religion. First the theorist of religion must find some common denominator in the religions which unites them all as candidates for his preferred mode of explanation. Without this presumption of a common denominator, which is part of an essentialist view of religion, there will be no reason to think that all the manifestations of religion call for the same treatment by a radical theory. Second, it will have to be a common denominator which calls for explanation in terms other than the reasons ostensibly offered for believing it. The theorist must be committed to finding this common denominator grossly false, or absurd in some other way, which is why religion as a whole requires external explanation. These two presumptions bear on the importance of the philosophical critique of religion mounted by secular thinkers of the Enlightenment, of particular importance for some of the chosen theorists of religion to be considered in Part Two of this book. For it carried sufficient conviction in the minds of some writers to show that belief in the sacred must be absurd. This belief is interpreted in one way – as belief in an ideal, metaphysical world behind the material – and then is written off as delusive in the light of the radical Enlightenment's 'demonstration' of the truth that no such metaphysical world could be the subject of rational, grounded hypotheses.

Belief in the sacred need not necessarily be written off as obviously false to yield damning diagnoses of how religious beliefs are acquired. A radical theorist of religion could concede that it is theoretically possible that religious beliefs are true. But, influenced by another strand of the radical Enlightenment, he might argue that of their nature they are so remote from experience that no one could believe they are true *with reason*. Many writers (for example, Southwold, 1978) take as typical of the sacred that it can only be described in terms of what Evans-Pritchard defines as 'mystical notions':

> These are patterns of thought that attribute to phenomena suprasensible qualities which, or part of which, are not derived from observation or cannot be logically inferred from it . . . [He completes the sentence 'and which they do not possess'.]
>
> (Evans-Pritchard, 1937: 12)

The logic of saying that only mystical notions can depict the sacred flows from the transcendent character of alleged sacred objects. This transcendent character might give grounds for saying that belief in the sacred must be an illusion in Freud's technical sense: a belief which though it might conceivably be true can only be firmly held by anyone on grounds other than reason. (Compare Freud, 1978: 26–7; positively, for Freud, these beliefs must be the outcome of wish.)

The fact that religious systems abound in paradox is another ground for thinking that belief in the sacred is inevitably delusive or illusory. Typically religious systems embrace and acknowledge seeming contradictions in their theoretical dimensions to a degree not matched (it is alleged) in non-religious schemes of thought. This characteristic provides an open invitation to the radical theorist to see absurdity and hence unreason at the heart of religion. We are familiar with such seeming contradictions from the developed theologies of Western monotheisms with their emphasis on the incomprehensibility of God. But they would appear to be part of the generic feature of belief in the sacred. Their presence in tribal religions has encouraged some writers to refer to something called 'the primitive mind' and to characterise it as pre-logical. The precise significance of this inclination to paradox in religious utterance remains to be assessed in the philosophy of religion. The radical theorist of religion seems to be committed to seeing it as a potent indicator of the inherent irrationality of religious thought.

If the radical theorist of religion can find something at the heart of religion that is grossly false or absurd or self-contradictory then he has good reason for abandoning methodological agnosticism. Methodological agnosticism involves taking seriously the reasons believers give for their beliefs and taking seriously (though not endorsing) the concepts they use to describe the object of their beliefs. To conclude that the outward form of religion is irrational as such in the manner of a Feuerbach gives ground for dismissing both the reasons believers offer for their beliefs and for the descriptions they offer of the objects of belief. If the beliefs fail of a minimal rationality, then the reasons offered for them are rationalisations and don't in themselves provide explanations for why they are held. If beliefs about the sacred are absurd, then we would have good reason to reinterpret accounts of what they are allegedly about. This follows a pattern observed in ordinary discourse: if someone's descriptions of an object are sufficiently confused or incoherent, we may say 'What you really wanted to talk about was . . .' On occasion we properly claim to know better what someone is trying to talk about than he does himself. In these ways the observer of a human institution may offer interpretations of its beliefs that set aside what participants understand as their meaning. So radical theories of religion tell us what 'really' moves religious beliefs and actions, and what beliefs and actions are 'really' about and aimed at. In the area of rationality lies the ground for when such re-description of the objects of cognition and action is appropriate. We can now see that many of the issues involved in deciding upon the truth of radical explanations of religion can be summed up in the question 'When is it proper to abandon methodological agnosticism?'

Rationality and its links with the content of belief appear to provide a way out for the radical theorist's attempts to subvert internal explanations of religion. One obvious weakness in the route is to be found in our objections to essentialism in the definition of religion (outlined in Chapter 1 above). Another must now be aired briefly, though we cannot discuss it properly. The argument that the scientist of religion must examine the rationality of religious belief and action so as to determine how they are to be explained presupposes that judgements of rationality can be made about whole genres or systems of thought. If rationality, however, is relative to theories, world-views, systems or the like, then there is no room for anyone to say of religion as such that it is irrational. Particular religious beliefs and actions might be irrational relative to the standards of rationality found within religion itself, but religion as a whole could not be said to be irrational.

Peter Winch is normally taken to be affirming relativism of this sort when he writes:

> Criteria of logic are not a direct gift of God, but arise out of, and are only intelligible in the context of, ways of living or modes of social life. So within science or religion actions can be logical or illogical . . . But we cannot sensibly say that either the practice of science itself or that of religion is either illogical or logical.
>
> (Winch, 1958: 100–1)

Winch applies this point when considering anthropological descriptions of primitive religions. Winch undertakes a sustained critique of Evans-Pritchard's account (in *Witchcraft, Oracles and Magic among the Azande*) on the ground that Evans-Pritchard ignores the principle that 'standards of rationality in different societies do not always coincide' (Winch, 1970: 97). Evans-Pritchard wishes to show how the irrational beliefs of the Azande can be maintained despite the fact that they are not in accord with reality. A key concept in his explanation of Zande thought and behaviour is that of a 'mystical notion' (as defined above). It is significant that, as we saw, mystical notions are defined as ones which are *founded on* irrationality. Winch's chief objection to this way of proceeding appears to be that it ignores the fact that what is the case, and what may be inferred from what is the case, are relative to society, its language and belief systems (Winch, 1970: 82; whether Winch has anything so crude in mind is open to question).

The very summary sketch of relativism offered so far is enough nonetheless to show the importance of its challenge. Not only will it stop radical explanations of religion in their tracks. It also constitutes a major objection to our endorsement of MacIntyre's thesis that rationality is a key category in the understanding of human acts and beliefs.

We cannot discuss the challenge of relativism at any length and shall assume for the sake of argument that it can be met. We shall thus allow that it is in principle possible to attribute irrationality or gross falsehood to religion as such.

The precise question to be settled in any final determination of the truth of relativism as a theory of truth and rationality concerns the degree to which rationality and evidence are contextually determined factors. We have argued that to some degree they are. We have supposed that they are to some degree, in that we have accepted that whether a subject is rational in holding a given belief is dependent on his background beliefs. What is evidence worth accepting depends to some extent on time, place and the context of specific intellectual traditions. All this may be conceded while holding that there are non-contextual factors which make the rationality of a belief independent to some degree of the specific system of which it is a part, and which might enable us to say of a large-scale system of belief and action (such as witchcraft in seventeenth-century Europe) that it was irrational. Candidates for non-contextual determinants of rationality would be: some basic beliefs of common sense, the laws of logic, some at least of the formal and informal principles of inductive reasoning.

The arguments for the wholly contextualist account of standards of rationality and evidence would start from the accepted difficulties in demonstrating that a large-scale system of belief is irrational. Each has great power to deflect criticism through reinterpreting evidence against it. The arguments for a partly universalist, non-contextual account of rationality would be that relativism leads to a sceptical account of knowledge and truth, where error may be allowed to live unchallenged, and takes insufficient account of the demands on common understanding imposed by the requirement that we be able to understand and translate alien systems of thought and action. (Readers may find full discussions of relativism which support our setting aside of its claims in MacIntyre, 1988, Mitchell, 1973, and Skorupski, 1976.)

In our discussion of MacIntyre's 'Rationality and the Explanation of Action' we endorsed the point that the nature of historical and social explanation demands the making of philosophical judgements because it rests in part on the notion of rationality. Even greater stress can now be placed on the use of philosophical understanding in the appraisal and construction of theories of religion. The radical theorist of religion may, of course, rest his theory on nothing more than empirically observed correlations which suggest that religion changes, rises and falls quite independently of the 'rationalisations' of the religious. But we have seen that the comprehensiveness of any such theory can be extended significantly if it can rest on philosophical judgements affirming the essential irrationality of religion. Whether religious beliefs are grossly false or inherently beyond empirical verification or contradictory is in large measure a matter for philosophical judgement. The radical theories of religion examined in Part Two will be found to rest on philosophical assumptions. We do not make this point so as to condemn them. It is part of our argument that philosophical understanding is involved in all historical and social explanation.

In many respects reflection on the underpinnings of influential theories of religion entails consideration of the radical Enlightenment's critique of religion. It is this which we have said convinced many thinkers that religion was grossly false and absurd. And the epistemological doctrines of the radical thinkers of the Enlightenment must not be forgotten in this connection. One important ground, visible in Feuerbach, for wishing to reinterpret references to the transcendent and denying the rationality of any beliefs about it lies in the empiricism that accompanies much secularising thought. It is plain that a severe doctrine about the limits of reason could suggest a priori that, however people arrived at beliefs about the gods, it was not through reasoning.

INTERNAL, EXTERNAL AND RELIGIOUS EXPLANATIONS OF RELIGION

Our aim in the remainder of this chapter is to offer further clarification of types of explanation of religion. In previous chapters we have relied on a distinction between internal and external explanations of religion. Internal explanations have been associated with conservative, contextual, participant-based accounts. External explanations have been linked to radical, comprehensive, observer-based accounts. Both types of explanation will have room for non-religious facts and factors in the explanation of religious phenomena. In the ordinary, non-controversial business of writing the history of religion the contextual character of explanatory narratives means that religious facts will be connected with facts from the larger life of the society in which the religion is embedded. The ground for distinguishing these two broad types of explanation of religion rests on the *degree* of explanatory power attributed to non-religious factors in the account. It is characteristic of external explanations of religion that they seek to explain the very existence and the fundamental character of religion by reference to allegedly more basic facts about the workings of human society or the human psyche. In an external explanation no religious facts are allowed to appear as proper termini of explanation, for the very existence and character of religion needs to be accounted for. Facts outside the life of religion are held to provide full, sufficient conditions for the occurrence of religious ones.

We have pointed to rationality as the key property that might make a system of religious belief, thought and action independent of external explanatory factors. For the reasons set out above, a rational institution cannot be represented as a mere result of causal mechanisms operating outside it. Its independence of external factors remains a matter of degree, however. For the exercise of rationality in a human institution will always depend on a background of enabling conditions provided by the larger life of the society of which it is a part. In the same way, if we say that the explanation of the start of a fire is the dropping of a lighted match, we take for granted the other necessary conditions (such as the presence of oxygen in the atmosphere) which contribute to the result and enable the 'cause' of the event to be operative. Rational explanations of religious facts and developments pick out decisive necessary conditions for the things they explain, but they too are dependent on background enabling conditions.

The relevance of external factors to internal explanations of religion is even greater than suggested so far. The historian of religion intent on conservative, contextual explanations of religion does not necessarily have a stable background of enabling conditions against which he can explain one religious fact by citing others. Changes in the background of enabling conditions may become important as they suggest radically different circumstances in which the operations of religious modes of thought and understanding must take place. Internal explanations of religion show religion to be independent of extra-religious factors only by revealing religious reasons and norms to be necessary conditions for the occurrence of religious belief and behaviour. The weaving together of foreground from religion with background from wider history is the stuff of which the discipline of the history of religions is made.

We have set out the reasons why radical, comprehensive theories of religion cannot accept religious norms and reasons as indispensable, necessary conditions for the explanation of the facts of religion. We have connected their radical, comprehensive character to a number of other features they possess. They do not appear to be compatible with a continued commitment to religion. They depend on attributing irrationality, and most likely gross falsehood, to religious belief. They are incompatible with methodological agnosticism. Such features of theories offering radical comprehensive explanations of religion will be further explored below. They collectively show why the explanations of religion they offer are well summed up as 'external'. In Part Two we shall illustrate varieties of external explanation of religion. Theories of religion which display forms of external explanation will be grouped under the following headings: philosophical, socio-anthropological, socio-economic, and psychological.

Now we turn to a third category of explanation of religion, alongside internal and external explanations, one that shares with external explanations the property of departing from methodological agnosticism.

Internal and external explanations of religion differ in the role they allot to the beliefs, reasons and norms of the religious in the interpretation and explanation of religion. In internal explanations such intra-religious factors occur as at least necessary conditions in the account of major, salient religious facts and developments. In external explanations intra-religious factors are not allowed this power and explanations typically terminate in facts external to religion. Our third category of *religious* or *theological* explanations includes those attempted explanations of religion which make reference to the actual existence and operation of divine realities in accounting for religious facts. While agreeing with internal explanations on the point that religious beliefs, reasons and norms can have explanatory power, proponents of religious explanations go further. They contend that at least some of the objects of those beliefs must be assumed to have real existence and causal power if explanation is to be adequate. Thus religious explanations are as much opposed to methodological agnosticism as external explanations.

In endorsing the stance of methodological agnosticism, outlined by such writers as Ninian Smart, we have suggested that two tasks in the critical study of religions are initially to be kept separate: describing and explaining religion in history on the one hand, and judging its truth on the other. Those who oppose methodological agnosticism will distinguish between a level of description in the study of religions, which can proceed without raising the question of religion's truth, and a level of explanation, which cannot be under-taken without deciding upon the reality of religious objects. The radical theorist of religion can present a case for making this distinc-tion if he can provide grounds for overturning the normal pattern of rational and normative explanations of religious behaviour. We have seen in the earlier sections of this chapter how this case can be mounted. The radical theorist of religion has one kind of ground for removing the 'brackets' (see p. 51 above) from the referring expres-sions within religious affirmations. The proponent of a religious explanation of religion feels that there are other kinds of grounds for assuming that the referring expressions of religion actually pick out real entities, and that only the assumption that religious entities exist enables us to offer an adequate interpretation and explanation of religion. Whereas external explanations are based on the assumption of methodological atheism or scepticism, religious or theological explanations are based on the assumption of methodological theism. 'Methodological theism' means that the existence of the sacred and its interaction with human beings is a premise in the interpretation and explanation of religion offered.

We use the labels 'religious' and 'theological' to describe this departure from a neutralist approach to the explanation of religion to distinguish two ways in which this particular mode of theorising about religion can be conducted. Religious theories of religion are those theories which are not neutral as to the existence of sacred, transcendent reality, and not neutral about the truth of a wholly naturalistic account of human affairs and the world in which these affairs are set. They are committed to the existence of some sacred reality or other and to the falsity of a wholesale naturalism. On the other hand they are not committed to the account of the sacred offered in any particular religion. They assume that, for the purposes of explaining religion, neutrality between the faiths is in order. They typically claim that the differences and conflicts between the faiths are unimportant for the purpose of explaining what religion is and how it arises. There are numerous detailed versions of such pan-religious interpretations of religion. In Chapter 4 we shall explore that offered in the recent writings of John Hick. But we might have equally selected W. Cantwell Smith's account in *The Meaning and End of Religion* or such important historical pioneers of this approach as Schleiermacher and F. Max Mueller. (For outlines of their theories of religion see Chapters 6 and 7 of Byrne, 1989.)

By theological approaches to the explanation of religion we intend to point to the accounts of humankind's religious history offered by particular religious faiths, such as Buddhism and Christianity. It is typical of those religions which are historically sophisticated and aware to provide a theology of religions: some account of the place of itself in human history and of its relation to other forms of human religion. A theology of religion usually involves an account of how the religion behind it is the goal of human history or the end of human striving; how this religion emerges as a true perception of the sacred; and how other religions are at best intermediate stages in history or misleading apprehensions of the sacred. Particular religions frequently, then, teach that they are unique in some important respect and use this premise of uniqueness to explain the whole of religious life.

There are temptations from within a commitment to the truth of religion (or to a particular dogmatic standpoint) to abandon or ignore neutralism and agnosticism in explaining religion. The consequences of so doing will be explored further in Chapter 4.

Part Two

Part Two

4

A Religious Theory of Religion

THE BASIS OF A RELIGIOUS THEORY OF RELIGION

It is a significant fact about 'world' religions such as Islam, Christianity and Buddhism that their dogmatic structures generate theories about the religious life of humankind. Sometimes in the history of the theory of religion it has appeared that its proponents face a stark choice between either accepting one such dogmatically inspired account of religion, or embracing a radically naturalistic, external explanation of religion of the kind we shall illustrate in later chapters. We have argued that the choice is never as stark as that, because a case can be made for internal explanations of religion which are nonetheless methodologically neutral. In this chapter we shall explore another way of avoiding this stark choice through the possibility of a religious, yet non-theological, theory of religion. We shall do so through discussion of the theory of religion contained in John Hick's writings, notably his recent *An Interpretation of Religion* (Hick, 1989). Hick is agreed by many to be the leading contemporary exponent of this approach and *An Interpretation of Religion* remains his fullest attempt to expound his ideas.

John Hick's theory of religion stems from the thesis that all religions worship the same transcendentally real focus, albeit under the guise of different culturally conditioned *personae* and *impersonae*. There is a unitary, if unknowable, object behind the world's religions and all religions present humanly based and influenced means of grasping this object or focus and of orientating human life toward it. Hick thus has a pluralist view of religious truth and of religious history. Pluralism is the negation of the thought that any one religion is unique in truth, in salvific effectiveness, or in relation to the meaning of history. Truth, at least in grasping aspects or genuine appearances of the transcendent Real behind all human religious thought and action, is granted to all faiths (or at least the non-

79

animistic, 'post-Axial' ones that arose in the period 800–200 BCE: see below).

This assumption about the common object of all religions, and hence denial of the uniqueness of any one of them, is styled 'the pluralist hypothesis'. It is important to note that Hick offers no strict proof of it. The thesis about the unitary, if unknowable, focus of religion is presented as a hypothesis which, in the nature of the case, cannot be demonstrated (Hick, 1989: 1). The major thrust of Hick's study is to show what might follow for the interpretation of religious life and history if it were true. In other words, Hick is mainly concerned to show that a viable theory of religion follows from this philosophical, pan-religious belief and what form this theory must take. Hick states that his interpretation of religion aims to fulfil aims normally thought to be incompatible: namely to understand religion both scientifically and religiously (1989: 1–2). His theory can take into account all that history and the human sciences can teach about the origins of religion because it assumes that specific religions are humanly conditioned responses to the transcendent. But the retention of the thought that there is a real, transcendent focus of religion allows him to present religious life and experience as essentially non-illusory. The basic thrust of Hick's ideas shows him to be a distinguished representative of a mode of theorising about religion that goes back to at least F. Max Mueller. His religious theory is not yet a theological one, for it is not committed to the theology of any particular faith.

Though Hick makes no attempt to prove his pluralist hypothesis he obviously regards it as superior to one based on the belief in the uniqueness of any particular faith. There are a variety of grounds he might offer against beginning the description and explanation of religion from the standpoint of any such claim for uniqueness.

One such ground, relating to justice in salvation, is made much of in his earlier writings, particularly *God and the Universe of Faiths* (Hick, 1973). It is directed specifically against Christian claims for uniqueness, but evidently applies to other religions as well. If any one faith, such as Christianity, is uniquely related to the sacred by way of truth and salvific power, then the justice of the sacred reality is called into question. Not all members of the human race will enjoy an equal (or any) chance in learning of this sacred entity and of its plans for salvation. For any particular religion in human history is almost inevitably going to be known to only a portion of the human race and so cannot be the only or essential means of human salvation. This is a theological objection to the dogmatic claims for uniqueness made from within the faiths. Its strength rests upon the possibility of seeing uniqueness claims as unjust. Some contend that Hick's use of the appeal to cosmic and divine justice cannot be consistently used to overturn reliance on a particular set of dogmas to interpret religion. The inconsistency allegedly arises as follows: it is only by relying on the dogmas of a particular faith, such as Christianity, that Hick can know that God is good and therefore must intend to deal justly with all mankind (see D'Costa, 1986: 102ff). But Hick can defend his claim that any account of the status of human religions must be compatible with a view of the sacred as just on a priori grounds: the requirements that the sacred be worthy of worship and devotion entail by definition that we cannot have a picture of it that makes it out to be partial in its relations to humanity. And he can point to the *common* testimony of the post-Axial faiths that the object of religion is worthy of devotion, praise and the like. We cannot pursue these points about justice and uniqueness further, but we note that appeals to justice do provide prima facie difficulties for uniqueness claims.

Hick can also appeal to the futility of attempts to offer theological theories of religion. Such theories appear to have an advantage, for religious believers, over external theories in that they avoid using categories like illusion and delusion in the interpretation of human religious life. In fact, a theological theory, while it grants non-illusory status to one tradition, will find itself using categories that belong to external, radical explanations of religion of other traditions. For example, on the crudest, Christian portrait of human religion, while Christianity is a response to genuine revelation, other faiths are mere human inventions, motivated by superstition. On more sophisticated views, such as those of Karl Rahner (see Richards, 1989: 60–2), non-Christian faiths are vehicles for genuine divine grace, but describe the source of this in misleading form. There are truths and insights in non-Christian faiths but Christianity remains the absolute religion and the absolute truth. But the essential terms of these theological explanations are similar to those of the philosophically, sociologically or psychologically inspired theories we consider in later chapters. Religion (or non-Christian religion for the dogmatist) exists as a misleading response to a genuine reality, a misperception of real truths. It is judged in the light of an account of the truth external to it, unguessed at by its participants. It remains to be completed and achieve a true knowledge of itself. A large part, perhaps the major part, of the religious life of mankind has not escaped from the categories used by external explanations of religion. We have the same, familiar gap between the participant's understanding of his faith and the true interpretation offered by a favoured, external theory. In this respect, dogmatically inspired theories of religion are the ancestors of all external, radical explanations of religion.

Another difficulty with which Hick can press theological theories of religion is their arbitrariness, which can be argued for on philosophical and historical grounds.

We might contend on philosophical grounds that if a version of Christian dogmatics uses the categories of truth to interpret Christianity and those associated with error and illusion to interpret Buddhism, there is no reason why Buddhist dogmatics cannot reverse the process (and so for other forms of faith). In fact we do find that many forms of faith claim uniqueness and develop accounts of religion as a whole which turn around their own finality and normativeness (for detailed description of a Hindu attempt see Richards, 1989: 129–32). Each dogmatic scheme will find its attempt to explain religion as a whole fitting, illuminating when judged in the light of its own presuppositions. However, failing any independent criteria for judging one dogmatic theology or one faith better than another, these appear to present the theory of religion with merely a plurality of arbitrary starting points for its work. If it has to begin its task of constructing interpretations of religion on the basis of one of these accounts then it is difficult to see how it can get started.

A theological theory of religion will tend to relate the religion it favours to the explanatory factors of human history in a way different from the way non-favoured forms of faith are so related. Consider how the non-favoured forms of religion come to misperceive the sacred: because they are too deeply embedded in culturally conditioned, historically limited forms of human understanding, while the favoured faith rises above these. In traditional Christian explanations of religion this distinction is made in terms of revelation. Christianity is genuinely revealed. Other forms of faith are not. The Christian epochs (or at least the founding epochs of Christianity) are not simply forms of ordinary human history. The promulgation of the Christian message and the formation of its Church and Scriptures stand out from the normal ebb and flow of history. It may be alleged that no consistent historiography of religions can allow the kind of contrast between epochs of religious history that a theological theory of religion demands. The history of religions, it may be argued, must be constructed on the same working principles. If one religion can be made intelligible by reference to the facts of ordinary human history, then so must all. There must be common presuppositions behind all applications of historical enquiry to religion. The defender of a theological theory of religion might reply that this appeal to consistency merely masks a dogmatic refusal to admit that one religion might be unique in its place in history in relation to the others.

It is difficult to judge where the truth lies in such controversies over the presuppositions and character of history (see Byrne, 1989: 241–55). However, there is a strong case for saying that the actual course of historiography of religions shows no clear case for regarding one religion as distinct in its relation to human history when compared with others. Indeed, particular claims for uniqueness, such as those for the uniqueness of Christ as revealer, look weak in the light of detailed historical investigations of religious origins. It is with this in mind that we must read Hick's implicit claim that a theological interpretation of religion will not be compatible with a full appreciation of the data of the historical, scientific study of religion. For example, in Chapter 20 of *An Interpretation of Religion* Hick contends that we know that some of the claims about historical matters made from within the faiths are literally false (see 1989: 371–2 for the discussion of Christ's divinity). To accept a picture of religious life and history from within one of the faiths may thus be incompatible with the critically established data of religious studies.

Through his appeal to impartiality, consistency and the awareness of the historical, human-rootedness of all faiths, Hick is able to make the choice of a theological interpretation of religion appear distinctly unattractive. His exposition of the rival religious theory of religion is divided into five parts. The first dwells on the historical and phenomenological similarities between post-Axial religions. Hick hopes to show how concentration on their soteriological and ethical aspects reveals parallels between them which make the hypothesis of a common object or focus reasonable. The second part of the argument clears the way for his religious epistemology through the contention that the universe is religiously ambiguous. The character of the world yields, neither by observation nor proven inference, any religious truths. The unprovability of the sacred and of particular human claims about it follows, as does the impossibility of proving or disproving atheism. The third part of Hick's case presents an account of religious experience and the rationality of religious belief in the light of the religious ambiguity of the universe. This stresses the character of faith as free human response to the discernment of religious significance in the world. The emphasis on faith as being derived from the human subjects's own free interpretation of reality becomes particularly important for his overall theory of religion. The fourth element consists in an outline of the pluralist hypothesis. It develops his account of the nature of the focus of religious faith and his distinction between the way in which this is experienced through various forms and images in the traditions and the manner in which it exists as an unknowable reality behind all religious experience. It stresses the manner in which different religions are human, culturally influenced responses to a transcendent reality which none can describe as it is in itself. Hick finally sets out the criteria which we must use to judge which human traditions are to be counted as linked by a common ultimate focus and which not. These place greatest stress on there being a common soteriology or ethics linking those faiths which are genuine responses to the transcendent.

Hick's emphasis on the religious ambiguity of the universe and the unprovability of the pluralist hypothesis behind his theory of religion leads to a question about the status of his religious explanation of religion. He notes the power of external, radical explanations of religion of the type discussed below, which tend to assert that religion is ultimately illusory (or more precisely: radically false and acquired irrationally). There is no way, Hick states, that such radical explanations can be proved to be invalid, even though he has specific points of criticism to raise against some of them. Religious life remains ultimately ambiguous between its religious and naturalistic explanations (1989: 114). We must ask what is gained by adopting a religious explanation if none of the scientifically established data about religion show it to be correct, for this implies that it is in no clear sense a better interpretation than its rivals. Further, ambiguity in the phenomena might argue for a methodologically neutral interpretation of religion, one that was uncommitted in its descriptions and explanations of religion. However, for Hick ambiguity is not a reason for agnosticism but an opportunity for religious faith as a free cognitive attitude toward an alleged level of meaning in things whose existence no one may prove or disprove. So the possibility of a religious explanation of the facts of religious life must exist and is there to be spelt out. In thinking about how John Hick tackles this job we shall concentrate on: how far his theory is possible, the definition of religion it contains, and the extent to which it is a realist theory of religion.

IS HICK'S THEORY OF RELIGION POSSIBLE?

If Hick can produce a religious but non-theological theory of religion, he must be able to register a commitment to a transcendent, non-human source of religion while being agnostic, and sceptical to a degree, about all specific, historically located affirmations of the existence of transcendent beings and states. Some will wonder how he can have this commitment alongside his agnosticism. This query relates to how, if at all, his own references to the transcendent can remain free of the factors which make those found in the faiths unusable in a critical theory of religion. It also relates to the kind of content Hick can give to his reference to a religious source of religion while distancing himself from what the faiths say about this object. It would not seem to be possible to have a religious but non-theological interpretation of religion unless these questions can be answered.

It is common to find the following criticisms of Hick's underlying thesis that none of the immediate objects of worship in the world's religions is real, while there is one, unknown Real-in-itself of which they are the humanly based images. How can Hick claim to know that all religions have this identical, focus when (a) he asserts that none of the belief systems of the particular faiths can be relied on as literally true, and (b) he preaches a thorough agnosticism about the sacred in order to undermine reliance on the theology of any particular faith? Implicit in *An Interpretation of Religion* is a distinction which serves to found a reply to these objections, namely one between theological and philosophical truth.

The confessional statements about the transcendent that belong to particular religions are informed by a naively realist picture of religious truth, and pay little attention to the human contribution to the formation of faith and the culturally based nature of that contribution. Philosophical statements about the transcendent are informed by knowledge that faith is a free, cognitive response to a religious dimension to reality whose existence and nature cannot be proved by external facts. Philosophy realises that any human instance of faith is always expressed through the filters provided by the concept-set of a particular tradition and therefore knows that no naively realist view of religious language will do. All these second-order truths about the nature of religion are revealed in Hick's analysis of the nature, origins and basis of faith. It must be an assumption of religious pluralism that the character of philosophical statements about the transcendent is such as to escape the relativising factors which infect theological, confessional knowledge. Just as when Kant tells us that certain universal truths of which we are sure, such as that every thing is in time, apply only to the world as it appears and not as it is in itself, this 'transcendental knowledge' is not affected by the very subjectivity in human knowing that it is pointing to. This theme of the distinction between first-order religious and second-order philosophical statements about God runs through various parts of Hick's book (see, for example, 258–9). It allows Hick to avoid the charge that he has taken the ground from under his own feet in stressing the human-centred nature of talk about the transcendent. This stance is strengthened by another distinction implicit in the crucial chapter on 'The Pluralist Hypothesis' (1989: 233–51). The statements that the critical philosopher of religion makes about the transcendent are on a different logical plane in being largely negative and relational (1989: 239). Thus Hick avoids the alleged subjectivity that comes with the infection of humanly based modes of perception when *substantive* concepts are used of the transcendent in the faiths. The critical philosopher of religion can also escape the charge that he introduces exclusivism by the back door in condemning all those who believes in the *personae* or *impersonae* of traditional faiths to falsity. Hick's assertion that, ultimately, the transcendent real is unknowable and beyond any substantive human concepts is meant to be on a different level from a specific, traditional claim such as that God is three persons in one substance. This gives Hick prima facie room for arguing that the truth of the philosophical statement leaves the traditional one untouched.

Questions remain concerning how the philosophical claims about the ultimate focus of religion can be established and about whether these claims are rich enough to allow content to be given to a religious but non-theological theory of religion. These claims must be free of any particular traditional religion if the philosophical account is to stand above the relativities of the particular faiths. (Compare Gavin D'Costa's criticism that Hick's inference from the benevolence of God to His desire to give salvific value to all religions depends essentially on what *Christ* reveals about God's love – D'Costa,

1986: 102ff.) Hick's examination of the phenomenology of the world's religions is meant to provide data which are not confined to particular traditions, while the succeeding philosophical parts establish the appropriate critical sense to be made of them. Hick is aware of the charge that his critical strictures allow too little to be said about the transcendent to make a difference between his own position and that of a radical, sceptical theorist of religion such as Feuerbach. Both Hick and Feuerbach posit an element of human projection and falsehood in the gods men have actually worshipped, while agreeing that there is *something* real on which this projection gets to work. Hick contends, however, that his view does avoid the conclusion that human religions are based on delusion. There is a non-mundane, non-human focus and source for human religion. The immediate foci of religion (God, Allah, sunyata, etc.) are not finally real, but we can hypothesise on good grounds that they mediate a real beyond all human projection. Later we shall have to press the question of what this hypothesis adds to the survey of religious life, but let us note for the present that Hick thinks it avoids the twin dangers of positing wholescale delusion in the faiths, on the one hand, or plumping for confessional exclusivism entailed by reading all religious history in the light of one religion, on the other (1989: 249).

Hick's debt to Kant is, of course, immense (as acknowledged – Hick, 1989: 240–6), and it is only through understanding the Kantian basis of his argument that we can judge the coherence of his postulation of a transcendent Real behind all religions.

It is a common criticism of Kant that any postulation of a Real-in-itself within a critical philosophy which has acknowledged the human basis of all thought must be inconsistent: it at once sets limits to the human understanding and then makes an assertion that goes beyond those limits. If human religious thought has inevitable limits set by the constitution of religious knowledge, how can we both acknowledge those limits and think beyond them? This, however, is to misunderstand the way in which the thing-in-itself can be introduced into a critical philosophy. Knowing that how things appear to us reflects to some degree how they must appear to beings with our cognitive constitution, we can acknowledge that this does not set absolute limits to the nature of reality considered in itself. By entertaining the thought of the thing-in-itself we leave open the possibility that reality might have quite other properties than the ones our cognitive constitution allows us to perceive. In this way we stop a number of dogmatic claims in their tracks. The ideal of reality as it is in itself essentially leaves a place open for speculations about the ultimate nature of reality, which must be unprovable, but which may be of use in the ordering of human knowledge. Kant specifically allows for such a negative, critical use of speculations about reality as it is in itself, by suggesting that the categories have a purely formal meaning which remains after their application within experience is left behind (Kant, 1933: A147/B186).

Kant's procedure does not appear to be inconsistent and Hick can be seen, so far, to follow it, down to distinguishing the substantive predicates applied to the immediate foci of the faiths and the rather more formal attributes applied to the postulated Real-in-itself which may lie behind them. But to make the analogy work, and to preserve a purely critical use of the appearance/thing-in-itself distinction that does not involve thinking both sides of a necessary limit of the human understanding, Hick's postulation of the transcendent Real has to obey certain conditions. It has in the first instance to remain a purely regulative one. It can involve no claim to *knowledge* and must be offered as merely heuristically required by the purposes of human reason – here the purposes of bringing a certain advantageous order into our enquiries into religious life.

As a Kantian style regulative postulate, Hick's use of the idea of a transcendent Real behind the faiths has to be governed by strict limits. It is a moot point how far he remains within these (see Ward, 1990, for critical discussion of this). In the final section of this chapter we shall raise the question of whether the demotion of the immediate foci of the faiths accomplished by Hick's postulation of a single transcendent Real beyond them goes too far for him to remain a realist about actual religion and the sacred entities it postulates. This is also relevant to the Kantian basis of his argument. Hick cannot be true to a critical use of the thing-in-itself and claim the coherence established for that use and at the same time present the apparent objects of faith as unreal in the manner of a sceptic.

HICK'S DEFINITION OF RELIGION

In *An Interpretation of Religion* Hick explicitly supports a family resemblance definition of religion. He states on p. 4 that it is '. . . illuminating to see the different traditions, movements and ideologies whose religious character is generally agreed or responsibly debated, not as exemplifying a common essence, but as forming a complex continuum of resemblances and differences analogous to those found within a family.' There are oddities in this which strike us immediately when we ask how, if the class of religions has no essential unity, can it be the subject of the generalisations that Hick so obviously wants to make about it? The pluralist hypothesis is after all a large-scale general statement about how to see all religions (or at least all those that matter). If the class of religions is irreducibly diverse Hick's project appears to be in jeopardy. This point connects with the previous section on the postulation of a transcendent Real behind the faiths. One of the advantages of postulating a single, ultimate focus for religions is that it enables certain kinds of unity to be seen in them.

A sense of tension in Hick's account is confirmed when we examine what he suggests about the character of the post-Axial religions later in the book. What unites them is not simply that they arose coincidentally. They exhibit a strikingly similar soteriology. They all preach the transformation of consciousness from self- to reality-centredness as the means to gain salvation/liberation. (Other, earlier religions don't have the same emphasis on soteriology and tend to stress other forms of devotion (Hick, 1989: 36–55).) The first paragraph of Chapter 5 (p. 56) seems unequivocally to assert a common core to all post-Axial faiths in a certain type of soteriological structure. When described at the right level of generalisation they can be said to have the same soteriology. By the time we move onto Part V of the work ('Criteriological') we find Hick wielding the characteristic weapon of core or essence theorists of religion, namely a distinction between genuine and fake versions of the kind 'religion' (1989: 300). The boundaries of the class are not in the end to be settled by the tracing of an open-ended list of similarities but by the detection of the presence/absence of the soteriology that is the core of true religion (compare the discussion of Marxism as religion on p. 36). Since Hick has to accept variety in the beliefs of religion as the inevitable outcome of the subjective input into religion, the common soteriological core comes to be identified with ethics. Chapters 17 and 18 delineate a range of respects in which the practical dimensions of all genuine religions are alike. His discussion here is headed by these revealing words from Bunyan: 'The soul of religion is the practick part' (299). This shows Hick's essentialism and his closeness to the tradition which locates an essence to religion in ethics.

Hick does not play down other aspects of religion, such as modes of experience, doctrine and myth. The specific forms these take in particular faiths, however, varies according to how responses to the transcendent are shaped by tradition and culture, whereas soteriology as ethics is invariant if described in sufficiently general terms. The outward family resemblance structure of religion arises in Hick's theory according to a common pattern we have found in other essentialist accounts of religion. Religion is in essence one, but in manifestation various, as its common essence reacts with the different historical and cultural circumstances in which mankind is placed. The family resemblance character of religion appears to be true only of its surface characteristics. And this must be so for Hick. If it were finally the case that religion was a polythetic class, then there would be no reason to look for a common origin or focus to all the post-Axial faiths. Similarly, even though the postulate of a single, ultimate and transcendent focus for religions cannot be proved, the use of this notion as a regulative idea must bear some fruit or it would be a totally gratuitous hypothesis. Convergence and shared characteristics between the faiths united by this postulate must be sought in order to give it some work to do. It surely bids us to seek common properties underlying culturally induced differences, and orders our awareness of such properties.

Hick is not in the position of having to prove that religion has an essence. But on the other hand implausibilities in the idea that it does suggest difficulties in maintaining the pluralist hypothesis of a common Real behind all faiths. Indeed the two fundamental objections to the postulation of an essence to all religions can easily be illustrated in *An Interpretation of Religion* (see Chapter 1 above). Accounts of religion's essence quickly attain a normative force, so that when presented with examples of religion that do not appear to exhibit it, we shall be told that these are not genuine or central examples of religion. It is evidently the case that Hick uses his account in just this way in Chapters 17 and 18. The common core of soteriology as ethics provides the norm of genuine religion (Hick, 1989: 326). But there is an inevitable hint of circularity about this. While all definitions of religion provide norms because they imply rules for the use of the word 'religion', not all are normative. Hick offers a normative definition of religion because he tenders an account based on the moral effectiveness of proposed members of the class. He must use the distinction between true and false religion more freely than we might feel ideal for a theory of religion. A second problem is that accounts of essence work by finding a feature(s) which can be asserted to be common when described at a given level of abstraction and generality. Hick's common core of soteriology abstracts from all specific 'myths' about the nature and location of salvation. It is reduced to ethics and that in turn abstracts from specific things which appear culturally influenced and idiosyncratic (for example, Jewish ritual law and Islamic *shari'a*). So it is altruism, compassion and the reciprocity of the Golden Rule that are the outward signs of identical turning away from self-centredness to reality-centredness. But now, if we can have an essence only through heavy abstraction from specific differences, does this not merely show that the supposed essence does not really unite? It is too general, some will argue, to create any great likeness. This is an objection of principle to the essentialist's project. In Hick's case the point would turn on whether the common ethical core is too thin to do the job. Moreover, some might argue that the facts Hick wishes to incorporate in his account of the common core of true religion are too easily explicable on other grounds to show that his hypothesis is doing real work. After all, on the most minimal view of natural law we should expect moral codes in various societies to have common features reflecting the requirements of benevolence and justice (compare Hart 1961: 189ff).

The essentialism underlying Hick's theory may just bring out the extent to which the philosophy that lies behind the theory is not derived from a neutral phenomenological survey of religions but comes instead from metaphysical postulates about the ultimate validity of all major faiths.

A REALIST THEORY OF RELIGION?

We have suggested that Hick must show that his hypothesis that all religions focus on one ultimate, transcendent reality has some work to do. In particular he must indicate that it has different consequences from the external, sceptical hypothesis that all religions are illusions without at the same time falling into a confessionally grounded portrayal of religious life and history. We can assume that the unique consequences of his theory will centre around the notions of truth and realism.

An external theory of religion such as Durkheim's appears to start from the premise that the key beliefs of religion are false if taken literally and that some non-rational explanation is required of how reality comes to be so radically misperceived by the religious community. Hick can avoid this and contends that he is offering a realist interpretation of religion. It is not a naively realist but a critically realist interpretation (Hick, 1989: 174–5). The foci of religion as actually conceived we (that is critical philosophers of religion) know not to exist outside the stream of human experience. But they do present, at one remove, humanly influenced images of a real if unknowable focus.

For someone like Feuerbach or Freud the logic of the acquisition of religious beliefs is a logic of illusion, of misperception. Processes other than rational, truth-seeking ones are at work in the generation of belief. One would assume in Hick that the logic of the generation of religious belief is a contrasting logic of truth.

To get to grips with this issue we might turn to the analogies provided by the difference between a realist and subjectivist account of the history of science and the generation of scientific theories. A subjectivist view will seek only a sociological account of the rise and fall of theory. Facts about the structure, needs and interests of the historical scientific community will account for it. There will be no need of reference to the idea of truth. Typically the subjectivist will adopt a philosophical view to the effect that scientific theories are so underdetermined by data that none can be judged truer than any other. 'Truth' in the sciences reduces to what works and no reference need be made to the thought that some theories are abandoned because they are discovered to correspond to reality less well than rivals. The realist on the other hand will maintain that many theories, though not all, are advanced or rejected on rational grounds because they are judged to be more (or less) true than alternatives. Rationally instigated theories need not be true in total, but judging in the long term theory change can be explained in terms of the human desire for truth producing a series of better approximations to the truth.

The subjectivist will appeal to variety in theory and the lack of any evident common features between theories as the marks that theory change is not motivated by reason and its concern for truth. The realist will counter that variety can be accounted for if we employ the notion that there are degrees of truth and that theories can show different approximations to it. He will then use this notion to show links between successive theories. Though much of what Newton and Hooke believed about gravity is false given contemporary understanding, they discovered some true things about it and may be said to have written and talked about the same thing as Einstein, while believing many false things about that thing. A common reference between the changing theories in the history of science can be posited by looking to (a) common intentions between proponents of theories and (b) overlapping propositions across theories.

The realist has to be a critical realist (in Hick's terms) if he is to be a realist at all. If he employs a correspondence conception of truth, then, in the light of historical and contemporary facts, he knows that there will always be some gap between how reality is conceived in even the best theory and how it actually is. Naive realism is a contradiction in terms. Only subjectivist accounts of truth can make it appear acceptable to hold onto a theory come what may – there being no external reality to falsify them and no truth to which they are only human approximations. Dogmatism belongs to subjectivism. Even the best theory of the present day will be proved false in the light of future discoveries. Our realism about science and commitment to the idea of truth and external reference still has force if we can maintain the idea that some portion of the truth is captured by each rationally motivated theory. We know that contemporary ideas about gravity will inevitably give way to further theory development but at the same time, if our theory has a realist intent and is moved by reasons, some of its beliefs will be preserved. Essential to the realist view here is the ability to see a slow, if fallible, accumulation of knowledge about reality through the history of the rise and fall of theories.

The above points should make us question how far Hick's approach to living religions genuinely captures the spirit of a realist attitude and makes any worthwhile use of the notion of truth in interpreting religion. Hick maintains once more the commitment to a cognitivist, realist understanding of religious language that he has shown in earlier writings (Hick, 1989: 175–7). The question remains how he can do this if he does not employ a notion of approximation to truth in explaining relations between religions. This question bears on the gulf between actual religions and truth that Hick postulates, the meagreness of his idea of verification in religion and the emphasis he places on a pragmatic conception of truth. We illustrate these three points briefly in turn.

The gulf between the content of the theoretical dimension of any actual religion and the truth is clearly presented in these words:

It follows from the distinction between the Real as it is in itself and as it is thought and experienced through our religious concepts that we cannot apply to the Real *an sich* the characteristics encountered in its *personae* and *impersonae*.

(Hick, 1989: 246)

That to which the religions truly refer – the Real in itself – is literally indescribable (Hick, 1989: 350–1). The only method of verification in religion relates to the practical effectiveness of the stories and myths we relate about the Real. This criterion is well illustrated in Hick's comments on his own doctrinal constructions in *Evil and the God of Love*. The theodicy outlined there is now said to be only mythologically true. That is, it is an untranslatable set of metaphors or stories, none of which are literally true of the transcendent, but which may be true in the pragmatic sense of evoking the right response to evil in the human readers of the stories (Hick, 1989: 359–60). There appears to be no sense in which religions could cumulatively yield knowledge of the sacred, or be judged as a series of linked approximations to the truth. Time and again Hick evinces his commitment to a pragmatic conception of truth as it applies to religions and their theoretical dimensions. Actual religions are culturally conditioned responses to a sacred reality which cannot be literally described. They are true in so far as they orientate folk practically in the correct way to respond to this sacred reality. The correct way is that shared by the worthwhile post-Axial religions (the transformation of self-centredness to reality-centredness). Non-pragmatic truth belongs only to the philosophical expressions of the account of negative and relational truth about the transcendent, an account that belongs to a critical perspective on religion.

If the analogies drawn from the philosophy of science are of use in placing Hick's thought, then it would appear that he offers an analysis of religion which is closer in spirit to an instrumentalist account of scientific theory. The instrumentalist sees truth in theory as effectiveness in certain practical tasks. Truth as correspondence to external reality plays no part in explaining the rise and fall of an individual theory or the relation between theories.

We have suggested that if Hick's religious realism is to make any difference in the explanation of religion it must allow different religions to be related as commensurable attempts to add cumulatively to a knowledge of some human-independent reality. The gulf he places between religions and non-pragmatic truth and the incommensurability of different mythologies may be too great for this. Where cumulative overlaps between traditions are allowed by Hick they appear to relate to two areas. One is ethics, for a knowledge of the path from self-centredness to reality-centredness is shared by the faiths. Another area of overlap is in the anticipations of the philosophical truths about the incomprehensibility and transcendence of the sacred which a critical philosophy contains more fully (see Hick, 1989: 236–40). This suggests one way in which the idea of truth and convergence could figure in an explanation of religion. The truth would consist of the critical philosophy of religion's negative account of the transcendent plus the anti-egoist ethics behind the particular faiths. Now this is one way in which the faiths might converge: on a syncretistic religious truth discovered by philosophy and proclaimed to be the culmination of religious knowledge to date. Religious history is then seen as the slow faltering discovery of this truth and the terms of a scientific realist's account of theory progress can be applied to religion.

If this is the way of giving realism and its associated notions some bite in this context, it achieves it only at a cost. The cost is signalled by Ward: the pluralist hypothesis itself becomes an exclusivist religious truth to which all other religions are the preparation. The philosophy which proclaims that hypothesis becomes the goal and source of meaning of the whole of religious history. Illustrations of this use of philosophical theory as the implicit goal of religious striving would not be hard to find: one only has to recall the Hegelian theory of religion. But such an approach denies what is needed to defeat Ward's strictures – namely a firm distinction between the *levels* at which the theologies of the religions operate, on the one hand, and that at which the critical account of the sacred operates, on the other. Hick appears to entertain no such thoughts about the role of his own philosophy as the culmination of religious history. Yet he does indicate points at which his interpretation may react with the theologies of particular faiths, ways in which first-order religion may now be influenced by a critical philosophy of religion.

CONCLUSION

Hick's 'critical realism' toward the *personae* and *impersonae* of the religions of history is supposed to avoid the disadvantages of a confessionally based theory of religious history and those of an external, illusionist theory. Trying to steer a middle path and retain some advantages from both approaches is bound to meet with the objection that no one can have his cake and eat it. Our remarks have tried to give substance to this thought. Hick is at one with us in questioning the dichotomies that frame established approaches to the explanation of religion. In *An Interpretation of Religion* Hick is suggesting that the dichotomy 'Either explain the history of religion as the history of illusion or explain it from the standpoint of a particular confessional account of religious truth' is false. While we join in that questioning, we are not convinced that a religious theory of religion is in the end viable. Combining some kind of commitment to the reality of the sacred while avoiding all first-order theological claims may in the end be an impossible task. We have endeavoured to avoid the dichotomy which is Hick's target by outlining the possibility of a methodological neutralism. But it cannot be denied that that has its problems too.

One important question for our defence of a methodologically neutral stance in the theory of religion, embodied in the idea of internal explanations of religion, has emerged in this chapter. For we have seen reason in discussing Hick to forge a further link between the concept of rationality and the concept of truth. We have implied that if we wish to see theories in the history of science as rationally generated then we should expect to see the history of science as the history of the slow accumulation of truths and theories as successive approximations to truth. Should this thought not apply to the history of religions as well? We noted in Chapter 3 that it is the mark of a rational belief that it is motivated by a concern for the truth and strives after truth even if it misses the mark. If human religions are a succession of rational institutions in human history, should we not see a movement toward greater approximation to the truth across human religious history? If so, then is not the person who accepts the rationality of religious life committed to some judgements about the presence of truth in it, and thus to the abandonment of methodological agnosticism?

We are inclined to accept the basic force of this objection, but to see it as entailing only modest departures from methodological agnosticism. We did make some connections between truth and rationality in Chapter 3: beliefs which are radically false cannot be rationally held. This entails that if a religion contains even minimally rational beliefs then there must be a basic fit between its theoretical dimension and the most obvious features of reality. The points about truth and reason made above entail further that, if the history of religions is one of the succession of rational institutions, then we should expect to see the accumulation of insights about the human condition in it. In that respect we cannot be wholly neutral toward it, even if committed to internal explanations of it. But all this is compatible with the widest divergence of opinion among those who accept the minimal rationality of religion about the kinds of insights and truths accumulated in the to and fro of human religious ideas. Believing in that minimal rationality they might have quite other ideas about the reality of the sacred than participants in religion. They need only be committed to the thought that belief in the sacred is minimally rational, and hence part of a network of beliefs which are in some manner striving toward truth.

5

Philosophical Theories of Religion

PHILOSOPHY AND RELIGION

Philosophical theories of religion grow out of the inheritance of the Enlightenment. In certain philosophers this inheritance shows itself in a commitment to the following combination of ideas: the unity of science, scepticism about the rationality of religious belief and the reality of the sacred. It thus provides the two chief sources for the radical theories of religion described in Chapter 2. If we concentrate on the role of philosophical scepticism, we may see how the philosophy of religion came to appear to some to be on a collision course with established faith.

Philosophy of religion in the West can be seen as the outcome of a long tradition in theology of natural reasoning (that is, unaided by revelation) concerning the doctrine of God. The aim of such reasoning has been to supplement revealed sources in the demonstration of truths about the being and nature of the Christian God. Thus philosophy might provide preambles to faith and assist in the development and exposition of doctrine. The freeing of philosophical and intellectual reflection from the control and service of the Church, aided by the discovery of new sources of philosophical speculation, allowed the possibility to emerge that the God whom philosophy could rationally support was different from the God preached by established Christianity. Thus philosophy took on two of its characteristic relationships to religion: that of its critic/destroyer and that of its replacement. As critic/destroyer some philosophers contended that the God of traditional belief was fabulous and unreal, with the upshot that no rational route to faith in that God appeared open. Philosophy then sought to replace traditional belief with its own creed and system of observances.

This stance toward religion depends on a certain metaphysical optimism. It has to be assumed that philosophy is capable of offering a definitive verdict on the rationality of traditional religions and substituting its own account of what is ultimately real. Given this optimism (which many philosophers of religion do not share today), it appears inevitable that philosophy will yield a verdict on whether religion is veridical or illusory.

The characteristic way in which this optimism showed itself in the Enlightenment was through belief that philosophy provided proof of the truths and duties of natural religion, while leaving much of traditional belief as it was encountered in the West, superstitious and delusive. (In what follows we draw upon the accounts in Byrne, 1989.) Belief in natural religion led to a characteristic two-layered view of the nature of living religion. Some strands in it were true reflections of the operation of reason and the legacy of a primal, pure, natural religion. A great deal of what remained was the outcome of priestcraft working upon human ignorance and fear, with the assistance of the authority of rulers, customs and institutions. The greater part of popular religion was not regarded as minimally rational. An array of superstitious factors could be cited to explain it away.

Assuming an inevitable opposition between religion and philosophy, the accommodation sought by deistic promoters of natural religion amounted to an unstable compromise. The God of natural religion was in many respects similar to that of traditional Christianity. Only a slightly increased dose of scepticism was required to suggest that belief in this God could not really be supported without reliance on the superstitions of established faith. The two-layered view of religion was vulnerable to the criticism that it made historical religions into an implausible mixture of disparate elements. If there was a pure rational core of religion how had it ever been overlain by fear and superstition? If natural religion was an original human possession how could folk ever be persuaded into accepting something obviously inferior? Where might the original source of the evil of priestcraft be if mankind's original rational nature remained unsullied?

A way out of these dilemmas was found by more radical wings of the Enlightenment, of whom David Hume is a good representative. From despairing of any possibility of philosophy demonstrating the reality of an absolute remotely like the God of traditional faith he moved to the conclusion that religion was through-and-through superstitious, wholly accounted for by the operation of fear and ignorance. (See notably his *Natural History of Religion*, whose contents are explored in Byrne, 1989.)

But it can be shown that this too is an inherently unstable and unsatisfactory philosophical stance toward religion. Out of this approach we can see the type of philosophical theory of religion emerge that is the main topic of this chapter.

Granted that there is a perceived gulf between philosophy's account of rational belief and ultimate reality, on the one hand, and the elements of religion, on the other, it will be seen that it is deeply unsatisfactory to explain this gap as the product of superstition. The shallowness of the appeal to superstition lies in part in its failing to account for the persistence and spread of religion. It prompts the continually disappointed expectation that religion will die where civilisation spreads. More importantly, this type of explanation fails to face up to the fact that on its own terms the gods of popular faith are exclusively human products. If they are nothing but illusions and the products of superstition, then the expectation that, by exposing their illusory quality, a better human future can be secured is bound to be cruelly disappointed. On this account nothing other than the human race can share the responsibility for creating the gods. If belief in them is obviously false and irrational, then human nature must be in dire straights to have given birth to such a monster. Even if philosophy could gain a hearing for its exposure of these illusions what expectation could one have that this would be listened to? The philosophical account already entails that humankind has an inveterate inclination to believe what is contrary to sense and understanding. This philosophical explanation of religion, then, condemns itself to futility (cf. Williams, 1973: 94).

The challenge to any philosophical theory of religion is to rise above 'superstition' as the major category in an explanation of religion and to find something of positive value in the alleged human process whereby the gods or the sacred are invented and manufactured. A crucial role in the development of accounts along these lines was played by Hegel (1770–1831). It is not our intention to offer a full survey of Hegel's contribution to theorising about religion in these pages (attempts along these lines will be found in Morris, 1987, Byrne, 1989, and Reardon, 1977). Of greatest importance for our purposes is his foundational attempt to show how the different phases in the evolution of religion represent the outcome of distinct stages of human self-consciousness. Tying an explanation of religion to the development of human self-consciousness has a number of important consequences. One is that it sees something of importance in the phases of religion. Even if ultimately false in the light of a true philosophical account of the absolute, each phase of religion can be seen to embody one stage in the development of humankind's knowledge about itself and to contribute to the completion of human self-understanding. The gods are not then simply illusions. Moreover, point is given to the philosophical exposure of the alleged truth about religion. If humankind is engaged in a journey toward self-understanding along which the religions are necessary steps, then philosophy, somewhat immodestly, can claim a role in the final steps of that progress. Its revelation of the true status of religion prepares the way for the coming of complete self-understanding. It is thus working with, rather than against, the grain of human nature as this is displayed in the life of religion. The appeal to self-consciousness entails that something at the very heart of human thinking is responsible for belief in the sacred. If belief in the sacred is mistaken in its characteristic manifestations, it nonetheless has a deep-rooted cause, one which promises to account for why believers can be taken in by the apparent reality of sacred objects. It is not their stupidity which makes them take the gods of their own devising to be real. It is rather processes integral to the operation of the psyche that produce this result. If we seek a radical explanation of religion this must be an advance in theory.

Hegel's detailed accounts of how different stages of religion arise, each with its characteristic account of the gods, is intertwined with its philosophy of *Geist*. An individual's attempts at self-knowledge are at the same time the vehicle for *Geist*'s self-realisation. Part of the significance of speaking of the realisation of *Geist* through human lives is that it represents simple philosophical abstraction: *Geist* is human nature in society (*Geist* being the German for 'mind'). But there are also strong metaphysical overtones of belief in a spiritual principle that undergirds the development of all reality to its ultimate goal. This spiritual principle uses human nature in society as its essential vehicle for reconciling all aspects of reality back into itself. *Geist* is then a philosophical, evolutionist, panentheist version of the God-idea. The ultimate truth about the absolute is that it is *Geist* and that *Geist* becomes fully real when it and human nature become one, a condition attained with the realisation of a fully free human society on earth in which *Geist*'s, and therefore humanity's, self-knowledge is complete. Whether this quasi-theistic understanding of *Geist* is fully intelligible can be doubted, but on any reading of Hegel his views have the clear consequence that up to the arrival of mature Christianity, the gods of religion are to a degree illusory. Even Christianity, which preaches the truth that the absolute descends into a person to become one with human nature, presents the truth about *Geist* in a partly misleading form. Yet somehow, the gods of the faiths in history are cloaked in an aura of reality which is the necessary outcome of the processes of self-consciousness. How this comes about is through the unavoidable use by self-consciousness of the processes of alienation and objectification.

One of the great themes of Hegel's work, as shown for example in *The Phenomenology of Spirit*, is that self-knowledge is an achievement attained only after a process of development. We do not have any magic inner eye which reveals to us a true self-understanding. We come to a knowledge of what we are as human beings through an expressive process. By means of this we, as members of a society, embody our ideas, aspirations and ideals in a world of external objects.

> The very essence of spirit is activity; it realizes its potentiality – makes itself its own deed, its own work and thus becomes an object to itself; contemplates itself as an objective existence. Thus it is with the spirit of a people: it is a spirit having strictly defined characteristics, which erects itself into an objective world, that exists and persists in a particular religious form of worship, customs, constitution and political laws, in the whole complex of its institutions, in the events that make up its history.
>
> (Hegel, 1956: 73–4)

Having objectified their consciousness through these forms of expressive activity, human beings can then take items in consciousness as objects for reflection and knowledge; only after expression in external form can they be known in their full reality. Thus at the heart of Hegel's account of self-consciousness is a paradox: human wholeness is achieved only through alienation. We alienate aspects of ourselves to the extent that we enthrone these aspects in a humanly created world around us. But through that process we come to a true knowledge of ourselves which enables us to re-absorb these aspects of our nature.

This process is exhibited in the progress of human religion. Thus in the second great phase of human religious development – the religion of spiritual individuality – the conception of the gods held by humankind mirrors that the knowledge of *Geist* then attained. The religion of ancient Greece, which is one manifestation of the religion of spiritual individuality, portrays the gods as a society of limited, localised individuals, still subject to an overarching, impersonal fate. This shows that *Geist* in human society at that epoch had risen to an awareness that it was possessed of a freedom which made it distinct from anything merely natural, but had not yet grasped the great truths about the unbounded nature of *Geist* that Hegel proclaims to be the end of self-knowledge. But the objectification of this mode of self-consciousness gives humankind a greater awareness of these partial truths about the nature of *Geist* which is vital in its onward progress. *Geist* in humankind will absorb and transcend these partial truths in the journey toward more adequate expressions of itself: thus one conception of the gods will give way to another. The final stage to be reached is mature Christianity, which as absolute religion presents in the pictorial, imaginative form of its mythic system the great truths about the indivisibility of *Geist*, the world and humankind declared in conceptual form by Hegel. When *Geist* has become absolute it will no longer need to alienate itself to know itself.

We have suggested that any radical, philosophical theory of religion must face up to a great challenge: how to make plausible and free of paradox the idea that human beings in large measure create their gods yet worship them in good faith as external realities. Our very brief excursis into Hegel indicates one likely way of measuring up to this challenge: (a) the 'invention' of the gods is related to the basic structures of self-consciousness; (b) it is said to be essential if important human goals are to be realised; (c) it is asserted to be part of the general processes of the human mind in society and in no way an aberration or departure from the normal operation of the intellect. Crucial in the Hegelian account is the active role given to the intellect as the, at least partial, creator of the world which it knows. This fundamental thought underlies these three points. Together with his quasi-theism, it places Hegel firmly in the idealist tradition in philosophy. The presence of this crucial assumption must soften the contrast, which otherwise creates the challenge we describe, between the gods as somehow invented, on the one hand, and ordinary, proper objects of knowledge which are genuinely real, on the other.

FEUERBACH ON RELIGION

The ambiguities in Hegel's account of *Geist* and his quasi theism
allowed him to be seen as an apologist for Christianity as well
as a critic of religion in general. It was left to the more left-wing
among his followers to produce an unequivocally radical theory
of religion. One such was Ludwig Feuerbach (1804–72). This
task he largely completed in *The Essence of Christianity* (Feuerbach,
1957). We shall also make reference to: *Lectures on the Essence of
Religion* (Feuerbach, 1967) and *The Principles of the Philosophy
of the Future* (Feuerbach, 1966).

   The general pattern of Feuerbach's approach in *The Essence of
Christianity* is to say that religious beliefs are plainly false and that
there are no good reasons for holding them. It seems clear that
religious beliefs are not actually held because of an awareness of
reasons. This creates our familiar demand for an explanation in
terms of something other than reasons to account for why people
hold them. Why don't people see that they are plainly false? This
question gains increased force in Feuerbach because he does not
want to dismiss religion as a passing, local aberration. He admits
that it is one of the characteristic marks of the human species. It
cannot then be simply an illusion. Feuerbach's explanation accordingly has two parts to it. One is the finding of something true in
religion. There must be a kernel of truth in religion which he can
bring out. Another element is an account of how this true element
gets overlain with falsity. What is true in religion is very different
from what believers and theologians say they believe, hence an
explanation is needed as to how they come to misperceive and
misdescribe this truth. Religion exists as the misperception of certain
truths. Feuerbach's explanation has to offer an interpretation of religion to reveal these truths and the description of a mechanism to
account for how these truths are misperceived and misrepresented.
His interpretation of religion does not just dismiss religion as an
opaque mass of error: it provides (for Christianity in particular) a
detailed correlation between theological claims and atheistic glosses
on those claims. His interpretation and mechanism both concern the
role of religion as containing an image of humanity and as a means
of presenting that image in misleading form.

   Feuerbach appears to be aware of the paradox humanistic explanations of religion can generate, so avoids the simplistic claim that
religion is an illusion. He is coy on occasions about admitting to the

charge of atheism (see Feuerbach, 1967: 282). His position is that affirmations of the reality of the gods sometimes do express illusions, but they can also express truths. In trying to pin down what is truthful and what is illusory in religion he sometimes uses the distinction between 'religion' and 'theology' (1957: xxxvi–xxxvii). The distinction between religion and theology parallels that made later between religion's latent nature and its conscious nature (1957: 247). Theology is humanity's conscious reflection on the meaning of religion. It is the explicit doctrines of religion (theology) that contain illusion that creates the error Feuerbach diagnoses. But religion in essence is true.

Feuerbach is by no means always faithful to the religion/theology distinction and it would be wrong to suppose that his radical theory debunks theology to leave religion intact. It is extremely doubtful whether any institution having the characteristic dimensions and differentiate of human religion could survive Feuerbach's theory. It would have no practical dimension other than the pursuit of human good. No characteristic sociological and experiential dimensions and no real object of worship or devotion. These points bear on his definition of religion, as we shall see below.

A brief account of Feuerbach's review of the error in religion must begin with his belief that religion is the form of humanity's reflection on its own nature. Religion generates illusion when this nature is thought of as something distinct from humanity and is contemplated and worshipped as a separate, other-worldly entity. In essence religion presents a series of truths about human nature. In its manifest form as theology it presents these truths as accounts of the nature of a divine being distinct from the world:

> It is supposed that we have here unfolded to us the life of a Being distinct from us, while nevertheless it is only our own nature which is unfolded, though at the same time again shut up from us by the fact that this nature is represented as inherent in another being.
>
> (1957: 89)

So each theological claim, such as 'God suffers' (1957: 60, 62) presents a truth about humanity (here, the role of suffering in the realisation of virtue and compassion) in the form of claim about a non-human subject. If we take away the dummy-subject 'God' and substitute the true subject 'suffering', we get a true claim about the importance of that subject in the realisation of human aspirations. 'God' then functions as a predicate term, indicating the crucial centrality of the true subject (the human attribute) in human development.

Sometimes Feuerbach's basic thought about religion is summarised in the slogan 'theology is anthropology'. As a distinct statement this does not occur in *The Essence of Christianity*, the closest approximation being 'The secret of theology is anthropology' (1957: 270). Feuerbach's actual words fit in better with the theology/religion distinction. Behind theology lies religion, which in essence is anthropology, a form of human self-reflection and consciousness. Religion is formally defined as having its basis in 'the essential difference between man and the brute'. Human beings have consciousness, and particularly consciousness of their own natures as members of a species. The human being's nature can be an object to itself, an object of reflection; not so for the animal (1957: 1). Religion then in essence is the form that humankind's reflection on its own nature takes. It embodies our conceptions of what facets of human nature we take to be important and of what is of value to human living. So it is in essence a form of human self-consciousness and human self-affirmation. As such it is true and valuable.

We must note that Feuerbach's thought here involves a particularly strong form of the distinction between the surface and the essential meaning of 'religion'. As we shall see below it is reasonable to see Feuerbach's account of the surface meaning of religion as agreeing with Hume's description of the propensity to believe that 'there is invisible intelligent power in the world' (Hume, 1967: 37); that is, it is the disposition to accept non-human, non-material but conscious agents as responsible for the world and its workings. But it appears to be only in certain circumstances that religion's essence will manifest this surface characteristic. It will not do so after philosophy has successfully exposed the illusion-bearing character of this surface. Thereafter religion will exist in essence, yet, as indicated above, will display hardly any of its typical features as a human institution. Here we see how the option of producing an essentialist or theoretical definition of religion may lead to a radical, stipulative re-definition of it.

Feuerbach's belief that religion is in essence a form of human consciousness and affirmation entails, as we have seen, that statements about God are indirectly statements about humanity's species nature. One obvious objection to this interpretation is that since God is an infinite subject and humanity only a finite one, statements about the former cannot be translated into statements about the latter. Feuerbach's reply is that, while individual people are limited and finite, the nature of the species is inexhaustible and infinite. He substitutes a contrast between limited individual and unlimited species for that between finite human and infinite God. Our talk about the infinite God is a way of expressing the 'mystery of human nature as infinitely, varied, infinitely modifiable' (1957: 23). Our conception of the divine being is reached precisely by purifying, and freeing from the limits of individual human beings, our conception of human nature (1957: 14). Thereby we show our knowledge that the history of mankind is the history of its conquest of limitations and commit ourselves to a future in which the limits of the species are shown to be unreal (1957: 152–3). This quasi-Platonic and rosy, optimistic vision of human nature was to attract later marxist criticism for introducing religious faith in by the back door (see pp. 128–9 below).

Feuerbach offers as evidence for his thesis of the identity of God and the human essence the Incarnation doctrine in Christianity. Like Hegel and other thinkers of the period, he appears in *The Essence of Christianity* to be committed to an evolutionary view of religion which sees Christianity as its highest manifestation. In Christianity, therefore, we should see a growing awareness of religion's latent nature. Christianity, in its teaching that God became man in Christ, asserts the identity of the human and divine natures and all but betrays out loud the essential nature of religion (see 1957: 50–7).

Now that the heart of Feuerbach's radical theory has been expounded we can turn to the question of why he was so confident that there is error in the theological account of religion. This is down to three reasons: empiricism, materialism and the alleged contradictions of theology.

According to the theological account of religion the word 'God' in a statement such as 'God is omnipotent' refers to a transcendent entity, radically different from human beings. Feuerbach's empiricism tells him that we could not know anything about such a being: the limits of our thought and knowledge are set by the limits of sense experience. He affirms (1957: 200) that we can make no sense of an existent that we cannot potentially perceive. As with the later logical positivists Feuerbach affirms that claims which are beyond possible verification by sense experience are not only unknowable but senseless. To this kind of point Feuerbach adds the thought that religion itself demands the truth of a certain kind of empiricism. It needs definite conceptions, certain knowledge of its object if it is to exist. It is the end of religion, because of the abandonment of any definite object of worship and devotion, if we give up the claim that we can know what God is like. The God of religion does not merely have to exist, he has to exist in a way which makes a difference to human experience, so that he can function as the centre of a human institution. But no transcendent God can do this (1957: 14–15, 17). This thought – that mystery and agnosticism is the end of religion – is a familiar one in the philosophy of religion. Feuerbach's empiricism leads him to say that for us human experience and human life is the measure of what is real. Empiricism entails anthropocentrism. What is radically unlike the human and unconnected with human life can have no reality for us. So belief in the transcendent God of theology must be an illusion (1957: 22).

Feuerbach's materialism is connected with his attack upon idealism and will be more fully explored when we consider his relationship to idealist thought below. At bottom, Feuerbach asks us to reflect on and generalise from our experience of the relationship between the material and the ideal/mental. In our experience we find that ideas only exist because there are flesh and blood creatures to bring them into existence. They only have effects in the real world because embodied beings act upon them. The theological interpretation of religion would have us believe that something non-material, ideal (that is God-as-spirit) is the true reality on which all other real things depend. This contradicts the only warranted generalisation we can make about the relation between the material and the spiritual. Making it, we must come to the conclusion that material human beings are the creators of the spiritual God, not the other way round (1957: 100–10).

Feuerbach is confident that the theological interpretation he attacks is an illusion because he thinks it falls into numerous contradictions. These contradictions are not only intellectual but also emotional and practical. Abstracting from Feuerbach's extensive discussions of the contradictory nature of theology in *The Essence of Christianity*, we may note that his attention fastens both on the traditional paradoxes or mysteries of Christianity (such as the Trinity doctrine, in 1957: 235) and on alleged contradictions he finds unguessed even by theologians. Of the latter kind we instance his discussion of the apparent contradiction in the doctrine of creation, which tells us both that the world is real, not part of God (because material while God is spirit) and that it is absolutely dependent on God for its very existence from moment to moment (1957: 297–8).

Feuerbach's case for the illusory character of the manifest content of religion is crucial. He is one of the few authors of radical theories of religion who see the importance of demonstrating *from the very nature of religious belief* that an unreflective, participant-based interpretation of religion cannot be taken seriously (see Chapter 3 above). However, his attempt to do this illustrates the weakness of such wholesale verdicts on religion. For each item in Feuerbach's critique is philosophically controversial and it is by no means clear that a reasonable interpretation of his demands cannot be met by much less radical adaptions of religious belief than he himself favours. On empiricism: many authors throughout the history of Christian theology have agreed that rational belief and meaning in theological discourse demands that such discourse be anchored at some points in human experience. But it does not follow at all that what is anchored in human experience can only speak of realities that are to be found in human experience, merely that experience provides the basis of reasonable inferences to those realities. Feuerbach's empiricism only yields his conclusion if interpreted as the strong demand that statements about transcendent realities be *reducible to* (not merely *anchored in*) statements about human experience. This strong demand is, however, unacceptable on other grounds: if followed consistently it creates havoc for natural science and produces the conclusion that much of its theories are no more than myths useful in the ordering of our knowledge of observed matters of fact. This has been the Achilles' heel of empiricist critiques of religion this century: if the demand for anchorage is strong enough to rule out theological discourse it is strong enough to rule out much else as well.

Similar things may be said about Feuerbach's other challenges. An extreme materialism will yield the swift conclusion that the theological interpretation of religion can contain no truth, but such an extreme position is not obviously true. More modest forms of materialism do prompt intellectual questions about how a material world can be created by a spiritual God, but it is not obvious that theology cannot be developed to take account of these doubts. There are problems surrounding the coherence of theistic belief (and Feuerbach has acute things to say about many of these) but it is not obvious that they cannot be overcome and force us to conclude that religion is downright self-contradictory, rather than merely paradoxical to a degree. Feuerbach has assembled powerful weapons for a philosophical critique of aspects of theological discourse. But recall (from Chapter 3) that he needs to show more than that it is reasonable to refuse assent to religion from the standpoint of this or that philosophy. He must show that living religion is an illusion in its manifest meaning – so that its manifest meaning cannot be taken seriously and as a living institution it cannot be given an internal explanation. He must not simply show that he can find no credible route into it. He must show that it is so obviously wrong-headed in its theological interpretation that the typical participant in it cannot be credited with entering it rationally.

If religion really is about humanity how does humanity come to think it is about a being distinct from itself? Feuerbach gives an answer to this question by outlining the unconscious, non-rational processes by which we project our own nature onto reality and then think of it as a separate existent. To understand how and why projection takes place we need to see its twofold nature as a union of imagination and desire. Feuerbach has numerous passages where he comments on the power of the human imagination. Indeed, he argues that merely to make our species nature an object of thought we have to treat it as if it were an object. So by an involuntary reflex we initially think of our nature as separate from ourselves.

> Man, by means of the imagination, involuntarily contemplates his inner nature; he represents it as out of himself. The nature of man . . . thus working on him through the irresistible power of the imagination . . . is God.
>
> (Feuerbach, 1957: 208)

But why should the imagination prove irresistible here? There appears to be a gap between the periodic treating of human nature as if it were an object for the purposes of reflection and the permanent view of God as an external object to be worshipped. Feuerbach's account, therefore, has to lean heavily on the notion that human feelings demand that our nature be enthroned as a deity to rule over us: 'Religion is the mind's light, the rays of which are broken by the medium of the imagination and the feelings, so as to make the same being [humanity] appear as a double one [humanity and God]' (Feuerbach, 1957: 225). It is our inability to resist the pull of our desires that makes us give free rein to the imagination in enthroning human nature as the ruler of the universe. The thought of something analogous to human nature as responsible for the universe's existence and development proves too flattering to human feelings to be resisted. Many passages in *The Essence of Christianity* celebrate this union of desire and imagination. Notable is the statement in Chapter 18 that the end of religion is the 'welfare, the salvation, the ultimate felicity of man' (1957: 105).

It is because of the link between imagination and desire in the mechanisms of projection that Feuerbach is able to call religion 'the dream of the human mind' (1957: xxxix). This comment relies on the fact that dreams are often imaginary wish-fulfilments (that is they are mental operations where desire and imagination hold complete sway). In dreams our wishes can be granted omnipotence. They gain a satisfaction though nothing material is done to effect that, since in dreams thought can create its own objects. All this is possible only because the satisfaction exists only in a world of the imagination. One who lives a life of dreaming has forgotten to distinguish the subjective from the objective.

> Religion is a dream, in which our own conceptions and emotions appear to us as separate existences . . . The religious mind does not distinguish between subjective and objective.
>
> (1957: 204)

It is in this spirit that Feuerbach describes the fundamental dogmas of Christianity as 'realised wishes of the heart' (1957: 140).

Why should Feuerbach wish to disturb those caught up in the illusions of religion/theology? The answer must be that we have here a harmful illusion. It is generally wrong to let people live in a world of make-believe. Those who live in dreams will not actually do anything to improve real life. A fuller answer to the question posed is that religion is a form of human alienation, in that it separates humanity from its own nature. It leads to a false view of that nature, leaving us unhappy with it. To destroy the illusory aspects of religion is to return humanity to itself, to unite humankind once more with its own nature. Religion as alienation has a twofold movement: it represents human nature as if it inheres in a being beyond the world and then judges humanity as impoverished in the light of this ideal representation of itself. So it is vital that the misleading representation of humanity in theology is replaced by the true representation given by a reformed philosophy of human nature. Thus will the dreaming element of religion be left behind and humankind will realise the truth that the fulfilment of its nature can only be accomplished if worked for in the real world. By this means also will the knowledge of our nature concealed in the misleading forms of theology be returned to us.

The Essence of Christianity says very little about non-Christian religions. It is clear despite this that Feuerbach does think that religion has an essence: religious phenomena have an essential unity, being everywhere the expression of the same powers and propensities of the human mind. So he speaks of the 'common nature of all religions' and of the 'necessary and eternal laws which constitute the essence of all religion' (1957: 13). It is plain too that he takes Christianity to be typical of a class of religions. It serves as the model of the spiritual, ethical monotheism. While this might suggest generalisation of his account to fit Judaism and Islam, he says little about polytheistic or tribal religions.

For more extended comment on non-monotheistic forms of faith we must study a later work: *Lectures on the Essence of Religion* (originally published in 1848). Here Feuerbach appears to divide religions into two types: moral/spiritual and natural. The latter have nature as their focus. They are typically polytheistic, though not invariably so – it is possible to have a single god who is the personification of the forces of nature. His explanation of the first type of religion is essentially unchanged. It is the result of the deification of the human personality in its moral and spiritual aspects. This deification is the result of the work of the imagination fuelled by feelings and desires. At first sight the second type appears to reflect, not the deification of the human personality, but of the forces of nature, either as separate gods or as the attributes of one god. So he begins his exposition by saying that theology is either anthropology or 'physiology' (that is natural philosophy; Feuerbach, 1967: 20). But the continuation shows the essential theory of *The Essence of Christianity* being carried out.

When Feuerbach comes to the question 'Why does humankind personify the forces of nature and why does it select the ones it does?' his answer makes reference to human nature once more. We personify as gods those forces which human feelings select as important. So, crudely, a tribe will make a god out of water (venerate a water-spirit) because of the importance of water in the satisfaction of human needs and the support of human life. Such deification secures *in the imagination* the continued gratification of human needs. So all religion is a projection of the human essence, albeit some is so only indirectly. Natural forces and objects are deified only in so far as they relate to human concerns. And what is thus deified is as much the human need that gave rise to the concern with nature as the natural object which is the object of that concern. Religion, he affirms, is the art of life, giving expression to the forces and drives which govern the life of humanity. The underlying principle of all religions is that humanity unconsciously takes its life to be divine and consciously, therefore, makes a god out of that which is the origin and support of that life (1967: 53). Human nature remains the criterion of divinity (1967: 54).

Feuerbach rounds off this picture by describing the way in which human beings are connected to the world around them by all manner of needs, desires and feelings. Feelings of this kind make human beings dependent on the world around them, so, in conscious echoing of Schleiermacher, Feuerbach contends that human life is characterised by a 'feeling of dependency' (1967: 31). This is not the name of a specific mode of feeling but is a generic title for many distinct feelings of need and desire that link us to things outside us. The first object of such feelings is the natural world, so the first objects of religion are aspects of nature (1967: 25). But among the chief, and enduring, forms of the feeling of dependency is the fear of death and the sense of human finiteness (1967: 33), and more sophisticated conceptions of deity are required to cope with these manifestations of dependency. As the *Lectures* develop Feuerbach brings his account of the sense of dependency to a head by describing the basis of human life as resting on egoism. What characterises human life is the 'striving for happiness' (1967: 198). Religion is the result of the clash between this basic egoistic striving and a world which is at best indifferent, at worst hostile, to this striving. The striving for happiness marks out the world as something separate from the basic thrust of human nature and yet as something on which we are inextricably and continually dependent. It reveals the gulf between what is essential to the ego (namely its desires) and what surrounds the ego, while at the same time insisting that something must be done to bridge this gulf. Religion arises out of this fundamental gulf between ego and non-ego and the one thing which can bridge it: the imagination. The gods are projections of the human imagination: 'A god . . . is merely the hypostatised and objectified essence of the human imagination' (1967: 136). Through the imagination the gulf can be overcome by objectifying a facet or facets of the striving for happiness as a divine being. Thus, in the imagination, that aspect of the striving for happiness is granted control over the world. What was non-ego becomes a reflection of the ego. Feuerbach sums up the process in these words: 'a god is nothing other than man's striving for happiness fulfilled in the imagination' (1967: 230).

The notions of the feeling of dependency, the striving for happiness and the centrality of the gulf between self and reality introduce fresh nuances into Feuerbach's theory of religion. There remain fundamental continuities with the earlier theory of *The Essence of Christianity*. The gods are still projections of human nature. Projection still works through the operation of the imagination fuelled by desire. The later theory obviously builds on the appeal to wish-fulfilment and dreaming prominent in the earlier. Significant differences appear with the downplaying of the theme of self-consciousness in the *Lectures on the Essence of Religion*. In the earlier work it is asserted to be essential to consider human nature as an object of reflection if it is to be known at all, and thus to some extent as a separate entity. As one recent commentator notes, the earlier theory still uses to a degree the Hegelian idea that we must objectify and therefore alienate our nature if we are to know it (Harvey, 1985: 316). This is how in the earlier account religion can be presented as inescapable, and as the bearer of knowledge. In the later theory it appears more as a passing phase of human weakness which we may be expected to grow out of. His account of religion and his exhortations to be rid of its baleful influences are close to pre-Hegelian accounts of it as weak superstition than to a vision of it as the inevitable outcome of the processes of self-consciousness (compare Harvey, 1985: 316). He announces his intentions in *The Lectures on the Essence of Religion* as being to oppose the oppressive results of religion, which may be removed once we see that in religion we are worshipping creatures of our own imagination. Once we have a clear vision of the origin of the gods we may in future take the human essence to the determining ground of our political and ethical life (Feuerbach, 1967: 22–3). He denies the fantastic structures of theology so as

> to transform theologians into anthropologists, lovers of God into lovers of man, candidates for the next world into citizens of this world, religious and political flunkeys of heavenly monarchs and lords into self-reliant citizens of the earth.
>
> (1967: 23)

Criticism of Feuerbach's theory of religion must begin with the points made above concerning how far he has demonstrated that religion's manifest meaning cannot be taken seriously. Feuerbach certainly realises that if an account of religion is to be based on the assumption of methodological atheism or scepticism some grounds must be offered for that assumption. We doubt if those grounds are conclusive, for the reasons outlined. Those who follow Feuerbach in supposing that explaining religion as a human phenomenon entails adopting a standpoint of methodological atheism generally welcome him as a pioneer of this approach who nonetheless failed to turn it into an adequate, detailed theory (compare Kamenka, 1970: 60–3). From within this perspective he offers valuable elements of a general programme: an alleged exposé of the theological interpretation of religion, and a pointer to general sources from which the god-idea is moulded (imagination, desire, human nature). His deficiencies are then seen to lie in lack of detail in the matching up of elements of religious belief and behaviour to the cultural and historical life of mankind. The explanation is then overly general and abstract, in particular it abstracts human nature from details of historical and cultural context. This in part is the major criticism of Feuerbach from Marx and Engels (to be outlined in Chapter 6).

Our, more radical, questioning of Feuerbach's account not only relates to his case for methodological atheism, but to the basis of his account of projection. It strikes us that the very empiricism which plays such a large part in that case seriously disables his account of projection in his positive theory of religion. This point can best be drawn out after a brief account of his relationship to idealism.

Many commentators note that Feuerbach's critique of religion is intimately bound up with a 'new philosophy' that will reverse the movement of idealistic metaphysics characteristic of German philosophy in the early nineteenth century (Wartofsky, 1977: 200). Criticism of religion and idealism are interlinked: exposure of the illusions of either one leads inevitably to criticism of the other. What is characteristic of any idealist system of thought for Feuerbach is the inclination to make the object of human knowledge – reality – dependent for its existence and/or character on the mind that thinks it. This is the essential premise of post-Kantian German idealism, which followed in varying ways Kant's thought that reality-as-known consists of appearances, which are at least in part constituted as objects by a contribution made to their character and reality from the resources of human cognition. This premise is also concealed in religion, which has it that what is real depends for its existence on the will of a spiritual being or beings. Religion is but a form of idealist thought: 'In theology things are not thought and willed because they exist; they exist because they are thought and willed (Feuerbach, 1967: 117). Hegelianism is the final stage of idealist philosophy, because, in a manner said to be self-contradictory, it tries to save the idealist premise while half acknowledging the truth that defeats idealism – namely that material existence is the ground of ideal representation (see Feuerbach, 1966: 31–4). It teaches that for the non-material ground of the world (that is, *Geist*) to know itself fully, it must alienate itself by producing a world separate from itself in which its own being can be contemplated. It is only through a process of interaction with this alienated being in creation that *Geist* is eventually able to reach fulfilment and re-absorb all reality back into itself. Hegel, on Feuerbach's reading, advances a step away from pure idealism, by making a material creation necessary for the ideal ground of being to exist and develop. Hegel thus wishes to incorporate a materialist premise into his idealism and the result is contradiction: 'the negation of theology from the viewpoint of theology or the negation of theology that itself is again theology' (Feuerbach, 1966: 31). It is left to Feuerbach to reveal the way out of the resulting 'mishmash of belief and unbelief, theism and atheism' (Feuerbach, 1967: 168) by removing the idealist premise. Hegelianism and idealism, and the religious theory of creation, are then set in reverse: material humankind to know itself must alienate part of its being in the form of theistic conceptions. Through interaction with these alienated forms it comes to know itself fully and then re-absorbs its creation (the gods) back into its own nature.

As revealed in *Principles of the Philosophy of the Future* the truth we must oppose to idealism is that of empiricism. What are real are the objects of the senses:

> Truth, reality and sensation are identical. Only a sensuous being is a true and real being. Only through the senses, and not through thought itself, is an object given in a true sense. The object that is given in thought or is identical with thought is only idea.
>
> (1966: 51)

This gives us a criterion of reality: what can be present to the senses is real. In turn this fuels the critique of religion and the search for an object of perception (human feelings, desires and the like) which can stand as real things for ideas of the gods to refer to. But it also makes the human subject not a creator of its objects of knowledge, but a passive percipient of those objects. It is designed to banish once and for all the idealist tendency to make us part or whole creators of the objects of knowledge. However, the net result of this empiricism must be to stress the differences between the ordinary objects of knowledge and the contents of religious consciousness. At the beginning of the chapter we noted how the move toward projectionist accounts of religion could get over the paradoxes of humanism by locating the human origin of ideas of the sacred in processes integral to the general exercise of self-consciousness. But as Feuerbach's account develops the passivity of the subject in relation to non-illusory objects of consciousness is matched by the stress placed upon imagination and the desires in relation to the false objects of consciousness revealed in religion. Where Feuerbach's account of religion promises depth it tends in actuality to reveal only shallowness in the idea that religion is wish-fulfilment and the dream of the human mind. Feuerbach leaves too much room for his readers to associate the origin of religion with fear and intellectual laziness: for only those who are fearful and lazy will be content to give up distinguishing dreams from reality and to live in a dream world. Consider what is said about the origin of religion in the manner in which the striving for happiness is met by the gulf between self and not-self. This looks like a fundamental problem but at the end of the day it seems to be only a temporary truth that this must be overcome by the resources that produce the idea of gods. That is, it appears to be weakness and ignorant lack of confidence in human powers that makes human beings bridge this gulf with imaginative and desire-driven perceptions of gods. There is a remedy for this disease, we read Feuerbach's programmatic statements in the *Lectures on the Essence of Religion* as telling us: namely hard work and self-confident devotion to the triumph of human nature over a recalcitrant world.

We suggest that Feuerbach has missed an opportunity in his account of the feeling of dependency. This is in large part due to his preoccupation with religion as wish-fulfilment.

Let us grant for the sake of argument that Feuerbach is correct in the *Lectures on the Essence of Religion* in asserting that the felt gulf between the human self revealed in the striving for happiness is a powerful force over human conceptions. According to Feuerbach what religion does in responding to that force is offer an imaginary fulfilment of the desires that create the gulf between self and reality. Its way of coping with the gulf between ego and non-ego can always be contrasted with an obviously more appropriate way of doing the same job, namely working in and upon the real world so that it reflects the human will and gives real satisfaction to human desires. Looked at in this light, religion appears to be an aberration, and a temporary one at that.

The truth that there can be quite other ways in which our feeling of dependency is met in religion is indicated in Feuerbach's own statement that the fear of death, and the general sense of our own finiteness, are among the most important of the feelings that constitute dependency (Feuerbach, 1967: 33). Whatever religion offers by way of coping with the threat to the self's conception of meaning provided by these particular feelings cannot be *continuous* with ordinary efforts to make the world bend to our will. For such facts which threaten the ego cannot be sensibly tackled by human projects of action in the real world. Indeed, all human projects will be governed and limited by such facets of our finiteness. So these facets can never be overcome.

At this point we are driven to see the merits in the functionalist interpretation of religion in Yinger's *The Scientific Study of Religion* (1979: 5–16, and see Chapter 1 above). Yinger's distinction between ultimate and utilitarian problems/concerns now comes into play. The latter are problems which we have some hope of overcoming in action (either individual or cooperative). In so far as these problems throw up the gulf between ego and non-ego, then that gulf is not absolute or finally threatening to us. Ultimate concerns are those such as: the fact of death, the fact that all human projects fail in some measure, the fact that all cooperative arrangements give way to disagreement and hostility to some degree. These and other facts about our finitude cannot be overcome by even the most clear-sighted and whole-hearted human endeavours, because they will accompany and condition such endeavours. All endeavours will be limited by them. Here we see an ultimate gap between self and not-self, the ineradicable way in which the ego, once out of the womb, is in an environment which is separate, divorced and, to some extent, hostile to it. As we noted in Chapter 1, Yinger's account stresses the threat to life's meaning posed by ultimate concerns and the manner in which religion copes with the emotional paralysis which these concerns might occasion. It does so by providing symbols which putatively refer to absolute or transcendent values. In the light of these postulated values the facts of finitude are relativised and their emotionally threatening and paralysing aspects removed. It is thus that religion exists as a way of overcoming the gulf between self and not-self.

To illustrate this process consider in very broad outline the manner in which Buddhist symbolic structures cope with threats to the self. As is well known the cardinal tenet of many forms of Buddhism is that all life is suffering and that suffering is occasioned by desire. Desire convinces us of the reality and importance of the self, on the one hand, and of the gulf between that self and its fulfilment in the external world, on the other. It is not part of this system to give us a rosier view of the self's capacity to satisfy its many needs. On the contrary, it attempts to convince those happy with their conventional lot that the satisfactions they enjoy are illusory. It positively heightens our sense of the gulf between ego and non-ego, yet at the same time deals with the threat such an awareness might pose through teaching us to re-value the ego and its concerns. The path of liberation through *nibbana* is not continuous with the normal self's goals, but is radically tangential to it. Seeking the path is synonymous with regarding the normal self as illusory and its fixation with desire as false and misleading. Far from coping with the ego's anxieties generated by the striving for happiness by fulfilling the ego's wishes in the imagination, it offers a radical transformation of our sense of the value of the ego and its strivings.

That the idea of wish-fulfilment in Feuerbach is a fundamentally wrong turn has also been cogently argued by D.Z. Phillips (1976: 87). He illustrates the theme of the re-evaluation of desire in religion through the example of prayer in Christianity. If a believer confesses his desires before God, this may be with the purpose of seeing their true status in the light of the divine providence. That in turn involves seeing why they are unimportant, or need modifying or replacing by more religiously appropriate desires. Such confession of desire in prayer *is* a way of coping with the problem that the pursuit of desire satisfaction creates for the ego. But the 'solution' consists in bringing the ego's desires before a standard of what is truly worthwhile. This standard must then be thought of as something independent of and transcending human wishes.

We have reached the point where we can follow and learn from Feuerbach's opening out of a deep source for human religion in the ultimate gulf between the human ego and its setting in reality. But his account, via the wish fulfilment idea, of how religion copes with that gulf appears to be highly questionable. The crucial issue which readers of Feuerbach must resolve concerns his treatment of the sacred or transcendent in relation to his portrayal of the anthropocentric basis of thought. Feuerbach's epistemology in *The Essence of Christianity* moves from the unexceptionable premise that meaningful notions must have some anchoring in and relevance to human experience to the conclusion that human experience is the sum and measure of reality. This in turn demands the wish-fulfilment interpretation of the values religion brings to bear on the human feeling of dependency. It tells us positively that human wishes must be the criterion of what is really valuable, and negatively that we could make no sense of symbols of value independent of human wishes. But our discussion in this chapter has indicated the weakness of this epistemology and the dubious nature of its consequences. Yinger's symbols of absolute value are anchored in human experience. They have a real role to play in the ordering of our emotional and valuational experience. To play that role, however, they have to be assumed by the social actor to refer to values which are independent of human desires. The human, social role of sacred symbols actually demands that they be perceived to have a transcendent reference.

Yinger's interpretation of religion in the opening pages of *The Scientific Study of Religion* suggests one way in which we might part company with Feuerbach's anthropocentric reinterpretation of religion. We see a distinction in reflection on Yinger between two jobs a theory of religion might do: offering an account of the socially based human needs that give rise to religion (which Yinger does) and reinterpreting religious symbols so that they refer to realities in human, social experience (which Yinger does not do, but Feuerbach does). This distinction must be born in mind when considering other theorists of religion.

Note that Yinger's account is compatible with saying that religious symbols are false and do not succeed in referring to anything real. It is compatible with an external explanation of the basis of religious symbols. His core account describes the facts of human finitude, the emotional needs these create, and the ways these needs give rise to religious symbols which provide a residual way of dealing with the emotional needs. Now if 'give rise to' here means 'sufficiently, causally explains', then religious symbols have a sufficient explanation in factors independent of reason and any correspondence between them and reality would be the merest accident and of no importance in their explanation. A yet more radical departure from Feuerbach would question whether Yinger's functionalist apparatus sufficiently explains allegiance to putative transcendent values. Yinger may be taken as referring to non-rational factors which *predispose* religious folk to believe in the sacred, but cognitive factors must be mentioned in any complete explanation. It is merely that it is not the province of the sociologist or social psychologist to explore these cognitive factors.

The 'cognitive factors' that might be involved in any full explanation of the awareness of putative transcendent values would only be revealed through the study of religio-ethical systems such as Christianity and Buddhism. To bring them out would be to lay bare the traditions of thought in such systems which have persuaded men and women of the view that human experience of finitude can only be made sense of if transcendent values are postulated. It is Feuerbach's implicit claim that such exploration would reveal no rational structure at all (unless it be a rational structure of reasoning about Feuerbach's favoured values in transmuted guise). But as we have seen it is not obvious that if we take the transcendent interpretation of religious symbols seriously we will be left with religion as a mass of contradictions and unfounded metaphysical speculations.

Feuerbach's account of religion throws up its own paradox. It points to an area of human concern in the feeling of dependency which can be seen to give rise to an experiential basis for belief in realities which transcend the human (see Byrne, 1985).

6

Socio-economic Theories of Religion

MARX AND PHILOSOPHICAL MATERIALISM

The most widely known and most controversial of socio-economic theories of religion is that provided by Marx and Engels, which will often be referred to here simply as the marxist account of religion, an account which, as will be seen, explains religion largely in terms of alienation and ideology. While the focus of this chapter is on this explanation of religion there will, none the less, be some discussion of Max Weber's interpretation of religion which comes much closer to the marxist one than is sometimes realised.

In designating the marxist theory of religion socio-economic it is not the intention to suggest that it is purely that and nothing else for this theory clearly contains a number of philosophical themes which underlay Marx's sociological and economic analysis of society. It was, of course, with society rather than religion – which in any case, they argued, had no independent existence of its own – that Marx and Engels were mainly concerned, and more precisely with an analysis and interpretation of what they saw as the contradictory nature of capitalist society. It was only as part of this analysis and interpretation that they considered religion and even then not in any systematic and coherent fashion. It is primarily for this reason, therefore, that the materialist interpretation of religion provided by Marx and Engels has to be considered within this wider socio-economic context.

As is well known, theirs was not the first attempt to account for religion in materialist terms and a brief outline of the impact of Enlightenment materialism on the thinking of Marx and Engels will serve as a useful background to our discussion of the marxist theory of religion showing how, among other things, it both feeds off and seeks to reinterpret in the light of its own understanding of matter this materialist perspective.

Although they were eventually to be highly critical of its limitations both Marx and Engels were well aware of the debt that they
owed to Enlightenment materialism, indeed to the precursors of this
movement – and to no one more so than Francis Bacon (1561–1626)
who according to Marx was 'materialism's first creator' in that he
pointed out that the senses were 'infallible and the source of all
knowledge' (Padover, 1979: 301). From this it followed, Marx maintained, that:

> Conception, thought, imagination etc., are nothing but phantoms
> of the material world more or less divested of its sensuous form.
> (1979: 300)

Both Locke and Hobbes also contributed to this materialist view of
the world, the former by, in Marx's words, proving 'the principle of
Bacon' and the latter by 'divesting Bacon's materialism of its theistic
prejudices' (Padover, 1979: 302).

This 'detheisisation' of materialism was further advanced in France
by the sceptic Pierre Bayle whom Marx credited with preparing his
country for the reception of atheism by:

> . . . proving that a society consisting only of atheists is possible,
> that an atheist can be a respectable man, and that it is not by
> atheism but by superstition and idolatry that a man debases
> himself.
> (Padover, 1979: 300)

The *Philosophes* and *Encyclopaedists* of eighteenth-century France
also found favour with Marx and Engels who praised their critical
spirit:

> Religion, concepts of nature, society, political systems, everything
> was subjected to the most merciless criticism; everything had to
> justify its existence at the bar of reason or renounce all claims to
> existence.
> (Selsam and Martels, 1973: 27)

The views of the *Philosophes* and *Encyclopaedists* on matter as eternal and in possession of the power of self-motion were regarded as
extremely important to the advancement of scientific thinking for
they enabled the world to be seen and understood from within,

making any resort to supernatural explanations redundant. But they were not the first to think in this way about matter for, Marx tells us, Duns Scotus had asked 'whether it was possible for matter to think' and Bacon strongly maintained that natural philosophy was 'the only true philosophy, and physics based on the experiences of the senses . . . the chief part of natural philosophy' (Feuer, 1969: 88).

However, the materialism of the Enlightenment had its limitations for as Engels characterised it 'it was predominantly mechanical', as opposed to dynamic, and, therefore, incapable of understanding the universe

> . . . as process, as matter undergoing uninterrupted historical development . . . Nature, so much was known, was in eternal motion. But according to the ideas of that time, this motion turned, also eternally, in a circle and therefore never moved from the spot; it produced the same results over and over again . . . This same ahistorical conception prevailed also in the domain of history . . . Thus a rational insight into the great interconnection was made impossible, and history served at best as a collection of examples and illustrations for the use of philosophers.
>
> (Selsam and Martels, 1973: 232–3)

The marxist understanding of materialism, by way of contrast, rejected any idea of it as 'crude, mechanical motion', as 'mere change of location', and defined it more dynamically as 'heat and light, electric and magnetic tension, chemical combination and dissociation, life and finally consciousness' (Selsam and Martels, 1973: 171).

Marxism believes that matter has its own inner, opposing forces, so to speak, which move it along toward qualitative transformations reaching its highest expression in the form of human consciousness. Therefore, rather than seeing the universe as consisting of a mere aggregate of various parts, matter, energy and consciousness are regarded as integrated and inseparable. Thus, matter is not simply acted upon from outside but is driven forward by its own internal, opposing forces, and it is the struggle between these forces that, over time, gives rise to series of interelated changes that will, at a given moment, erupt in a sudden transformation of society. This 'dynamic' interpretation of historical development is analogous to the notion of biological evolutionism according to which an accumulation of small changes is understood to lead to the emergence of a new species.

Marxism believes in the historical inevitability of a totally new society brought about by a slow process of social and economic change and then suddenly coming into being through violent revolution in which the proletariat overthrows the bourgeoisie and forever puts an end to the exploitative capitalist system.

The initial importance of Marx's materialism for his theory of religion is at least twofold. In the first place it makes him assume without question that methodological atheism or scepticism is the correct approach to the interpretation of religion. It is not just a matter of excluding divine intervention in accounts of religious development. It is a matter of assuming the fictional nature of the gods as the premise and problem for theorising about religion. In the second place materialism gives marxism a bias to dismissing reason-based explanations of human actions and beliefs. In this respect marxist theory illustrates very well the tendencies to link the ideas of explaining, accounting for, and cause to scientific paradigms of explanation. If we find these two consequences of materialism implausible in themselves, then we will have reason to reject fundamental aspects of Marx's approach to religion.

Before completing this account of dialectical materialism, as the marxist doctrine of matter is known, we need to discuss briefly the influence of both Hegel and Feuerbach not only on the development of this theory but also on the related subject of the marxist theory of religion. (For a more detailed view of Hegel's and Feuerbach's ideas see Chapter 5.)

Hegel, as already indicated, was an idealist. He understood the intellect to be at least part-creator of the reality it knows, and he also implied that reality depends on a non-material, spiritual principle (*Geist*) that exists outside or beyond the world of the senses. He was not, however, a subjective idealist; he did not accept, like certain of his contemporaries, that what is ultimately real are the personal thoughts and sensations of each individual. His idealism is better referred to as absolute idealism according to which upon completion of history all reality will be re-absorbed into one mind or spirit.

This was a view Marx once accepted when a student of Hegel's and which he was later to abandon due, in no small measure, to the influence of Feuerbach. Marx, however, held onto Hegel's dialectical method as transformed by Feuerbach.

Hegel, as understood by Marx, offers the following portrait of the process of dialectical development: the first stage of development is the *thesis* which was followed by its negation, the *antithesis*, after which came the *synthesis* which ended the developmental process by reconciling stages one and two. It is important to note that these stages are simultaneously both opposites and the same, and that their 'reality' is seen to consist of a movement toward and apart from each other, in other words in *becoming*. The marxist idea of matter just discussed clearly echoes this insight, as do a number of other marxist notions.

As already indicated, Hegel's notions of *alienation* and *self-consciousness* also exercised an important influence on marxist thinking. As we noted in the previous chapter, self-consciousness, Hegel maintains, requires an external object from which it could differentiate itself in order for it to be realised in turn. A further aspect of the notion of externalisation developed by Hegel that Marx found valuable was his idea of labour. According to Hegel the one who works invests his labour with his thoughts and emotions as well as his physical efforts, and in this way becomes externalised. It is through the embodiment of thought in external objects that thought can become properly self-conscious. Here the notion of thesis and antithesis comes into play giving rise to a synthesis which emerges in the form of a self-consciousness which is in full possession of itself. Thus, there is in Hegel a key idea that Marx was to make use of even after he turned his back on idealism, namely that mind or spirit is self-creative activity.

Marx interpreted Hegel as arguing that the state of estranged consciousness in human beings would only be overcome through the external operation of a god-like absolute – *Geist*. Marx on the contrary asserted that alienation not only could but would be eliminated by human effort. Indeed, according to Marxism the fundamental meaning of historical development was to be found in the ending of alienation and the emergence of the totally integrated individual through the efforts of mundane forces. We will return to the marxist notion of alienation below.

Meanwhile we can note here his main criticism of Hegel. Marx came to regard Hegel not only as incorrigibly abstract and metaphysical but also as dangerously misleading and even harmful on a whole range of issues not only of a philosophical but also of a political, social and religious nature. For example, Marx, following Feuerbach, a fellow 'Young Hegelian', attacked Hegel's critique of religion on the grounds that it simply provided another way of justifying the phenomenon. What Hegel wrongly believed, Marx insisted, was that an individual, providing he or she recognised that religion exists as a consequence of self-alienation, could turn it into a means of self-integration. This, according to Marx, was a basic flaw in Hegel's logic and one that had serious adverse political consequences; particularly it supported an oppressive state:

> After annulling and superseding religion, after recognising religion to be a product of self-alienation, he yet finds confirmation of himself in religion as religion. Here is the root of Hegel's false positivism, or of his merely apparent criticism: this is what Feuerbach designated as the positing, negating and reestablishing of religion or theology. There can, therefore, no longer be any question about an act of accommodation on Hegel's part *vis-à-vis* religion, the state, etc.
>
> (Padover, 1979: 289)

Despite the strength of his own attack Marx suggested that it was to Feuerbach that one should turn for the most devasting critique of Hegel's philosophy of religion. But while they greatly appreciated his work in this area Feuerbach's own ideas on religion were also to come in time under fire from Marx, and Engels.

Feuerbach's role not only in undermining the hold that Hegelian idealism exercised over his many students but also by enabling them to provide what was considered to be a soundly based materialist understanding of reality was crucial. Engels referred to Feuerbach as 'an intermediate link between Hegelian philosophy and our conception', and went on to state that his influence on both himself and Marx was 'more than that of any post-Hegelian philosopher' (Feuer, 1969: 236–37). Feuerbach's principal achievement was the virtual completion, as far as Germany was concerned, of the criticism of religion by demonstrating that religion was a human construct by means of which people worship their human essence in the guise of a supernatural being.

As pointed out in the previous chapter Feuerbach did not dismiss religion out of hand. It had performed a positive role in the development of human consciousness. However, it also had alienating effects in that it encouraged people to take a mistaken view of their essential human nature, and this point was not lost on Marx. But even more important to them was Feuerbach's transformative method. This was used to great effect in his *Essence of Christianity* and which in essence consisted of applying Hegel's dialectical method while abandoning his idealism. As Engels remarked:

Then came Feuerbach's *Essence of Christianity*. With one blow it pulverised the contradiction (that reality derives from thought) in that without circumlocution it placed materialism on the throne again. Nature exists independently of all philosophy. Nothing exists outside nature and man, and the higher beings that our religious fantasies have created are nothing other than our own essence.

(Feuer, 1969: 251)

Once, like Marx, a student of Hegel, Feuerbach, Engels continues, had used the latter's dialectical method to illustrate that:

Matter is not a product of mind, but mind itself is merely the highest product of matter. This is of course pure materialism.

(Feuer, 1969: 251)

However, after their initial enthusiasm for what they considered to be his 'devastating' attack on Hegel's idealism had waned and their own materialist perspective had begun to develop Marx and Engels were to become highly critical of Feuerbach's understanding of materialism. They criticised in particular his failure to bring the historical and philosophical sciences into harmony with what they saw as that 'natural, scientific materialism' which he had correctly identified as the basis of all knowledge. Feuerbach failed to realise that 'it is not the consciousness of men that determines their being but their *social* [our emphasis] being which determines their consciousness' (Padover, 1979: 241).

The shortcomings in Feuerbach's understanding of religion arose from the fact that he continued, according to Marx and Engels, to treat the realm of the abstract as if it were the real world. He demonstrated that the Christian God was but a fantastic reflection, a mirror image of man, and on every page of his writings 'preaches sensuousness and absorption in the concrete', but for all that his realism is 'an empty shell' for he makes no mention of the world in which people live, 'historically come into being and historically determined.' Feuerbach explains what it is to be an individual by recourse to abstractions such as 'human nature' and 'human essence' without ever considering the historical and social context in which people actually live (Feuer, 1969: 278). Feuerbach's criticism of religion was in no sense an account of the concrete process, social and economic, by which it came into being and has been sustained. As a consequence his notion of religion as a projection constituted little more than a search for a device to explain rather than undermine the phenomenon. As Engels wrote:

> The real idealism of Feuerbach becomes evident as soon as we come to his philosophy of religion and ethics. He by no means wishes to abolish religion, he wants to perfect it. According to Feuerbach, religion is the relation between human beings based on the affections, the relation based on the heart, which relation until now has sought its truth in the fantastic mirror image of reality – in the mediation of one or many gods, the fantastic mirror image of human qualities – but now finds it directly and without any mediation in the love between 'I' and 'Thou.' Thus, finally with Feuerbach, sex love becomes one of the highest forms, if not the highest form, of the practice of his new religion.
>
> (Feuer, 1969: 257)

Marx and Engels also went on to call for Feuerbach's cult of abstract man to be replaced by a science of real people in their historical development.

These are the main criticisms expressed by Marx in his *Theses on Feuerbach* and here we can cite a number of excerpts from these for purposes of illustration, beginning with 'Thesis IV':

> Feuerbach starts out from the fact of religious self-alienation, the duplication of the world into a religious, imaginary world and a real one. His work consists in the dissolution of the religious world into a secular basis. He overlooks the fact that after completing this work the chief thing still remains to be done. For the fact that the secular foundation detaches itself from itself and establishes itself in the clouds as an independent realm is really to be explained only by the self-cleavage and self-contradictoriness of this secular basis. The latter must itself, therefore, be understood in its contradiction, and then by the removal of the contradiction, revolutionized in practice.
>
> (Feuer, 1969: 284)

And in 'Thesis VI' Marx provides what is perhaps his clearest statement of how Feuerbach failed to complete what he had started:

Feuerbach resolves the religious essence into the human essence. But the human essence is no abstraction inherent in each single individual. In its reality it is the ensemble of human relations. Feuerbach who does not enter upon a criticism of this real essence is consequently compelled:

1. To abstract from the historical process and to fix the religious sentiment (*Gemut*) as something by itself, and to presuppose an abstract-isolated-human individual.
2. The human essence, therefore, can with him be comprehended only as a 'genus', an internal, dumb generality which merely naturally unites many individuals.

(Feuer, 1969: 285)

This criticism is continued in 'Thesis VII':

Feuerbach, consequently, does not see that the 'religious senti- ment' is itself a *social product* [our emphasis], and that the abstract individual whom he analyses belongs in reality to a particular form of society.

(Feuer, 1969: 285)

For Marx all life is essentially practical and it is from this perspec- tive that everything else including religion, philosophy and all forms of knowledge must be assessed. He was strongly opposed, as should be evident from what has been said so far, to what he considered to be 'pure' speculation, emphasising instead the necessity for *praxis*, that is action as opposed to philosophising, as 'Thesis XI' makes clear:

Philosophers have only *interpreted* the world in various ways; the point, however, is to change it.

(Feuer, 1969: 286)

The essence of Marx's rejection of Feuerbach should now be clear. While appreciating Feuerbach's materialist critique of Hegel, Marx wanted to retain Hegel's view of the self as creative of its own being. Contrary to Feuerbach, in such works as *The Principles of the Philoso- phy of the Future*, the self is not a passive subject of sensation. There- fore there is a basic mistake in Feuerbach's implicit claim that if only one removed the false ideas of theology, human beings would sud- denly see the true human essence. If they could not see their essence truly it was not because they were the victims of false ideas. Rather there must be something wrong in the creative processes whereby they fashioned, through work, the world in which they lived. It is the contradictions in those processes which need to be addressed. But contrary to Hegel, these contradictions are ones that can only be understood materially. They are contradictions in and between the various material circumstances (that is: the forces of production, their relationships in an economic system, the legal and social institutions built on this system) which give birth to contradictions in the ideas that beset and befuddle our understanding of ourselves.

Praxis, then, was the vantage point from which, Marx believed, all thinking about society should begin, and this was consistent with his doctrine of dialectical materialism, meaning here, as previously noted, the acceptance of the human world as the primary datum of all knowledge, as opposed to idealism which posits a world of ideas as both the source of our knowledge and the model of the real world which is experienced through the senses. On this point Marx wrote: 'Since only what is material is perceptible, knowable, nothing is known of the existence of God (Padover, 1969: 301). Thus, 'objective reality' is the basis of all knowledge, of religious beliefs, and aesthetic, moral and spiritual values and, indeed, all 'mental' products derive from a material basis. This should not, however, lead one to conclude that a marxist world is a world without philosophy, an anti-intellectual world, a world in which ideas, ideals and values have no place, for dialectical materialism holds, as already seen, that matter is dynamic, that it contains within itself the potentiality for life, thought and consciousness, and that it evolves from lower to higher forms reaching its pinnacle in human consciousness. Marx commented:

> The first and most important of the inherent qualities of matter is motion, not only mechanical and mathematical movement, but still more impulse, vital life-spirit, tension or to use Jakob Boehme's expression, the throes of matter. The primary forms of matter are living, individualizing forces of being inherent in it and producing the distinctions between the species.
>
> (Padover, 1979: 301)

MARX, CAPITALISM AND RELIGION

An exposition of Marx's materialism gives a basis for understanding his ideas on religion. It is worth noting that one can find points of overlap with religious ideas, as well as hostile diagnoses of them, in marxist thought. For example, the understanding of matter as permanent motion suggested to Zaehner the existence of a close parallel between Marxism and Buddhism. He likened Marx's notion of matter in 'tension' and his talk of 'the throes of matter' to the key Buddhist concept of *dukka*, pain and sorrow, in the sense of unease (Zaehner, 1977: 397). Further, he compared Engel's idea of the body as being 'at each moment the same and not the same . . . so that every organic being is at all times itself and something other than itself' to the Buddhist idea of *anatta* or void of self (1977: 397). Again, Engel's statement that 'everything is and also is not . . . is constantly coming into being and passing away' provides Zaehner with his marxist counterpart to the Buddhist idea of *anicca* or impermanence.

Zaehner concludes what is the first stage of a more detailed comparison of the two systems of ideas with the comment:

> Thus, the materialist premises from which Buddhism starts can be seen to be identical with the Marxist interpretation of existence.
> (397)

Viewed from another angle Marxism would appear to share a good deal in common with the Christian understanding of the world for, like the latter, it is convinced that history is purposeful, that it is moving toward a climax in the form of a paradise or 'land without evil', a perfect society. However, such comparisons can be misleading for, although according to both the Christian and the marxist view of things, concrete, human history *per se* has a deep layer of meaning to it, they differ in that the former believes in a salvation beyond history while the latter believes that it is within history that nature and human beings reach total fulfilment. As history makes progress through the emergence of new economic and social systems so also does the human race. Personal, individual fulfilment for its part is linked to this historical development which will culminate in the advent of the classless society.

There is no notion in Marxism of an external saviour from 'above'; a marxist understanding of human beings portrays them as intrinsically social beings who attain self-fulfilment by creating for themselves the freedom to exercise their human capacities to the full, the chief of which is their productive capacity. Individuals invest their mind and imagination, their emotional life as well as their skills and physical energy in their labour, and that is why productive activity mirrors what they are and constitutes that process of self-objectification necessary to personal integration and development. And since such activity reflects what in essence human beings are it is by recognising a real association between themselves and their products, something that is impossible under capitalism, that individuals come to discover themselves and come to exist as subjects.

What individuals produce is their externalised or objectified self without which they cannot exist as human beings, for as Marx expressed it, following a Hegelian line of thought:

> A being which does not have its nature outside itself is not a natural being and plays no part in the system of nature . . . [It] is a non-being.
>
> (Harvey, 1985: 303)

The marxist theory that individuals fulfil themselves through their productive activity maintains that their material and 'spiritual' development will be hindered where the socio-economic system militates against the full and free exercise of this capacity. Modern capitalism is the prime example in the marxist view of such a system. On the one hand it deprives productive activity of its meaning by turning such activity into a necessity and thus making it unfree, and on the other it reduces it to a mere commodity or commercial object over which the individuals who produce it have no control and which they no longer appropriate. The result is the alienation of labour which Marx regarded as the most basic form of alienation consisting, he wrote, in:

> . . . the fact that labour is external to the worker, i.e. does not belong to his intrinsic nature; that in his work, therefore, he does not affirm himself but denies himself, does not feel content but unhappy, does not develop freely his physical and mental energy but mortifies his body and ruins his mind. The worker, therefore, only feels himself outside his work and in his work feels outside himself.
>
> (Lukes, 1987: 81)

Therefore, becoming human requires a process of self-objectification and self-estrangement through productive activity. However, when this process results, as it does under capitalism, in individuals seeing their labour as a commodity like any other to be bought and sold,

this leads to a complete distortion both at the level of self-understanding and in terms of their relationships with others. In such a
world nothing is seen for what it is.

Capitalism generates the desire for false needs and panders to
'inhuman, sophisticated, unnatural and imaginary appetites' are
encouraged, above all, by an 'obsessive need for money' (ibid: 82). It
gives rise to basically instrumental kinds of relationships, that is
relationships of a conflictual and non-reciprocal nature, and as a
consequence, people are turned into 'forsaken' and 'despicable' beings confronted by an 'alien force existing outside them' in the form
of the institutions and social relations of capitalism – the exchange of
commodities, capital and money.

Capitalism and self-development are mutually exclusive. Under
the capitalist system what individuals produce no longer leads to
self-realisation for their products, now valued solely in terms of their
market worth, no longer provides them with the mirrors in which
they can see reflected their own essential nature. Rather capitalist
methods 'mutilate the labourer into the fragment of a man', alienating the person from the 'mental and spiritual potentialities of the
labour process' (Lukes, 1987: 83). Under capitalism, what should in
principle provide the precondition for and the means of attaining
self-fulfilment at every level, in practice gives rise to the situation
in which people's productive activity becomes an 'alien power'
in opposition to their interests and makes 'their conditions of life
something extraneous, something over which they as separate
individuals have no control' (Lukes, 1987: 84).

People in these circumstances not only experience alienation in its
socio-economic form but also what Plamenatz has called 'spiritual'
alienation which, of course, from a marxist perspective, is inextricably linked under capitalism with socio-economic alienation; it is that
form of alienation that consists in that experience of the self as
'fragmented', as 'unfree and valueless and robbed of all life content'
(Plamenatz, 1975). This is the condition, referred to by Marx in his
Theses on Feuerbach, which produces the 'duplication of the world
into a religious and secular one' and at the same time blinds one to
the fact that 'religious sentiment is in itself a *social product*' (Feuer,
1969: 285).

Thus, alienated people turn to religion to alleviate the pain they
feel as a result of the absence of meaning, purpose and value in their
life. It is for this reason that religion can be said to be 'the self-
awareness and self-regard of man who has either not yet found

himself or has already lost himself again', and the 'fantastic realization of the human being because the human possesses no true reality' (Padover, 1979: 206).

Religion is essentially both an expression of and a protest against real human misery created by an alienating socio-economic system that for its success requires the existence of a world that is essentially antagonistic.

Marx, of course, not only accounted for religion in terms of alienation but also in terms of ideology, and his religion as ideology thesis can be considered from two angles: that of the dominant group in society and that of class position. In *The German Ideology* and elsewhere Marx and Engels wrote of how, in a class structured society, the dominant group, the bourgeoisie under capitalism, controls the means of mental and cultural production through its control over the means of material production:

> The ruling material force of society is at the same time its ruling intellectual force.
>
> (Feuer, 1969: 289)

Engels, writing of religious belief in the Middle-Ages, made the same point by maintaining that because the ideology of the ruling class, the clergy, was religious, the total ideological system was religious. This explains, he argues, why opposition to the authorities took the form of religious protest and why so often it was transformed into a passive form of millenarian fervour as the dominant class made use of religion to mystify and control the masses (Padover, 1978: 210).

It is not only the religion but also the morality of society that is ideologically determined by the dominant or ruling class. By controlling the churches and schools this class can teach what will serve its interests, the chief of which is the accumulation of wealth which is nothing other than the fruit of labour and therefore done at the expense of the worker's material and personal well-being. Workers likewise when the opportunity arises look after the interests of their own class. According to Engels:

> As society has hitherto moved in class antagonisms, morality was always a class morality; either it has justified the domination and interests of the ruling class, or as soon as the oppressed class has become powerful enough, it has represented the revolt against

this domination and the future interests of the oppressed . . . we have not as yet really passed beyond class morality.

(Feuer, 1969: 313)

This, then, is the marxist view of the way in which religion functions as an ideology in a society where the dominant class controls cultural and intellectual activity.

Religion can also be seen as ideological if considered from the perspective of the class-based nature of society. As already pointed out, the idea of class is central to the marxist theory of the development of history. In the *Communist Manifesto* all history is presented as the history of class struggle with oppressors against oppressed. When the latter seizes power, as it inevitably will, class antagonism will naturally disappear with the disappearance of the class system itself. Meanwhile, religion will continue to serve to integrate society around a set of 'false' ideas that serve to maintain the status quo.

This view of religion is consistent with the idea already referred to that it is the 'social being that determines consciousness' and not the converse, and with the interrelated notion that it is people's location in the class structure that is the most important aspect of their existence. It is this location that forms a person's opinions, attitudes and expectations. As Marx and Engels expressed it:

Upon the social conditions of existence rises an entire superstructure of distinct and peculiarly formed sentiments, illusions, modes of thoughts and views of life. The entire class forms and creates them through tradition and upbringing.

(Marx and Engels, 1968: 117–18)

There would, however, seem to be a contradiction here between this class ideology view of religion and the dominant ideology view already discussed. Among other things it would seem to follow that if there is more than one class in a society there must be more than one ideology and in capitalist societies there must clearly be a separation between the ideology of the dominant class and that of the subordinate class, the proletariat. This point was made by Engels with regard to nineteenth-century England where, he observed:

The bourgeoisie has more in common with every other nation of the earth than with the workers in whose midst it lives. The workers speak other dialects, have other thoughts and ideals,

other customs and moral principals, a different religion and other
politics than the bourgeoisie.

(Engels, 1968: 124)

Leaving aside for the moment the apparent contradiction, it is
clear that in the marxist view of it, religion is solidly grounded in
class and seen to serve class interests, a view that many believe Max
Weber strongly opposed.

MARX AND WEBER COMPARED

Weber clearly wrote at times as if he intended to counter Marx's
opinions:

> It is not our thesis that the specific nature of a religion is simply a
> 'function' of the social situation of the stratum which appears as
> its characteristic bearer, or that it represents the stratum's 'ideol-
> ogy' or that it is a 'reflection' of a stratum's ideal or material
> interest-situation . . . However decisive the social influences may
> have been on a religious ethic in a particular case, it receives its
> stamp primarily from religious sources.

(Weber, 1969: 22)

Weber stressed the contribution made by ideas to human action and
behaviour and to the development of history. However, he was
careful to point out that it was a combination of ideal and material
interests that governed human conduct and the course of history:

> Not ideas but material and ideal interests govern men's conduct.
> Yet very frequently the world images that have been created by
> ideas have like switchmen determined the tracts along with ac-
> tions have been pushed by the dynamic of interests.

(Weber, 1969: 34)

But was Weber consistent and was his account of religion so different from Marx's? There is considerable evidence that Weber was far
more of a materialist than the above quotations suggest. While stressing that religious ideas are never simply a function of the particular
social stratum where they are found he, nevertheless, on occasion
accounts for the content of religious belief in terms of the material

and ideological interests of social groups. For example, he gives as the main reason why monotheism failed to emerge in certain cultures 'the pressure of the powerful material and ideological interests vested in the priests who resided in the cultic centres and regulated the cult of particular gods' (Weber, 1969: 411–12). Moreover, he also accounts for religion in ideological terms while at the same time rejecting any suggestion, though not always convincingly, that it is based purely on class interests. One example is his account of the carriers of the world religions whom he portrays as the propagators of an ideology in keeping with their social position. He writes:

> If one wishes to characterise succinctly in a formula so to speak the types representative of the various classes that were the primary carriers or propagators of the so-called world religions they would be the following: in Confucianism, the world organizing bureaucrat; in Hinduism, the world organizing magician; in Buddhism, the mendicant monk wandering through the world; in Judaism, the wandering trader; in Christianity, the itinerant trader. To be sure, all these types must not be taken as exponents of their own occupational or material class interests, but rather as ideological carriers of the kind of ethical or salvational doctrine which most readily conformed to their social position.
>
> (Bendix, 1966: 91–2)

Furthermore, he explains 'modern' Lutheranism, as opposed to the Lutheranism of Luther himself, as predominantly a struggle against 'the rationalism of intellectuals and political liberalism' (Bendix, 1966).

Weber's proximity to Marx can also be seen in his notion of theodicies of privileged and non-privileged groups. Central to Weber's thinking on religion was his conviction that people, whatever their socio-economic status or condition, needed to make sense of their life and religion was one of the principal, if not the principal, providers of meaning. In this sense it could be seen, he believed, to cater for a genuine psychological need by providing different social strata with explanations adapted to their particular needs and ones that gave meaning and purpose to experiences which otherwise may have seemed completely senseless. Of such explanations or *theodicies* he wrote:

> Since every need for salvation is an expression of some distress, social or economic oppression is an effective source of salvation

beliefs, though by no means the exclusive one. Other things being equal, classes with high social and economic privilege will scarcely be prone to evolve the idea of salvation. Rather they assign to religion the primary function of legitimizing their own life pattern and situation in the world. When a man who is happy compares his position with one who is unhappy, he is not content with the fact of his happiness, but desires something more, namely the right to this happiness, the consciousness that he has earned his good fortune, in contrast to the unfortunate one who must equally have earned his misfortune . . . What the privileged classes require of religion, if anything at all, is this psychological reassurance of legitimacy.

> (Weber, 1965: 107)

Thus, one type of theodicy, the theodicy of good fortune, serves the ideological function of legitimating privilege and success which cover all the 'good' derived from honour, power, possession, status and pleasure. Such a theodicy was, Weber believed

> The most general term for the service of legitimation which religion has had to accomplish for the external and inner interests of all ruling men, the propertied, the victorious, the wealthy.
>
> (Weber, 1969: 24)

The polar opposite to such a theodicy is the theodicy of misfortune which for its part serves to make sense of why the just seem to suffer while the wrongdoers prosper by offering compensation and better prospects in a future life. Examples of theodicies of this kind given by Weber include the Christian idea of paradise and the notion of *karma* and *samsara* in Hinduism.

The similarities between Weber's and Marx's position on the general character of modern capitalist society are also worth noting. Both pointed to the social and cultural costs of capitalism, the former using the term 'rationality' to describe this and the latter, as we have seen, employing the term 'alienation' (Gellner, 1974: 189). Furthermore, on the question of its future, both Marx and Weber foresaw a time when religion would cease to exercise any serious influence either on the functioning of the social system or on individual thought and behaviour. However, they looked at this demise of religion differently. Marx was optimistic that communism would more than adequately meet the needs and desires that the capitalist system gave rise to and which were once expressed in an illusory form in religion and superficially satisfied, thus making religion redundant. Weber, on the other hand, was pessimistic, maintaining that the ongoing process involving the rationalisation of every aspect of the social system and of everyday life would leave little or no space for religion, giving rise to a 'disenchanted world', to the 'iron cage' of modern civilisation.

By no means everyone is convinced that Marx and Weber are as close in their ideas on religion and its effects as has been suggested so far. The marxist scholar Lukács believed, like others, that Weber gave much more autonomy to ideas than Marx by allowing 'ideological formations such as Law and Religion an equal role to (that of) the economy, and even the attribution of a "supervisor" causality to them' (Lukács, 1972: 390). And this view is reinforced when one considers Weber's *The Protestant Ethic and the Spirit of Capitalism* (Weber, 1984) and his explanation as to why modern capitalism failed to emerge in regions outside the influence of Protestantism. Weber concluded, for example, that Hinduism was greatly responsible for this in that it lacked the kind of ethic necessary for 'rational worldly capitalism' to emerge (Bendix, 1966: 172ff).

Marx, for his part, attributed this failure to a stagnant form of social organisation which he called the 'Asiatic' mode of production, a form of production based on the domestic industry of small-scale village communities under despotic leaders. And the religion of such communities was but a reflection of this socio-economic context. He wrote:

> We must not forget that these little communities . . . subjugated man to external circumstances instead of elevating man to be the sovereign of circumstances, that they transformed a self-developing social state into never changing natural destiny, and thus brought about a brutalising worship of nature, exhibiting its degradation in the fact that man, the sovereign of nature, fell down on his knees in adoration of Hanuman, the monkey, and Sabbala, the cow.
>
> (Feuer, 1969: 518)

However, although there can be little doubt that Marx provided a much more thorough-going materialist account of religion than Weber and that some of the latter's statements can be read as a clear rejection of the marxist attempt to reduce beliefs to material class interests, the gap between the two theories of religion is not as wide as is usually believed. In his account of religion Weber very often directly related its content to systems of social stratification. And it would seem that, like Marx, he also was persuaded, despite his many disclaimers to the contrary, that human actions were largely determined by interests in conjunction with socio-economic conditions. However, unlike Marx, Weber often strongly argued that it was not only economic interests that operated in this way, and was also convinced that people's beliefs and ideas influenced their perception and interpretation of their interests and so channelled these into relevant action.

Thus, overall, Marx and Engels provide a more radical socio-economic explanation and interpretation of religion than Weber, reducing it to the status of an epiphenomenon. Their primary focus was, of course, on Christianity under capitalism and, thus, they pay little attention to religion in other cultures and in other periods of history, whereas Weber provided a comparative study of the ethical orientation of several of the major world religions (Bendix, 1966: 172ff). Marx and Engels also provide, it is true, an outline of the history of Christianity, some brief comments on other religions including Hinduism, and a brief account of the origins of religion, which, while for the most part unexceptional, derived, as it is, from the writings of Frazer among others, has some unusual and interesting features.

The marxist view of the origins of religion bears all the marks of the evolutionist, positivist outlook of many other nineteenth- and early twentieth-century theorists including Durkheim and Weber. And like so many of their contemporaries Marx and Engels traced the origins of religion to the fear that comes with ignorance and lack of control over nature. Marxism also accepted the view long current in materialist circles that religion's origins lay in the dark, unenlightened minds of primitives. According to Engels, it arose in very early times from erroneous, backward conceptions people had about their own nature and the external world which surrounded them (Feuer, 1969: 278).

Following Tylor, Engels maintained that the idea of the immortality of the human soul originated in dreams: primitive peoples allegedly believed that during sleep the soul left the body and experienced what they had been dreaming about while asleep, and that it would behave in the same way after death. This, among other things, was evidence that religion derived from the animism of primitive peoples who personified all natural things and endowed them with souls, thoughts and desires. Religion was at this stage simply magic but went on to pass through various stages of development, in accordance with the 'material conditions of life' of different generations of people and will continue to do so until its eventual demise with the advent of the classless society. Engels described the first stages of this development in what were clearly positivist terms:

> All religion is nothing but the fantastic reflection in people's minds of those external forces which control their daily life, a reflection in which the terrestrial forces assume the form of supernatural forces. In the beginning of history it was the forces of nature which were first so reflected and which in the course of further evolution underwent the most manifold and varied personifications among various people.
>
> (Feuer, 1969: 278)

This marxist materialist explanation of the development of religion is, however, in some respects different from accounts provided by other theorists in that religion's origins are directly related to the emergence of classes. The passage from food gathering to agriculture saw, we are told by Engels, the emergence of a class-based society and an 'unproductive' priesthood, and with this came the transition from magic to institutionalised religion. At this point both natural and social forces combined to control people from without – as they are said to be controlled from without under capitalism – and hence the persistence of religion. Under the weight of imperialism innumerable community, ethnic and national gods eventually give way to one, all powerful divinity:

> Side by side with the forces of nature, social forces begin to be active – forces which confront man as equally alien and at first equally inexplicable, dominating him with the same apparent natural necessity as the forces of nature themselves ... At a still further stage of evolution, all natural and social attributes of the numerous gods are transformed to one almighty God.
>
> (Marx and Engels, 1977: 148)

Weber's view of the development of religion, at least the early stages in this development, is similar: magic turns to religion with the emergence of a priesthood that begins the process of 'rationalising religious life'. However, the rise of a priesthood, which tends to have an affinity with the bourgeoisie, is not explained, as in Marxism, in class terms, but more in terms of status interests (Bendix, 1966: 86–7).

CONCLUSION: A CRITIQUE OF MARXIST THEORY OF RELIGION

The marxist account of the origins, development and content of religion, like others of the period, is highly speculative. Indeed, regarding Marxism as a whole, Popper saw it as an excellent example of the historicist fallacy in that it claimed to provide a scientific prediction of the future course of whole societies, basing itself on the assumption that they change along a predetermined path (1957). Popper supports this claim with evidence such as the following from Marx's writings:

> When a society has discovered a natural law that determines its own movement, even then it can neither overleap the natural phases of its evolution, nor shuffle them out of the world at the stroke of a pen. But this much it can do: it can shorten and lessen the birth pangs.
>
> (1957: 51)

Popper argues that the theoretical basis of this understanding of change is seriously flawed for it confuses laws of nature with what are no more than trends and is, therefore, inadequate as a foundation for scientific prediction (1957: 120).

This kind of criticism turns Marxism into little more than a form of secular messianism. However, while there is undoubtedly a messianic dimension to Marxism – indeed it has, as previously noted, many strands including a philosophical, economic, political and a 'religious' strand – this should not be allowed to obscure the fact that it is a serious attempt to provide a thorough sociological and economic analysis of the capitalist system, of its evolution and functioning, which constitutes, as already pointed out, the framework for any assessment of the marxist account of religion.

However, granted the seriousness of the enterprise as a whole, Marxism does not appear to offer a serious, intellectual critique of religion. Indeed, its account of religion is largely anti-intellectual and shot through with contradictions. For example, its explanation of religion as ideology, as already indicated, is highly contradictory for it points to religion as the basis of working-class solidarity, on the one hand, and as a device used by the bourgeoisie to legitimise their interests and keep effective control over the proletariat, on the other. Moreover, the marxist view that religion and socialism and, therefore, religion and progress are opposites is not supported by the historical evidence. As Chadwick pointed out, history could have shown both Marx and Engels that religion had been more than the symbol or reflection of alienated society (Chadwick, 1975). And, indeed, their own personal contacts with communists of their time had shown both Marx and Engels that religion was not necessarily incompatible with communism.

Furthermore, the central tenet of Marxism, historical materialism, seems to raise a number of difficulties. As frequently pointed out in the foregoing, this doctrine maintains, for example, that ideas are a direct reflection of social and economic conditions, and that religious and moral values are directly related to and dependent upon the prevailing mode of production and the social relations based upon it. Evidently modes of production and social relations derived therefrom can and do influence ideas: the way they are developed, interpreted and passed on. They can also influence what ideas are acceptable and what are not. But ideas plainly can and often do transcend the particular social and economic conditions in which they originate to embrace a much wider world.

There are numerous examples of this in all fields, including the philosophical, the scientific and the religious. However, it is not only difficult to accept that religious ideas are no more than a direct reflection of a particular material condition but it is also difficult to accept the marxist view that religious, and moral, values are simply reflections of class position for here, likewise, there is evidence of such values transcending class boundaries. There is every reason to see Marx and Engels as embroiled in a similar, and therefore questionable, view about the limits of consciousness as that found in Feuerbach.

As noted in the previous chapter, Feuerbach is inclined to assume that human thought cannot transcend the limits of what is given in experience, whereas all that he is entitled to believe is that all human thought must be anchored in experience. The marxist version of this idea is that all human thought is limited by class interest. As a reminder of the *starting point* of human ideas in a given social context this is a valuable insight. As an assertion of the final destiny of human thought it is highly questionable. Both Feuerbach's and Marx's ideas about the necessary anchoring of human thought could provide valuable principles of criticism of some of the sillier pretensions of idealism and metaphysics. Marxism's materialist vision of history has also given a worthwhile stimulus to the search for appropriate socio-economic contexts for religious ideas. But the marxist–feuerbachian principles can yield conclusions about the necessarily illusory character of religious ideas only if taken as dogmatic, uncritical claims about the inability of human beings to transcend immediate experience and social circumstances in their beliefs, ideals and actions.

These difficulties with the marxist account of religion are related to another more general problem arising from the notion of religion as symptomatic of alienation and false consciousness. There is, clearly, much that is a priori about this interpretation. The idea, for instance, that there is a superstructure which contains such epiphenomena as religion and philosophy – both of which, according to Engels, stand furthest away from material life and seem most alien to it (Feuer, 1969: 278) – has the appearance of assuming that what has to be proved is in fact the case. It has the appearance of a deduction from principles already given in the marxist theory rather than a conclusion reached on the basis of the evidence.

Marxist theory of religion provides a paradigm of the idea that religion is a 'masking institution' and thus contains a denial of priority of the appearances in this part of the human world (as discussed in Chapters 2 and 3 above). It is of the essence of religion that it disguises from folk the true meaning and motives of their actions and the true state of their social relationships. It is of the essence of religion that at the conscious level its beliefs and actions are supported by rationalisations and not reasons. Here we confront the major point about method in the theory of religion stressed repeatedly in this study. How is the theorist of this type to know that religion is a mask and an illusion? The marxist theory could be based on an induction, in which case it would be a generalisation from discoveries about specific forms of religion (such as modern Protestantism) being the expression of class consciousness. But then it should be a limited and tentative generalisation at best and not an assertion about religion *per se*.

It looks as though it is a deduction a priori from the ideas about the material, mechanistic basis of all causation, even causation in human action and belief, and the specific theses about the way ideas are generated in the human world. It is these which give marxists a determined methodological atheism which they then bring to bear on religion. It may be argued that the marxist explanatory scheme could be intermediate between an induction and a dogmatic, a priori account. It could be that the theses relating changes in the modes of production to changes in the relations of production, to changes in social relationships and finally to changes in ideas are but hypotheses proved by their worth in organising the data of religious history. As such their totalist quality matches that of other paradigms in the natural sciences. But without an initial acceptance of the core ideas of dialectical materialism (ironically, derived from a speculative philosophy of consciousness and history in Hegel) they would lack any initial plausibility as a governing paradigm. Far from introducing needed simplicity into the study of religion they involve acceptance of a major complicating factor in the interpretation of religious realities. If they are true, we can no longer rely on the reasons of the religious in gaining an understanding of what they believe and do, and why they believe and do it.

The endeavour to make every idea fit into an all-embracing, watertight system is one desideratum in explanation. Socio-economic (and other grand) theories of religion exhibit this feature. But granted, as we have noted in Part One, that explanation varies in its aims and demands from one context to another it is not always to be welcomed, and certainly not if it leads to forced and dismissive accounts of the empirical realities, producing what amounts to a closed system of thought. The marxist theory of *praxis* can have a very similar effect, as Berger and Kellner have pointed out (1981: 139). The notion of *praxis* also contains the controversial idea that fact cannot be separated from value. Marx, as we have seen, maintained that people's ideas could not be changed by criticism; the conditions that made people think as they did would first have to be destroyed. This lies behind his stress on the importance of the fusion of theory and practice. And, also, important in understanding the purpose of this fusion, is the fact that, as McIntyre explains:

> For Marx theory was to inform and direct the activities of a party and a class which had been brought into existence by social agencies which could be comprehended only by his theory.
>
> (1969: 122)

The idea of *praxis* which will not allow for the separation of fact from value highlights a very important difference between the marxist view of society and that view of society grounded in the political theory of 'possessive individualism' which underpins liberal democratic societies and, according to which, individuals are the proprietors of their own persons and capacities for which they owe nothing to society (Macpherson, 1962: 263). It was, of course, Marx's intention to provide a devastating critique of this liberal view which, he believed, led to a reification of the individual and of so many aspects of life.

Paradoxically, this insistence on the fusion of theory and practice, based on the belief that action and not speculation brings about change, also provides, as contemporary history has shown, ample room for reification, including the reification of Marx's own analysis of society. Moreover, taken to its logical conclusion, it renders almost impossible an empiricist understanding of social and economic data and, thus, virtually rules out any attempt at scholarly objectivity.

These limitations apart, their own antipathy toward it made it well nigh impossible for Marx and Engels to provide an objective explanation of religion. But this is not, however, to suggest that marxist analysis has not made a significant contribution to our understanding of history and to genuine theory construction in numerous fields of scholarship, including the sociology of knowledge, the context from within which Durkheim attempted to account for religion. Indeed, although far apart politically and in temperament, when it came to accounting for religion, Durkheim, like Weber, shared much in common with Marx. As Evans Pritchard observed, Durkheim, who as we shall see was to define religion as a 'social fact', might well have written the well known marxist aphorism already cited above:

> It is not the consciousness of men that determines their being but their social being which determines their consciousness.
>
> (1965: 77)

7

Sociological Theories of Religion

DURKHEIM ON RELIGION AND SOCIETY

From socio-economic explanations of religion discussed in the previous chapter we move to an examination of sociological accounts of the phenomenon. We concentrate on what is undoubtedly one of the richest of all such theories in terms of the insights it offers and the explanatory power of some of its ideas: that advanced by the French sociologist Emile Durkheim (1858–1917). It is equally one of the most controversial sociological accounts. Here again, as in Marxism, the essence of the whole theory is to be found in a single artefact. Marxist theory, as previously indicated, is encapsulated in the idea of the commodity; how something is produced, exchanged, attains its value is the key to understanding capitalism and, by implication, religion. In Durkheim's theory of religion it is the Australian totem which constitutes the essence of the phenomenon.

We shall not focus exclusively on Durkheim. Some attention will also be paid to more contemporary sociological explanations of religion which, while seeking to go beyond Durkheim and avoid some of his mistakes, nevertheless owe a great deal to his insights.

Durkheim was not unusual among his contemporaries in dedicating so much of his time to the study of religion. Religion was a central concern of nineteenth-century sociology and this for many reasons of both a theoretical and practical kind. Such study was considered essential to the development of sociological theory. Moreover, sociologists became preoccupied with the problem of providing a 'scientific' understanding of the effects on 'traditional' patterns of authority, morality, community life and culture, of which religion formed part, of rapid social and economic change. For Durkheim and his contemporaries the central question was how would the increasingly differentiated society of their time and of the future attain an adequate degree of solidarity, cohesion and consensus.

Religion it was generally agreed had provided the social cement of the 'old order' and for some nineteenth-century thinkers, including de Toqueville, it was also essential to freedom. Alexis de Tocqueville's *Ancien Régime* (1966) provides a classic example of that sense of everything breaking down that was so widespread in nineteenth-century social writings. There was serious doubt as to whether the old gods, myths, dogmas and rituals designed for a more integrated and simple world characterised by what Durkheim termed mechanical solidarity – that solidarity based on the common beliefs and consensus found in the 'conscience collective' – could operate effectively in the 'new' more industrially based and scientifically and technologically oriented world.

Industrialisation and urbanisation were accompanied by an increasing division of labour which, Durkheim believed, undermined mechanical solidarity and with it moral integration, thus rendering social order problematic. However, Durkheim was persuaded that a new form of order would arise in advanced societies the basis of which would be organic solidarity, a form of solidarity which would comprise the interdependence of economic ties arising from the differentiation and specialisation within the modern economy, a new network of occupational associations linking individuals to the state and the emergence within these associations of collectively created, moral restraints on citizens.

Durkheim remained concerned, nonetheless, about the danger to society of individuals who did not feel that social norms were meaningful to them and who, as a consequence, experienced that condition which he termed *anomie*, and embraced socialism not out of a desire to abolish private property but because it constituted a protest against the disintegration of traditional social bonds and values. Previously, religious culture consisted of the collective values which comprised a society's unity and personality, and religious ceremonies both reinforced those collective values and reaffirmed community among individuals. But in modern 'organically' integrated societies it was increasingly difficult to find such ceremonies and rituals and hence the far greater risk of *anomie*. Religion, however, would persist for, while he believed that its interpretative role had virtually come to an end with the arrival of modern science, Durkheim, nonetheless, was convinced that it remained indispensable. He wrote:

There can be no society which does not feel the need of upholding and reaffirming at regular intervals the collective sentiments and the collective ideas which make its unity and personality. Now this moral re-making cannot be achieved except by means of reunions, assemblies and meetings where individuals, being closely united to one another, reaffirm in common their common sentiments; hence come ceremonies which do not differ from religious ceremonies, either in their object, the results which they produce, or the processes employed to attain these results . . .

(Durkheim, 1915: 427)

Religion could not be dismissed as mere superstition, as an illusion, as the fabrication of simple-minded primitives. Indeed, Durkheim believed that by returning to simple, primitive society he could establish the solid, 'factual' basis on which the essence of religion rested and dispel once and for all those animist and naturist theories which treated it as the result of immature thinking, of a mode of thought unduly influenced by emotional considerations, as essentially a mistake. (How far these perceptions of Durkheim about the character of his own account are correct will be considered below.)

Like many of his contemporaries Durkheim held that there was a direct link between thought and social structure and on the basis of this assumption he went on to maintain that a religion could be said to be the most primitive

. . . when it is found in a society whose organization is surpassed by no other in simplicity; and secondly, when it is possible to explain it without making use of any element borrowed from a previous religion.

(1915: 1)

Durkheim not only assumes an identity between simplicity and evolutionary priority in matters religious, among other things, but also accepts that the essence of religion resides in its most primitive form and for this reason it is necessary to seek out the most primitive religion to explain the phenomenon in general. Thus he states:

What we want to do is to find a means of discerning the ever present causes upon which the most essential forms of religious thought and practice depend . . . these causes are proportionally more observable as the societies where they are observed are less complicated. That is why we try to get as near as possible to the origins.

(1915: 8)

In this quest Durkheim was greatly influenced by the opinions of Robertson Smith and particularly by two of his ideas: that the clan cult or totemism was the earliest and most elementary form of religion and his suggestion that it was best accounted for and understood by reference to its social character. Although Smith was at least indirectly indebted to the writings of Fustel de Coulange for his view of religion, including its essentially social character, Durkheim, nevertheless, credits him for 'having realised more than any of his predecessors how rich this crude and confused religion [totemism] is in germ for the future' (1915: 89). Durkheim was determined that his own explanation of religion would be scientific and begins by offering a set of largely positivistic, *ad hominem* arguments against the definitions of religion advanced by, among others, Mueller, Spencer, Tylor and Frazer. Mueller's account of religion as being essentially grounded in the 'sentiment of mystery' and the ability to perceive the infinite in the finite (see Chapter 1 above) is given very short shrift, Durkheim asserting that such a sentiment arrived very late on in the history of religions and is 'completely foreign, not only to those people who are called primitive, but also to all others who have not attained a considerable degree of intellectual culture' (1915: 25). Durkheim accused fetishist and animistic theories of religion of the kind found in Spencer, Tylor and Frazer as basing religion upon mere illusion. Religion, Durkheim maintained, must have a permanent underlying reality otherwise it would be impossible to account for its persistence, and it was this fact about it that allowed it to be examined scientifically. He wrote:

Our entire study rests upon the postulate that the unanimous sentiment of the believers cannot be purely illusory . . . we admit that these religious beliefs rest upon a specific experience whose demonstrative value is, in one sense, not one bit inferior to that of scientific experiments, though different from them.

(1915: 417)

Religion was a reality external to the individual, it was a 'thing' or 'social fact'. Moreover, like all 'social facts' or 'things' its essential nature could only be discovered if studied objectively. Introspection will yield no results in this field. Religion belongs to that class of social facts that includes established beliefs and practices which are the product of the collectivity or of a group within society. By interpreting it as a 'social fact' or 'thing' Durkheim insisted that he was not suggesting that it was the same kind of 'being' as a material thing but simply that it enjoyed the same degree of reality as the latter. His category of 'social fact' and/or 'thing' included:

> . . . all objects of knowledge that cannot be conceived by purely mental activity, those that require for their conception data from outside the mind, from observations and experiments, those that are built up from the more external and immediately accessible characteristics to the less visible and more profound.
>
> (Durkheim 1938: xiii)

It was in this sense and not in some crude materialistic sense that religion was to be understood as a 'thing' and/or 'social fact'. However, despite these qualifications Durkheim's strong emphasis on the idea of social facts existing outside the minds of individuals led to charges against him of hypostasising society, of postulating a group mind, of promoting a fanciful theory of social realism, criticisms that will be considered in detail later.

Durkheim for his part believed that by treating religion as a social fact he had given it a 'foothold in reality' as he put it. The reality behind religion was society and this meant casting to one side any alternative explanation of a subjective kind that believers themselves might offer. By explaining religion as a social fact external to the individual conscience Durkheim believed he could demonstrate the fundamental weakness of all those theories that presented it as some form of illusion, or error of the mind. However, it is important to bear in mind that he did not see himself as suggesting that believers themselves, who failed to see that it was society that was the moral force or power on which their beliefs rested and from which they received their inner spiritual and moral strength, were deceived, but rather that they had not ventured beyond the letter of the symbol by which this force was represented to uncover its hidden, deeper meaning (1915: 225). But before proceeding any further with his explanation of religion we should first of all examine Durkheim's equally problematic definition of the phenomenon.

As with everything else in his treatment of religion Durkheim was determined that his definition of religion would set new and objective standards. Previous attempts at defining religion were based on preconceived ideas that were formed 'without any method, according to the circumstances and chances of life' and consequently 'have no right to any credit whatsoever, and must be rigorously set aside in the examination that is to follow' (1915: 24). A definition moreover had to get away from all forms of ethnocentricity and incorporate what counted for religion wherever it was found. This led Durkheim to reject a definition that based religion on belief and practice centred on God or gods or some notion of the supernatural since this would have excluded such religions as Buddhism. Furthermore, it would have meant abandoning the attempt to provide a scientific definition of the phenomenon for to define religion in this way was to define it in terms of the non-real, as it were, thus making Durkheim's declared aim of demonstrating the scientific nature of religion an impossibility.

At the heart of Durkheim's own definition of religion are two key elements: the notion of the sacred and that of a moral community or church. It is the notion of the sacred which provides religion with its content and along with that of church – an idea said by Durkheim to be inseparable from religion and to distinguish it from magic – constitutes its most distinguishing feature. Durkheim states:

> A religion is a unified system of beliefs and practices relative to sacred things, that is to say things set apart and forbidden – beliefs and practices that unite into one single moral community called a Church, all those who adhere to them.
>
> (1915: 47)

There is much that could be said by way of criticism of this definition of religion, but before looking at the criticisms we can consider briefly its two main and equally important elements just mentioned, beginning with a sketch of the sacred.

The sacred is, as Pickering has shown, an ultimate category and one that is prior to such notions as the divinity (Pickering, 1984: Chapter 8). It takes precedence over all else including God or gods. It is to be discovered in society's collective representations or ideas. It is also irreducible in that it cannot be explained at some other level, be it at the economic or psychological level. It is also, as a general idea, universal and is extremely contagious, spreading itself to all that comes into contact with it. However, it remains indivisible even when it subdivides for as far as religion is concerned 'the part is equal to the whole; it has the same power, it is equally effective' (1915: 229). But the sacred does not stand alone; it is part of a binary opposition, indeed it only has meaning in terms of its opposite, the profane:

> All known religious beliefs, whether simple or complex, present one common characteristic: they presuppose a classification of all things real and ideal, of which men think, into two classes or opposed groups, generally designated by two distinct terms which are translated well enough by the words profane and sacred [*profane* and *sacré*].

> (1915: 37)

Durkheim clearly regards this dichotomy as a social construct, something devised by society; as a result of the way in which they think and of what they observe people divide all there is into one or other of these two fundamental categories and place an almost unbridgeable gulf between them only capable of being bridged by ritual. Thus, society creates what is sacred and although it is relative in terms of its content since societies will differ from age to age and people to people, the concept itself is eternal.

The profane, as has been implied above, is not as clearly defined as the sacred and the vagueness regarding its essential character may well prompt one to ask whether anything that does not have clearly definable characteristics can be said to be part of a binary opposition, in this case the opposite force to the sacred which, we are told, cannot be separated from it without losing its character. If it is nothing more than a residual concept then it is clearly of little or no use, despite Durkheim's claims on its behalf. It is also worth pointing out here that there would appear to be a certain lack of consistency about the way the two parts of this dichotomy are manufactured since Durkheim insists that it is only the sacred that is social while the profane is individual. Sacred ideas or representations, as he calls them, have been fashioned by society while profane things are those which each individual constructs from their own sense data and experience in the sense that the notions people entertain about profane things 'have as their subject matter unadulterated, individual impressions' (Pickering, 1984: 119). As indicated above, there will be further comment on this definition of religion later, and meanwhile we can turn to Durkheim's explanation of the phenomenon as a social reality. Society, Durkheim maintained, gave birth to religion: 'It is in the midst of effervescent social environments and out of this effervescence itself that religious ideas seem to be born' (1915: 218–19).

It would appear that what is being suggested here is that religion is the product of a form of collective delirium, and Durkheim would not have totally disagreed with this point. What was needed to give rise to a religious life of any intensity, he believed, was a degree of psychical exaltation little short of delirium, but not any sort of delirium. The delirium he had in mind was social and, thus, 'well founded' for it was one that corresponded to something in reality. He would not, as we have seen, accept the naturists' and animists' arguments that religion was pure illusion; rather it was the result of an 'intense social life' which naturally caused a 'sort of violence to the organism as well as to the individual consciousness which interferes with its normal functioning' (1915: 227).

It is during these moments of collective effervescence that another world is created above the profane, everyday world, and one which, although it only exists in thought, is held in much greater esteem than the latter. However, in an effort to be consistent and show that this ideal world which constitutes the sphere of the sacred is a proper subject for 'scientific' investigation, the main purpose of his study of religion, Durkheim attempted to demonstrate that it was open to investigation, that observation 'could touch' the foundations on which it rested, for it was, he claimed, 'a natural product of social life' and as such could not escape the attention of science (1915: 422). The ideal or sacred world, therefore, was an integral part of society and this could clearly be shown to be the case by investigating religion in its most elementary form, an investigation which would highlight the main ways in which it was social. It would also enable Durkheim to show the links between the features of the social structure and the content of belief.

Durkheim discovered the idea of totemism as the most elementary form of religion in, as already mentioned, the writings of Robertson Smith. Although he was to make sweeping generalisations about all Australian tribes, and indeed others, Durkheim, who relied entirely on ethnographic material which came to him second-hand in the form of articles and books, concentrated most of his attention on one Australian aboriginal tribe, the Arunta. At the basis of this and all other Australian tribes, he claimed, and wrongly, as will be seen, was the clan which was characterised by a bond of kinship, not of blood, but of a 'very special kind', which caused its members to see themselves as belonging to the same family.

What bound clan members together into a single family, Durkheim claimed, was the fact that each and every one of them had the same totem which, he defined, as a species of things, for example, of animal, or a particular object, which was used to designate the clan collectively, served as its emblem and from which it took its name. It is this that creates that bond of a 'very special kind' between members who 'imprint the totem upon their flesh so that it becomes a part of them' (1915: 115–16) and which gives rise to the same kind of duties incumbent upon blood relatives including, among others, mutual assistance, the obligation to marry outside the family unit, to mourn the loss of a member and to defend each other.

But the totem is much more than an emblem or a name; it has a religious character, indeed ' . . . it is in connection with it [the totem], that things are classified as sacred and profane. It is the very type of sacred thing' (1915: 119).

Durkheim in this connection makes much of the fact that on the instruments which they use in their rites Australian tribes engrave a design representing the totem of their group. The Arunta's use of the *churinga* – a wooden instrument and also the term used to designate all ritual acts – is singled out for special comment in this regard and its sacred character highlighted, sacred because of the way in which it keeps the profane at a distance. The *churinga*, replete with 'all sorts of marvellous properties', radiates its sacred powers far and wide. However, only the male initiates can have access to it as it remains isolated and hidden in a sacred cavern or deserted place, the *ertnatulunga*, 'the sacred ark of the clan', which must be at all times protected and guarded for the fate of the clan is bound up with that of the *churinga*. But what gives the *churinga* and other ritual instruments their sacred nature is the fact that they bear the emblem of the clan, the totem. It is that which is sacred.

The totem is also sacred in that it symbolises the totemic principle in the form of an impersonal religious force or *mana*, very similar to the *churinga* mentioned above. This force, moreover, is the object of the totemic cult and

> . . . the original matter out of which have been constructed those beings of every sort which the religions of all times have consecrated and adored. The spirits, demons, genii and gods of every sort are only the concrete forms taken by this 'potentiality' . . .
>
> (1915: 199)

The totem not only symbolises God but also, as previously mentioned, the clan and, therefore, society. And since it symbolises both these realities they must, clearly, be closely interconnected:

> Thus the totem is before all a symbol, a material expression of something else . . . it expresses and symbolises two sorts of things . . . it is the outward and visible form of what we have called the totemic principle or god. But it is also the symbol of the determined society called the clan. It is its flag . . . So if it is at once the symbol of the god and of society is that not because the god and society are only one?
>
> (1915: 206)

Durkheim also justifies the association of God and society by claiming that the latter in its ideal form has all the attributes of the former; society creates us, rules over us, gives us laws and in a general way

> . . . has all that is necessary to arouse the sensation of the divine in minds, merely by the power it has over them; for to its members it is what god is to his worshippers.
>
> (1915: 206)

However, the relationship between God and society is one of interdependence: while society cannot live without the gods for it is by worshipping and serving them that it regenerates itself and strengthens and renews its commitment to its core values, the gods for their part would die if there was no cult, for 'sacred beings though superior to men can only live in human consciousness' (1915: 347). Moreover, as already indicated, the way God is perceived and understood will vary somewhat depending on the features of the social structure of the society in question. In the Australian and American societies that Durkheim wrote about God was understood in a concrete, particularistic way, unable, as such societies were, to think of the totemic principle in its abstract generality as is the case in more advanced societies, a view that, as we shall see, has been strongly criticised by the social anthropologist Mary Douglas, among others. And while he agreed that this was due in part to the inability of these Australian peoples to 'reach the same degree of abstracting and generalising as more advanced societies', Durkheim was careful to point out that the more important reason was ' . . . the nature of the social environment which has imposed this particularism' (Durkheim, 1915: 196).

In societies where totemism is the basis of the social organisation the totem of the clan is only sacred for the clan in question and no one thinks of it as being universal in nature, as a manifestation of one and the same universal force. This force of a single and universal spiritual power could be born 'only at the moment when the tribal religion developed above that of the clans and absorbed them more or less completely' (1915: 196).

Religion, then, can be seen to be social in that society constitutes the very foundations and the content of the sacred realm, and in other ways too. In the past in particular it provided a convincing interpretation of reality. Its myths offered an explanation of the beginnings of the universe, of the causes of evil and suffering. Indeed religion provided a whole range of concepts which not only made explanation possible but were indispensible to the organisation of everyday life in society. As Durkheim expressed it:

> Before all, it [religion] is a system of ideas with which the individuals represent to themselves the society of which they are members, and the obscure but intimate relations they have with it. This is its primary function; and though metaphorical and symbolic, this representation is not unfaithful.
>
> (1915: 225)

Moreover, philosophy and aesthetics and pursuits such as recreation and leisure activities including games 'seem to have been born of religion' – recreation deriving from such rites as commemorative rites – and to have retained for a long time their religious character (1915: 318–19). Religion, then, not only displays social reality in its symbols and rituals, but also expresses it. The religious dimension to aesthetics, recreation, leisure and related activities would survive albeit in a diminished form for religion was in a sense all of these things. And even as an explanatory system it would always survive to some degree principally because of the length of time it takes for scientific understanding to influence popular beliefs and attitudes. But it was this explanatory dimension of religion in particular that would inevitably continue to decline in significance in modern society with the rise of science.

The social nature of religion can also be seen in the functions it fulfils, one being to integrate and already singled out as the main function of religion both when discussing Durkheim's definition of the phenomenon and his interpretation of the social origins of religion. In terms of its integrative role, religion in the first place makes communal life possible by encouraging through, for example, its 'negative' rituals individuals 'to do violence to their instincts'. It also teaches them to sacrifice their ego, to forget themselves by demanding from them great sacrifices. Freud, as will be seen in the following chapter, made a similar point in *Civilization and Its Discontents*. Religion, moreover, made possible the emergence of collective thought in that by means of it people were enabled to step outside their own minds so to speak – individual minds are closed to each other – and communicate with others, and this idea, as will be seen below, is one that Jurgen Habermas would appear to have developed.

The integrative role of religion could also be seen, Durkheim maintained, in the way it instilled through ritual and ceremonial the values of the community. There is, for example, a group of what Durkheim refers to as representative or commemorative rites or ceremonies celebrated ostensibly to remain faithful to the past, to tradition. But a rite of this kind Durkheim tells us also serves 'to revivify those most essential elements of the collective consciousness . . . to attach the present to the past or the individual to the group . . .' (1915: 375).

All rites, including what Durkheim termed positive and piacular rites, serve to integrate society by engendering a communion of minds among the participants. The sacrificial cult is among the best examples of a positive rite which sustains and unites the community, while the mourning cult is offered as an example of piacular rites that perform the same function (1915: Chapter 2 and Chapter 5 respectively).

As we have seen, the evidence provided by Durkheim for the social reality of religion was drawn from studies of pre-modern societies and in particular from Australian aboriginal societies, but what can be said about religion's future in more technologically advanced societies where organic as opposed to mechanical solidarity is reputedly the norm? While he believed that no one particular religion was immortal Durkheim, as was previously pointed out, postulated that religion *per se* was in some sense eternal and this would seem to follow from what has just been said concerning the ways in which, he maintained, it served fundamental human needs that were embedded in the lasting characteristics of society. Whether the context be primitive or modern society where people lived a common life the beliefs they shared would be 'religious' beliefs. Moreover, since religion was, as we have already seen, a 'social fact' and, therefore, related to the 'real' it would inevitably persist although not without undergoing continual change both in terms of its symbolic structure and the content of its beliefs.

As society changed religion would be recreated anew and while usually reluctant to forecast what kind of religion would emerge in modern society, Durkheim did, nonetheless, occasionally venture to suggest what the religion of the modern secularised world would look like.

Before developing its modern form in Western, technologically advanced societies there would be numerous religious revivals, some very transient, until the revival initiated and sustained by the working class (Pickering, 1984: 480). As to its content, Durkheim, like his predecessor Comte, believed that this modern religion would be a humanistic form of religion focusing on the cult of the individual and this, to a very large extent, would be in response to the process of secularisation. Once again this viewpoint has influenced to a greater or lesser degree much contemporary sociological reflection on religion showing through in, for example, the writings of Berger and Luckmann (1969) and Wilson (1971).

This 'new religion', furthermore, would be much more liberal, Durkheim argued, than the traditional ones, allowing for much more freedom of thought, and would enshrine the virtue of justice as its central concern. Moreover, there would be periodic ceremonies in which this and the fundamental values of the community would be given ritualistic expression, a line of thought that lies behind much of the contemporary sociological theorising about civil religion (Bellah, 1970, 1975).

Modern religion, however, would be in the grip of rationalism and its interpretative role, discussed above, would be greatly reduced as a consequence of the ever increasing influence of science on popular thought.

Was religion then false? While regarding it as an axiom that religious beliefs, though their appearance may belie the fact, contain a truth that must be discovered (1915: 438) and indeed that all religions contain some truth (1915: 417, 438) since they express social reality in the ways already indicated above, they were all also at another level false. They were false in their interpretation of reality, attributing causality, as they do, to an independent spiritual order. This much follows from his definition which has already been considered. God or gods do not exist in a world beyond this one giving the believer access to another level of reality than the non-believer.

Nor do rites in themselves have the physical effects they are believed to have; these are purely symbolic and of little or no instrumental value in this domain. Therefore, since religion is a genuine 'social fact', an empirical reality, its explanation of the world by reference to another world cannot be accepted – for this we must look to science – and in this sense it is false.

But it does not follow from this, according to Durkheim, that religion is an illusion. Although the believer may believe and act as if religion were supernatural in origin this does not imply, as previously noted, that religion is a pure figment of the imagination or a form of deception. Nothing so enduring as religion could be based on complete falsehood or deception. Failure to understand the reality that lies behind it can simply mean that the believer, rather than being the victim either of an acute form of neurosis, as Freud maintained, or of the marxist form of alienation, is unaware of the real foundations of religion, and understandably so, since it is far from being a simple, straightforward uncomplicated issue. On the contrary, for it has presented a challenge to some of the finest minds. How far this is a true picture of how Durkheim stands to the believer's understanding of his or her faith we shall examine below.

THE INFLUENCE OF DURKHEIM'S SOCIAL EXPLANATION

While highly critical of the substance of Durkheim's explanation of religion Evans-Pritchard rightly pointed out that it contained many valuable insights (Evans-Pritchard, 1965: Chapter 3). And Lukes has highlighted the use made of some of these ideas by contemporary social scientists – among them Robin Horton, whose explanation of ritual man in Africa as theory-building man (Horton, 1961) owes much to the Durkheimian notion of religion as a cognitive system (Lukes, 1973: 483). Likewise, Horton's thesis that African thought and Western scientific thought are essentially identical ways of thinking (Horton, 1967) recalls Durkheim's belief, based on his view of religion as a cognitive system, that:

The explanations of contemporary science are surer of being more objective because they are more methical and because they rest on more carefully controlled observations, but they do not differ in nature from those which satisfy primitive thought.

(1915: 238)

Horton's views on the nature of traditional religion will be considered again in the following chapter. Meanwhile we can take a brief look at the ways in which Durkheim's ideas have influenced the thinking on religion of three other contemporary social scientists, Douglas, Berger and Habermas.

Although perhaps less deterministic and overall less of a functionalist than Durkheim, Douglas, likewise, lays great emphasis on the collective nature of human existence and on how society's moral values are displayed in a dramatic form in ritual. Douglas, moreover, is of the opinion that social relations provide the foundations of religion and that as long as these exist religion will survive. It will not disappear with modernisation but will simply reappear in a new form. She sees, as did Durkheim, symbol and ritual as central to the shaping and reshaping of social relations (Douglas, 1970). She also looks to so-called primitive society, although not exclusively, to elucidate the essential character of this process.

Douglas, however, differs from Durkheim on a number of issues. She does not accept, for example, that there exists a sacred realm totally separate from the profane world. For her nothing is especially sacred where it is a question of providing a legitimation of the social or moral order; such legitimation is always derived from daily social relations (1970). Douglas, furthermore, rejects the idea that, while 'primitive' society is characterised by mechanical solidarity, modern society is organically integrated. This dichotomy distorts the facts since there is evidence of both kinds of solidarity in both types of society. And Durkheim's evolutionary position, that the movement from religion to science whereby the former becomes redundant as a system of interpreting society to its members, is also rejected by Douglas. Religion is not in conflict with science she insists; each has its own domain and deals with different problems and, thus, the explanatory power of religion has nothing to fear from science (Douglas, 1982: 8).

Moreover, the idea that religion is under threat from bureaucratisation and secularisation, themes associated more with Weber than Durkheim, are also dismissed by Douglas as being not only theoretically mistaken but also for being incompatible with the evidence. First of all it is particular patterns of social relations that produce secularisation, and secondly these can exist and indeed do exist in both primitive and modern forms of society. The evidence of secular cosmologies among the Pygmies of Central Africa and the highly bureaucratised states of parts of fifteenth-century Europe show that it is not the passage from primitive to modern nor from loosely centralised to highly bureaucratised states that gives rise to secular cosmologies. Secularisation, Douglas insists, is 'an age old cosmological type, a product of definable social experience, which need have nothing to do with modern life or social science' (1970: 36).

Secular cosmologies are, then, a possibility in both so-called primitive and modern societies, a cosmology being a product of a certain kind of social experience, and highly flexible and functional. Douglas speaks of it as 'a set of categories that *are in use* [our italics] and likens it to 'lenses that bring into focus and make bearable the manifold challenge of experience' (1970: 179).

Durkheim's influence on Berger appears less direct, less obvious than on Douglas. It is by looking in the area of the sociology of knowledge in particular that one can detect certain similarities between these two sociologists. For Durkheim, as we have seen, religion is a form of knowledge, among other things, and the means by which all things were once classified (1915: 141ff). For Berger, likewise, religion is one of the most important forms of knowledge by which society is made possible, knowledge here being defined as shared meanings about reality (1967: 25 and *passim*). Religion is theoretical knowledge – although not the only form of theoretical knowledge, philosophy being another example of this kind of knowledge – that reaches its highest stage in what are termed symbolic universes of meaning, that is 'bodies of theoretical tradition that integrate different provinces of meaning and encompass the institutional order in a symbolic totality' (1966: 113).

This understanding of symbolic universe and the identification of one of its main functions as the locating of 'collective events in a cohesive unity that includes past present and future' (1966: 120) suggests that Berger means by it something very close to what Durkheim meant by religion. Of course, for Berger, and his colleague Luckmann, religion is but one type of symbolic universe and is defined as the 'human enterprise by which a sacred cosmos is established' (1967: 34). The sacred here is not to be equated with the supernatural; it is a quality of mysterious and awesome power that is believed to reside in certain objects of experience and that exists within the realm of the supernatural. It is worth noting that, although less categorical than Durkheim about the nature of the relationship between the two concepts, Berger, nonetheless, implies that the sacred and profane are intimately interconnected and interdependent and essential to an understanding of religion. He states, for example, that 'the dichotomization of reality into sacred and profane spheres, however related, is intrinsic to the religious enterprise' (1967: 35–6).

Access is had to the sacred – and here also there are strong echoes of Durkheim – through its symbolisation which has been collectively produced. The supernatural for its part is not some infinite, nebulous realm but a limited sphere of meaning throwing a canopy over and even enfolding, so to speak, the world of everyday reality. Thus, as a symbolic universe of meaning religion becomes 'the audacious attempt to conceive of the entire universe as humanly significant' (1967: 37). In sum, Berger argues that it is principally through religion that society has provided a meaningful order of existence for the individual who without the protection of the sacred cosmos would be a victim of *anomie*.

The German philosopher and sociologist Jurgen Habermas who shares many interests with the marxist intellectual tradition, among others, is less Durkheimian in approach than either Douglas or Berger. Nevertheless, there are clear similarities with Durkheim. Believing, for example, that individuals need to live in a meaningful universe which provides them with a sense of personal integration and self-identity – both of which are much more necessary in the modern rational world than in other epochs such as the neolithic where the distinction between the individual and nature was not clearly perceived – Habermas suggests that Durkheim was correct in seeing that such integration and identity are derived from unified world-views provided by society (1975: 117).

From his evolutionary standpoint, moreover, Habermas sees religion as performing several crucial roles in more developed civilisations. In addition to furnishing individuals with their understanding of life in society and of their social role it also links their sense of self-identity with their assumptions about society as a whole. In this way it provides them with an assurance of their existence as part of something larger and greater than themselves. Religion can also provide a vindication and a form of compensation for suffering and misfortune that would otherwise remain totally without meaning. Here Habermas is closely following Weber's treatment of how people make sense of and give meaning to undeserved suffering and deprivation through the construction of a theodicy of misfortune (Weber, 1963).

But even where it is a question of providing a justification of suffering and of offering consolation Habermas seems to be convinced that religion's role in modern society is limited. While it continues to act as a means of subjective integration and a way of enabling people to cope with misfortune and even as a means of providing legitimation for social integration in the form of civil religion, religion, nevertheless, has become very much a private affair as society has stepped in to control areas of life which were once its concern.

But while arguing that its traditional roles have been drastically curtailed and that its assumptions make little sense in the modern world, Habermas does believe that religion, if properly understood, could assume an important role in modern society. Understood properly, religion could act as a system of communication concerned above all else with the symbolic expression of meanings and expectations. Seen from this functionalist perspective religion would serve to unite a community of individuals in the pursuit of a deeper sense and understanding of themselves and, in this context, God becomes

> . . . the name for a communicative structure that forces men, on pain of loss of their humanity, to go beyond their accidental, empirical nature to encounter one another indirectly, that is across an objective something that they themselves are not (1975: 121).

Thus, although variable in terms of the nature of the extent and the nature of their impact, Durkheim's views on religion have clearly had a profound influence on much modern social science thinking on the subject. However, despite the acclaim that his insights have received and the uses to which they have been put, Durkheim's theory of religion has, nevertheless, been subjected to many serious criticisms from sociologists and anthropologists, as already indicated, and from philosophers and ethnographers, and it is to a further look at such criticisms that we now turn.

CONCLUSION: A CRITIQUE OF DURKHEIM'S THEORY OF RELIGION

Many scholars have pointed out the ethnographic failings of Durkheim's account of Australian aboriginal society and these have been summarised by Evans-Pritchard (1965) and Lukes (1973), among others. One of the strongest criticisms made against Durkheim's theory on ethnographic grounds is that much of what he took to be characteristic of totemism – ceremonies, sacred objects and so on – the basis of his entire study of primitive religion is in fact atypical. Moreover, totemism cannot always be associated with clans, nor is it a religion or even a form of religion but a mode of social organisation, a theory of human descent from a plant or animal or some other natural object which can vary from one tribe to another. Furthermore, it is not the clan but the horde or tribe which is the corporate group and this mistake renders so much of the evidence on which Durkheim bases his theory of religion unusable.

Clearly, these assumptions about totemism greatly weaken Durkheim's position, as do others including his idea of Australian totemism as the first form of totemism and his belief that the most simple forms of social organisation were to be found among Australian aboriginals. Other assumptions also have to be treated with great caution for lack of evidence, including the idea that the gods of Aboriginal Australians are derived from ideas related to totems and the notion that *mana/wakan* comes from the totemic principle.

Some of his ideas about primitive peoples, such as their supposedly undifferentiated, uniform way of perceiving and interpreting the world, also damage Durkheim's theory. In primitive society there are often numerous rival gods competing for the attention and loyalty of followers by offering them divergent paths to health and success. Moreover, the notion that in so-called primitive society the world is divided into two diametrically opposed camps of the sacred and profane – a point already made and one that will be discussed in more detail below in the discussion of his definition of religion – does nothing to help Durkheim's case. But it is worth pointing out once again that these ethnographic weaknesses do not mean that there is nothing of value in Durkheim's account of Aboriginal life; a number of anthropologists, including Malinowski, though highly critical of it on many points, have found it illuminating, especially from a methodological point of view (1925).

But there are many criticisms of Durkheim's methodology also. For example, as Lukes points out, *petitio principii*, or begging the question, is a feature from the start to the finish of *The Elementary Forms*:

> For Durkheim begins it with his conclusion, building into it his very definition of religion and then seeking to prove it by finding examples.
>
> (Lukes, 1973: 481)

As was previously noted, Durkheim's definition singles out the sacred as forming the content of religion, as its distinguishing feature. There is also a strong emphasis on religion's communal character through the use of the term 'church'; it is this group or community aspect of religion that divides it off from magic. But the appropriateness of these precise terms of definition seems to depend on the theory of religion that follows. Durkheim then proceeds to demonstrate this theory by recourse to one test case – Australian totemism – that is deemed to support the thesis, although where his evidence does not come up to scratch other evidence from American Indian society is arbitrarily drawn upon to bolster the case. Experimenting in this way is not only unscientific but also – because done on such a small case – severely limits one's understanding of the phenomenon under review.

Durkheim provides a real or essentialist definition, one that seeks to identify what constituted the causally necessary elements of religion. His definition is hardly a neutral operational one. The extent to which the definition relies on the theory that comes later may be seen when we reflect on the inadequacy of the sacred/profane dichotomy. The sacred, as already noted, is presented in *The Elementary Forms* as the polar opposite of the profane, a dichotomy which some scholars, among them Malinowski, found useful, while others have attacked it on philosophical and empirical grounds. A rigid dichotomy of this kind, it has been argued, cannot exist where one of the categories, in this case the profane, is no more than a residual category (Pickering, 1984: 140ff). And at the empirical level it has been shown by Evans Pritchard among others that far from being opposites the two notions are often found to be inseparable (1965: 65).

If, as Evans-Pritchard and others maintain, sacred (that is religiously important) objects in many communities are not consistently set apart and forbidden, then this is not a good way of getting at their character as religious. Moreover, the general category of that which is set apart and forbidden would appear to include all that a society regards as taboo, frightening or unclean, and thus many things that have no particular connection with religion. Being set apart and forbidden thus appears to be neither a necessary nor a sufficient condition of being sacred. This way of getting at a common denominator in religion is no doubt present in Durkheim because he wishes to avoid getting entangled in any substantive definition of religion. He does not wish to make 'sacred' a shorthand for 'that which is connected with the gods', for this would be to exclude non-theistic religion at the outset. But 'being set apart and forbidden' does not help as an alternative to the alleged failings of a substantive definition of the sacred and so Durkheim is left to fall back on the socially unifying function of sacred things to do the real work. Hence, his definition has almost immediately to rely on his theory that the nature of social and moral ties is the source and meaning of the sacred.

The definition of religion that Durkheim provides not only singles out the sacred as the content of religion – it is the symbol of the collective entity which, in practice, is the object of worship – but also informs us of the nature of the relationship – a functional one, as pointed out above more than once – between the essential elements of religion and of their principal effect, the integration of society. This, however, is to assume what has to be proved: that beliefs and practices do in reality unite all who adhere to them into one moral community called a church. Indeed, Durkheim appears to have been so obsessed with the idea of religion as the principal means of integrating society that he failed to consider the possibility of it being a disruptive, destabilising force.

By assuming in these and other ways what has to be proved Durkheim turns his definition into a theory and when he does attempt to substantiate his theory of religion and show its worth in relation to other theories, he does so by turning to society and society only for his explanation. This not surprisingly has given rise to the charge of unilateralism. His discovery in society of a comprehensive, total explanation for religion has led some observers to speak of his 'sociocentric fixation' (Stanner, 1967: 238). As Lukes expresses it:

He was, indeed, quite obsessed by the vision of society as the unique and all-encompassing *fons et origo* of religion . . . seeing the former as causal determinant, cognitive and symbolic referent, and functional consequence of the latter.

(1973: 481)

Mary Douglas, however, maintains that in certain respects Durkheim was not sufficiently 'sociocentric'. She believes, for instance, that 'Durkheim did not push his thoughts on the social determination of knowledge to their full and radical conclusion' (1978: xi). Douglas suggests that Durkheim in a sense placed scientific truth above society and that this was due in large measure to certain assumptions he made, among them the existence of objective, non-socially determined scientific knowledge. However, she grants that this was only to be expected, stating:

> It is entirely understandable that Durkheim should have internalised unquestioningly the categories of nineteenth century scientific debate since he strove to have an honourable place in the very community from which the standards of conduct emanate.
>
> (1978: xvi)

Whatever the merits of Douglas's criticism, a strong case can be made for saying that Durkheim's social explanation of religion is inconsistent with his own stated aims and massively under-argued.

We have documented already Durkheim's claim that his theory, in contrast to those of others, accounts for religion by showing how it latches onto something real and is non-illusory. However, since he makes society both the cause and symbolic referent of religious beliefs it is questionable how far he succeeds in this. He states of religion that:

> It is a system of ideas with which men represent to themselves the society of which they are members, and the obscure but intimate relations which they have with it. This is its primary function; and though metaphorical and symbolic, this representation is not unfaithful.
>
> (1915: 225)

But what is this but the assertion that the *manifest* content of religious ideas is false, albeit they metaphorically refer to something true? And if the manifest content of religion is false, this implies that the participants in it are under an illusion, and not merely ignorant of the ultimate origins of their beliefs.

It is arguable that the entire shape of Durkheim's discussion of religious beliefs in Book II of *The Elementary Forms* is directed toward explaining how an illusion arises and is maintained. Sacredness is perceived in the Aboriginal communities under discussion as a peculiar force which resides in selected external objects, animate and inanimate. The task is to explain what this sacred force might consist in. Such sacred forces have a crucial 'ambiguity' (1915: 225): they are felt as external to the individual, are attached to external things, yet are not physical and not perceptible as physical things are. The ambiguity is resolved by diagnosing religious forces as nothing other than the collective, anonymous force of the clan projected onto external objects (223). It is because the force of the clan, excited in collective effervescence, does transcend and sustain the individual that sacredness has these attributes. What is explained is how a force comes to be projected onto external things by the human mind. Religious forces represent the way in which collective consciousness acts upon individual consciousness. This is saved from being pure illusion by the facts that: the social forces behind the process possess many of the formal qualities which sacred things appear to have, the projection is social in nature and not an individual illusion, and the social forces and their projection have real and necessary consequences for the maintenance of society.

To be set against these last-mentioned facts is the point that the manifest content of religious ideas is mistaken, a point brought home when Durkheim tells us that ' . . . the god is only the figurative expression of society' (227) and when he affirms as a consequence of his account of ritual in Part III of *The Elementary Forms* that sacred beings can live only in human consciousness (347) and that 'sacred beings exist only when they are represented as such in the mind' (345). A number of points need to be stressed here. We need to remind ourselves that no theorist can long pretend that there is no truth or insight at all in religion. Even Feuerbach claims that suitably reinterpreted religious ideas contain references to what is real. It matters, then, not so much whether a theory allows religion to refer to some real things as to *which* real things it allows it to refer successfully. On this will depend what we say about religion's content. If in a state of high drunkenness someone sees and describes his car as a battleship, he refers to something real but is under an illusion about its nature.

Durkheim clearly is offering the thought that the religious believers are mistaken (grossly so) about the nature of the sacred, even though there is something real behind their ideas of the sacred. In this light his assertions about religion having a future are to be taken with caution. Would it survive acceptance that the 'god is only the figurative expression of society'? A determined methodological atheism seems to underlie the choices Durkheim leaves himself with. Faced with the ambiguity of the sacred he can allow only two options: it has either physical reality or the reality of projected moral force. It does not have the former, so it must have the latter. That he excludes a third possibility (there actually is a non-mundane reality which is manifested through ordinary things) represents a *metaphysical* choice Durkheim makes in advance. There is no argument for it: its alleged necessity is hidden behind the presumption that we must have a 'scientific' approach to religion. We have explored this line of thought already in Part One above.

The illusory character of the projected sacred is perhaps mitigated by one additional factor in Durkheim's theory of society. There is a hint in the *Elementary Forms* that he holds that all realities are shaped by collective, social representations. Through 'collective representations' the human mind in society shapes the world in which it lives (1915: 435–41). This appears to be a sociological version of idealism (compare Chapter 5 above).

A number of writers have argued for yet deeper inconsistencies in Durkheim. They have attempted to establish the following conclusion (particularly in relation to the tribal religions Durkheim concentrated upon). How can religious ideas serve to cement social ties, roles and forces unless those who make use of them really think that they refer by them to non-human, non-mundane realities which provide an anchoring to social life? The point here is that the attempted referent of religious symbols must seriously be taken to be a non-human god or transcendent entity to explain why these symbols have the social effect they do. They serve to anchor, for those who believe in and use the symbols, the society in question in something more-than-human. They cannot be 'really about' society in that case. The beliefs of the believers must be taken at face value to account for their social function. An interpretive thesis does not and cannot follow from a thesis about the social efficacy of religious symbols (compare Skorupski, 1978: 173ff).

There is also the frequently expressed criticism that Durkheim totally neglected the subjective element in his account of religion, that Douglas herself and other contemporary cultural theorists, including Habermas and Foucault, have no difficulty leaving out this dimension altogether from their work. This they do on the grounds that for purposes of analysis a distinction can be made between the individuals who create culture and the cultural objects and artefacts themselves, and that the cultural theorist's concern is with the relations between the latter and not with purely subjective intentions or meanings. However, it remains one of the most common criticisms of Durkheim, and one which will be briefly examined here by way of conclusion to this chapter and as lead-on to the next, that he system-

atically ignored the individual, subjective dimension in his treatment of religion, and by way of corollary he is criticised for not
allowing any room for the mystic, the prophet, the shaman and so
on.

There can be little doubt about the fact that Durkheim saw religion
as pre-eminently social. And, as we have seen, he regarded it as a
'social fact' and saw it as 'the foundation of collective life' (1915:
419ff). However, he did not dismiss the individual as irrelevant to
the course of a religion's development. As Pickering points out,
Durkheim readily accepted the importance of prophets and religious
leaders although he did not examine this aspect of religion in any
detail due, he explains, to the complex nature of the subject (1984:
198). Moreover, he did accept the reality of individual religious and
moral experiences and wrote of the enabling effect that communicat-
ing with one's god could have on the individual.

It is, nevertheless, the case that Durkheim spent little time on the
individual element in religion. This, however, was not because he
regarded it as *per se* unimportant but rather because from the point
of view of the social scientist it was largely unmanageable. For
Durkheim the subject matter of sociology was, and indeed had to be,
the irreducible reality of social life which was located in the moral
force of collective ideas or representations. And although these ideas
were generated by individuals in community, they became trans-
subjective, taking on a 'real' life of their own. None of this, however,
was a criticism of studying the individual, as opposed, that is, to the
social. There was certainly room for research of the kind that Freud
and Jung would engage in, research that would scientifically examine those deeper recesses of the individual inaccessible to ordinary
perception, in the way Durkheim believed he had scientifically examined what had been the hidden, social foundations and the latent
social consequences of religion.

8
Psychological Theories of Religion

FREUD AND THE ILLUSORY BASIS OF RELIGION

This chapter is concerned largely with the theories of religion advanced by Sigmund Freud (1856–1939) and Carl Jung (1875–1961) for it was they who established the paradigms that have come to dominate the psychological, and psychoanalytical, understanding of and approach to religion. Their theories of religion, like those of Marx and Weber, have often been presented as if they were polar opposites, but as will be seen below, they share a good deal in common. Moreover, to maintain, as is sometimes the case, that Freud was anti-religion and Jung pro-religion is to oversimplify their attitudes toward and their interpretations of the phenomenon.

Although, as already indicated, the main focus of what follows will be on their own particular accounts of religion, some consideration will also be given to the influence of Freud's and Jung's ideas on present day psychological and psychoanalytical interpretations of religion and to a lesser extent on contemporary anthropological and theological writing on the subject. However, space does not allow us to address directly systematic studies of religious experience such as those of Leuba (1896), Starbuck (1899) and James (1985), who by contrast with Freud, among others, emphasised the positive contribution made by religion to 'healthy-mindedness'. All these studies continue to be regarded as classics in this field. This notwithstanding, many contemporary psychologists of religion would want to refine the way religion is defined in these studies by including a social component. This dimension is ignored by, for example, James who defined religion substantively in terms of the 'feelings, acts and experiences of individual men in their solitude, so far as they apprehend themselves to stand in relation to whatever they may consider divine' (1985). On the other hand, the pioneering psychologist

Wilhelm Wundt, who established what is regarded as the first psychological laboratory in 1879, was perhaps more concerned, like Durkheim who was one of his students, with the way religion integrates and is enforced by communities and societies, than with religious experience itself, a concern shared to some degree, as we shall see, by Freud.

Central to Freud's understanding of religion was his notion of it as a form of transference and, as such, something to be outgrown (Jones 1991). Transference, which Freud maintained was a form of neurosis, contained two basic ingredients: repetition and the primacy of instinct. The repetitive element consists of the re-emergence of the past to influence the present: during transference patients transfer or project on to the analyst their own feelings and anxieties generated during childhood in relation to someone else of significance and importance to them at that time. According to Freud what in essence we are in terms of our emotions is largely determined in childhood and provides a template, as it were, of our future relationships.

The repetitive element in transference is strengthened by instinct which, Freud insisted, was the prime determinant of behaviour. The fact that instincts and the desires they give rise to are repressed through being projected on to others or through being denied does not render them ineffective or inactive. On the contrary, for they are engaged in a constant struggle to escape from the region of the unconscious where they are held in check by the super-ego. It is this repression which gives rise to neurosis and which can be seen in the context of transference where the client projects on to the analyst, often put in the place of one or other parent, conflicting positive and negative thoughts, desires and feelings.

Instinct occupied the same central, pivotal role in Freud's theory of religion as the idea of the commodity did in Marx's theory and the notion of society in Durkheim's. Moreover, like both Marx and Durkheim, Freud was extremely concerned with presenting a scientific account of religion, a fact which determines his methodology. For example, his model of transference which has just been outlined is one that makes a clear separation between client and analyst, and insists that what has occurred and is occurring in the former's psyche be 'observed' in a detached, dispassionate, objective manner, as if the analyst were engaged in a Newtonian-type experiment. Weber's notion of *verstehen*, empathic knowledge, is not one that appealed to Freud.

Moreover, Freud was very much a positivist and when this is

taken into consideration along with the tremendous importance he attached to the idea of repetition in his model of transference in his everyday psychoanalytical activities, it is not hard to imagine why he began his account of religion by seeking out its origins. He sought out these origins in two ways: first of all he looked, like Durkheim, for an account of religion in its most primitive form and this he presented in his *Totem and Taboo* (1960) the subtitle of which, it is worth recalling, is: 'Some Points of Agreement between the Mental Lives of Savages and Neurotics'. This is noteworthy for a number of reasons, not the least of which is that for Freud the present is in a sense the past repeated and also because he saw the emergence of religion in childhood as paralleling the emergence of religion in the early history of the human race. It is in his account of the emergence of religion in early childhood that we have his second attempt to explain religion's origins and this is presented in his *The Future of an Illusion* (1978).

Thus, Freud explains the origins, development and function of religion in the context of two converging and reinforcing models, one of which, the first of the two mentioned above, is his phylogenic model of the human species and the other, also referred to above, is his infant prototype or model of personal development. We will begin this discussion of religion with an outline of the first of these models and then move on to a discussion of the second. But first of all we comment on the Freudian meaning of the key term which he used to characterise religion and which is not always correctly understood, *illusion*. Regarding this notion he wrote:

> An illusion is not the same thing as an error; nor is it necessarily an error. What is characteristic of illusions is that they are derived from human wishes. In this respect they come near to psychiatric delusions. But they differ from them, too, . . . in the case of delusions we emphasize their being in contradiction with reality. Illusions *need not necessarily be false* – that is to say unrealizable or in contradiction to reality . . . Thus we call a belief an illusion when a wish-fulfilment is a prominent factor in its motivation, and in so doing we disregard its relations to reality, just as the illusion itself sets no store by verification.
>
> (Freud, 1978: 26–7, our emphasis)

Freud's account of illusion in religion connects immediately with two elements in earlier parts of this study. One is the stress we saw in Feuerbach on desire and need as the source of religion (see Chapter 5). Another is our distinction, made repeatedly, between the truth and rationality of religious belief (see Chapter 3). Freud is clearly saying that whether religious beliefs happen to coincide with reality is not necessarily central to how we explain their provenance. A true belief is not inevitably the outcome of reason, nor is a false belief necessarily the outcome of unreason. In his account of illusion in *The Future of Illusion* Freud shows that he is not committed to diagnosing the irrationality of religious belief through one of the routes we have argued to be typical of the radical theorist of religion, namely that of first showing that they are obviously, radically false. He points instead to an independent source of evidence that they are illusory. And one important question to bear in mind when considering Freud's theory of religion outlined below is how can he be sure that religion *as such* is illusory?

If we examine the text of *The Future of an Illusion*, we find Freud complaining of the poverty of the avowed reasons for typical religious beliefs. These reasons fall into three categories: respect for our ancestors' beliefs, a memory of ancient 'proofs' for them, and a refusal to question what are now regarded as entrenched and sacred opinions (Freud, 1961: 26). Freud is in effect calling attention to the gap that exists between the degree of confidence these grounds really license and the actual hold of religious belief over culture. Moreover, he probably has in mind, implicitly, the thought that the remoteness of religious notions from any possible empirical confirmation makes this gap even more astonishing (compare Evans Pritchard on 'mystical notions' in Chapter 3 above). So it appears we can know from the nature of the case that religious beliefs must be motivated by something other than reason. Given *this* reading of the epistemological situation that surrounds popular religious convictions we *can* disregard the relation between these convictions and reality in seeking to explain them. Freud himself comments:

> Thus we arrive at the singular conclusion that of all the information provided by our cultural assets it is precisely the elements which might be of the greatest importance to us and which have the task of solving the riddles of the universe and of reconciling us to the sufferings of life – it is precisely those elements that are the least well-authenticated of any. We should not be able to bring ourselves to accept anything of so little concern to us as the fact

that whales bear young instead of laying eggs, if it were not capable of better proof than this.

(Freud, 1978: 23)

Hence psychoanalysis has a problem: how to uncover the real motives behind religious conviction.

Having in this way 'taken our bearings' as he puts it, Freud moves on to answer the question as to why religious doctrines, 'all of them', he notes, 'illusions', have exercised the 'strongest possible influence over mankind' (1978: 25).

Freud argues in *Totem and Taboo* and elsewhere that religion is born of fear and guilt (1960: 145). According to his phylogenic model of the origins of the human race the 'creation' of God consisted of an appeal by primitive man to his all-powerful father for assistance in overcoming the unsurmountable problems of life which he could not face alone. But this God, in the form of an all-powerful father-substitute, is not only a source of help and support and therefore to be loved, but also a jealous, violent and fear-inspiring figure who either castrated or banished his sons in order to preserve his authority over them and retain as his property all the females of the horde over which he exercised total control. In support of this version of the emergence of the idea of an omnipotent God Freud, strongly influenced by the writings of Durkheim, Frazer and Robertson Smith, looked to *totemism* which he regarded as the beginning of human morality, 'a first attempt at religion', (1960: 205–6), and even more than just an attempt, for he stated:

I think we are completely justified in regarding totemism, with its worship of a father-substitute, with its ambivalence as shown by the totem meal, with its institutions of memorial festivals and of prohibitions whose infringement was punished by death – as the *first form in which religion was manifested in human history* [and in confirming the fact of its having been linked from the first with social regulations and moral obligations].

(Freud, 1986: 326 [our emphasis])

Freud offers a number of examples of the moral and social regulations that had their origin in totemism, among them exogamy and the taboo on incest (1960: 143). He also, echoing Durkheim, lays great emphasis on religion's social character, stating that in general it was 'an affair of the community' and religious duty 'part of social obligation' (1960: 134).

In the context of the 'primal horde' which was the cradle of religion the sons experienced intolerable hardship and frustration and any intimacy between them and the female members of the horde not only aroused their father's jealousy but, as we have seen, resulted in them being either castrated or driven out of the horde, this latter punishment being possibly even a worse fate than castration. The youngest sons, protected by their mother's love, were safe. But it is important to note that those who were driven out not only hated and *feared* their father but also *honoured* him as a model and wished to take his place, so they joined together to overthrow him and then in an act of cannibalism, which they believed would ensure their identification with him, devoured him.

Nonetheless, a major problem remained, for given that each of the sons wished to take over their father's role, disagreements inevitably ensued. However, internecine strife was averted by the fact that the sons concerned were united by an unbreakable bond forged during the period of their banishment and the experience of liberating themselves from their tyrannical father's oppression. Moreover, they had come to realise that divided they would be unable to cope with the dangers and difficulties surrounding them. Therefore, instead of fratricidal strife what emerged between them was a 'fraternal alliance', or, 'sort of social contract' by which each individual renounced his ambition of acquiring for himself alone his father's position and of possessing his mother, sisters and all the other females of the horde. In this lies the origin of both the previously mentioned taboo on incest and the injunction to exogamy. By this contract, furthermore, some of the father's power passed over to the women and in time and for a time matriarchy came to be the norm. Moreover, in this way, and as a result of the 'renunciation of instinct' the first form of social organisation came into being with the recognition of mutual obligations, the establishment of definite institutions, regarded as inviolable and sacrosanct, and the beginnings of morality and justice.

However, in all of this the father was not forgotten: when forging the 'fraternal alliance' the brothers chose a powerful and feared animal as a totem animal and substitute-father figure. Moreover, the ambivalent emotional attitude which they had towards their real father was retained in relation to the totem which they regarded as the clan's blood ancestor and protective spirit, who must in turn be protected and worshipped. And to this end a festival was introduced which was celebrated at regular intervals and during which the totem animal was devoured and in this way made to experience the same fate as the real father. This totem meal or first act of communal sacrifice ('repeated in the rite of Christian communion' according to Freud) was one in which all the members of the horde participated and was performed to celebrate the sons' victory over their father and their liberation from his oppressive rule (1960: 126–46 and *passim*).

Here we have in outline the Freudian version of the first step in the evolution of religion. He did not, of course, intend to account for the total history of religion or for all its stages, but only to show how it emerged out of totemism and to trace the psychological development of what he considered to be its central belief, belief in God. For example, he explains the stages in the development of the object of worship. How it was once animal in nature before being humanised and worshipped in the form of male and then female and then male deities until the return of a 'single father-god of unlimited dominion' (1960: 146).

The 'determining cause' of this re-emergence of monotheism was the empire-building on a world scale of the Pharaohs. First Judaism and then Christianity, and we might add Islam which Freud does not mention, took over this monotheistic idea. In the case of Judaism the monotheistic idea which had reached it from Egypt had been latent for a long time – the re-emergence of the latent idea figures prominently in Freud's theory of the transmission of ideas – before it was finally taken up and preserved as its precious possession and one which gave the Jews pride in being a chosen people. Further it was:

. . . the religion of their primal father to which were attached their hope of reward, of distinction and finally of world domination.
(Freud, 1986: 329)

From Freud's story so far, we can at least see something of the way he understands the definition of religion. He is fundamentally concerned with religion as belief in gods, while allowing, in totemism, a pre-animistic stage to religion. But Freud concentrates for the most part on theistic religion using, tacitly, a substantive definition of religion, and he believed he had firm support for this, asserting with regard to the development of the monotheistic idea:

> There is nothing wholly fabricated in our construction, *nothing which could not be supported on solid foundations.*
>
> (Freud, 1986: 328, our italics)

Freud's theory of the origins of religion in early human history was not wholly dependent for proof on historical evidence about the character of primitive society or on how civilisation in fact developed, for, he insisted, we have it all confirmed at a very personal level when we analyse the development of the individual from birth throughout childhood. He states:

> For once before one has found oneself in a similar state of helplessness: as a small child in relation to one's parents. One had reason to fear them, and especially one's father; and yet one was sure of his protection against the dangers one knew.
>
> (1975: 13)

Moreover, he believed in the existence of what he termed a 'collective mind' in which 'mental processes occur just as they did in the minds of individuals' (Freud, 1960: 157). Thus, the phylogenic model of the origins and development of religion neatly dovetails into the infant prototype or model mentioned above and which we will now outline.

This last mentioned model of the relationship of psychology to religion essentially concerns the interaction between the *id*, the *ego* and the *super-ego*. The first of these three elements of the individual's mental and emotional make-up, the id, is composed of uncoordinated instinctual impulses, drives or wishes derived from the activity of conative trends, which in turn come from primary physical instincts and which have been so repressed that they no longer enter into one's conscious thoughts. These instincts are, nonetheless, still active, as we have seen, and in unrecognised and adverse ways continue to influence the individual's behaviour. We will return to Freud's ideas on the id, or *subconscious*, mind below, but first a comment or two on the third component of the mind, the super-ego, the old *preconscious* mind which Freud characterised as 'virtually conscious' or put another way 'capable of being conscious'. It differs from the *id* in that while one can be unconscious or unaware of the contents of this component of the mind one can call them to mind by simply directing attention to them. An example often given to illustrate what is meant here is that of the ticking clock which one might well become unaware of and by one act or other recall or hear its sound. A dripping tap would be another example. These analogies do not fully describe the notion of the super-ego for it does not depict that quality of harshness associated with it nor do they reveal the existence of a considerable tension between the super-ego and the ego.

The super-ego is a form of internalised external authority that has taken the place of the autocratic father. As just noted above, it is partly unconscious, in that it is a survival from infancy in the form of norms derived from early childhood, and it is partly conscious. It has components derived from the family, the school, the church and other associations and institutions, and by means of it aggressive impulses are repressed and civilisation allowed to develop and persist. The super-ego, the heir to the father and with all of his powers to command and correct, becomes for the individual the ideal to be attained. Not only does it insist on the renunciation of instinctual satisfaction but one is also aware that these instincts, even when renounced, still persist and proceed to demand punishment. In this way, like the primal father in the case of the primal horde and the father of the family in the case of any child, it induces fear and guilt, for if not obeyed it will withdraw its love and protection.

The autocratic, domineering father syndrome is, then, the basis of the authority of the super-ego, or conscience, which seeks to control and regulate the ego or conscious self with regard to the impulses arising from the id. And, in the formation of the individual's super-ego or conscience, we see almost the exact same process taking place as that which characterised the phylogenic development of conscience outlined earlier. We have in both instances a resolution of the 'Oedipus complex' as the basis of conscience.

The nature of this complex is well known: the child for a time wants the full attention of the parent of the opposite sex. The son, therefore, strongly desires the full attention of his mother and consequently would like to get rid of his father. But he eventually realises that his father will retaliate and castrate him and so from a motive of self-preservation the desire to propitiate his father emerges and takes over from the wish to dispose of him. Furthermore, as he becomes older, the son develops feelings of guilt and remorse on account of his previous desire to eliminate his father and for this reason he acquires a wish for forgiveness. This results in the emergence of a 'dual mind' or one which consists in part of the son's own desires and in part of the identification of himself and his own desires with those of his father. The son can now accept his father's commands and renounce his sensual desires for his mother.

Thus at the level of the individual and at that of the group an instinct is repressed out of fear and guilt and respect for the father. By reacting in this way to their instincts individuals are influenced by their very early experiences just as whole groups and societies in later times have been influenced by the action of primeval man. On this Freud wrote:

> It is quite certain that in the course of thousands of years the fact was forgotten that there had been a primal father with the characteristics we know and what his fate had been; nor can we suppose that there was any oral tradition of it, as we can in the case of Moses. In what sense then does a tradition come into question at all? In what form can it have been present? . . . In my opinion *there is almost complete conformity in this respect between the individual and the group: in the group too an impression of the past is retained in unconscious memory-traces*. In the case of the individual we believe we can see clearly. The memory trace of his early experience has been preserved in him in a special psychological condition . . . What is forgotten is not extinguished but only *repressed*; its memory-traces are preserved in all their freshness but isolated by 'anti-cathexes'. They cannot enter into communication with other intellectual processes; they are unconscious – inaccessible to consciousness.
>
> (1986: 329, our emphasis)

In the individual then there remains, albeit latent, this memory of a wish to dispose of his father which accounts for his idea of and about God and likewise in the life of the human race as a whole there remains latent the memory of primal man's response to his all-powerful father which gave rise to the notion of God in the first place. In conclusion to *Totem and Taboo* Freud wrote:

> I should like to insist that its outcome shows that the beginning of religion, morals, society and art converge in the Oedipus complex.
> (1960: 156–7)

Freud not only discussed the origins of religion in early childhood and showed how the process resembled and was indeed subconsciously interlinked with its development in early human history, but also addressed the questions of the role of religion in the creation and maintenance of civilised society, and its future. His ideas on the role of religion in the development of civilisation are found in several of his writings but more clearly presented in his *Civilization and its Discontents*. In his explanation of the origins of primitive religion he describes, as we have seen, how man becomes a social being by coming together and renouncing his instincts. This is the *decisive* step of civilisation, the essence of which lies:

> . . . in the fact that the members of the community restrict themselves in the possibilities of their satisfaction, whereas the individual knew no such restrictions.
>
> (1975: 32)

But however necessary civilisation may be for man's peace, enjoyment and freedom, this is by no means the end to his emotional, social and psychological problems. Individuals, in fact, while they find it almost impossible to live in isolation, also find it very difficult to live in common with others. In Freud's words they

> . . . feel as a heavy burden the sacrifices which civilization expects of them in order to make a communal life possible.
>
> (1978: 2)

Indeed individual liberty 'was greatest before there was any civilisation', even though it then had little or no value because the individual was not in a position to defend it. Civilisation is, further, an imposition on the majority, something created by a minority with the techniques and the power to enforce their will. Freud was not opposed to this in principle for he believed that leaders with superior insights, who have mastered their own instinctual wishes, are necessary to set an example. The masses would give them recognition and be induced by their example and by the coercion which they could exert over them to perform the tasks and undergo the renunciations necessary for the persistence of civilisation. Otherwise these same 'lazy, unintelligent' masses who show no love for instinctual renunciation, and who are not to be convinced by the argument of its inevitability, would support one another in giving free reign to their indiscipline. Not being spontaneously fond of work, they would seek to destroy civilisation which, he explains, is based on:

... the psychological discovery that man is equipped with the most varied instinctual dispositions, whose ultimate course is determined by the experiences of early childhood.

(1975: 5)

Nevertheless, Freud was not quite as pessimistic about human nature as, for example, Thomas Hobbes in *Leviathan*, for he did not discount the possibility that with improvements in education leading to the creation of a different cultural environment in which people would be susceptible to rational argument and fond of work, external coercion could be dispensed with. However, although some progress had been made in this direction there was still a very long way to go. Also, it was more than likely that 'a certain percentage of mankind, owing to a pathological disposition or an excess of instinctual strength, will always remain asocial' (1975: 5).

Thus, even Freud, one of the great believers in the power of reason, held out no higher hope for civilisation than the socialisation of the majority. As to the progress made to date, well there was evidence that coercion had been to an extent internalised as a result of certain mental advances, in particular the development of the super-ego, and this could be seen from the fact that the instinctual wishes of incest, cannibalism and lust for killing had been repudiated. These wishes, however, were still present and strong, and under certain circumstances some of them, for example killing, were even countenanced by civilisation. But the super-ego cannot censor all instinctual desires for these can only be controlled by external coercion, and this is true in particular of avarice, lust, lying, fraud, envy and calumny, all of which must be held in check if the moral fabric of a civilisation is to be preserved. The underprivileged classes, so long as they remain discontented, will envy the more favoured ones. Where the satisfaction of the better off depends upon the suppression of the underprivileged there will be no internalisation of the norms and values of the society in question and this last mentioned class will be prepared to go as far as destroying the culture itself unless their demands are satisfied.

Religion has a direct bearing on all of this although it is never very clear whether Freud regards it as distinct from civilisation, or an integral part of it, or simply as one of its techniques of survival. He seems to see it as all three. He also appears to regard it at one and the same time as both indispensable and an evil which he would like to see eradicated. The mental asset of the super-ego and other assets of civilisation in the form of artistic creations and cultural ideals and achievements provide, in their different ways, substitutive and narcissistic satisfaction and thereby help to combat hostility to civilisation. Religion, likewise, helps civilisation to do what it was created to do, that is to defend man against nature. However, as already indicated, civilisation is itself part of the problem, for in protecting individuals from nature it imposes restraints on them and causes severe injury to their 'natural narcissism' (1978: 11). This natural narcissism is under threat by our helplessness in the face of nature, and religion is 'born from man's need to make his helplessness tolerable' (Freud, 1978: 14). The longing for the divine father figure has a general motive in the desire to solve in the imagination the tensions that our helplessness creates, as well as in the more detailed workings of infantile sexual longings and jealousies. Hence comes Freud's threefold account of the functions of the gods in *The Future of an Illusion*: they exorcise the terrors of nature, reconcile men to the cruelty of fate and compensate them for the sufferings and privations which a civilised life has imposed upon them (Freud, 1978: 14).

Through the agency of religion civilisation enables man to tame and approach the impersonal forces or 'violent superman' of nature by endowing them with human qualities and passions and transforming them into humans. Moreover, as one of civilisation's techniques for accomplishing its purpose religion enables man 'to feel at home in the uncanny and [to] deal by psychical means with senseless anxiety' (Freud, 1978: 13). In addition religion contains historical recollections and, thus, provides society with historical truth where reason sometimes misleads. An example would be the introduction of the prohibition against murder which reason attributes to social necessity but which religion rightly tells us was issued by God in that the killing of the primal father evoked such an irresistible, emotional reaction with such momentous consequences that it gave rise to the commandment 'Thou shalt not kill'. It follows, therefore, that if the primal father was the original image of God, then God was responsible for this commandment which constitutes the foundation stone of civilisation, and it also follows that the religious explanation of this prohibition is the correct one. Furthermore, religion like art and music has acted to offset some of the negative consequences of civilisation itself. It has done so by providing individuals with consolation and compensation whereas civilisation, we have seen, by the restraints it imposes, causes them injury. Freud, then, while maintaining that religion is an illusion is prepared to enter a partial defence of it on the grounds that it 'has clearly performed great services for human civilization. It has contributed much to the taming of asocial instincts . . .' However, 'But not enough' (1978: 33): for religion has supported immorality as much as it has defended morality. Furthermore, it has failed to make many people happy and content with civilisation which they continue to see as a yoke which must be cast off.

Freud, nonetheless, seems to imply, as already indicated, that for the majority religion is still a necessity if civilisation is to survive without being despotically imposed. The few well educated people can replace religious motives for behaviour with secular ones without posing any threat to civilisation. On the other hand, the illiterate uneducated masses, unchanged by scientific thinking, must not come to realise there is no God otherwise they will have no reason not to kill, plunder and steal. To prevent this the masses must be kept from finding out that religion is an illusion otherwise the only other way of saving civilisation, if and when they are awakened to the fact that God does not exist, is through imposing it upon them by external coercion. He writes:

> Thus either these dangerous masses must be held down most severely and kept most carefully away from any chance of civilisation . . . and religion must undergo a fundamental revision.
>
> (1978: 35)

The irony here is that in modern society the more educated in a formal sense people are the more religious they tend to be, at least in terms of public practice.

On the question of religion's future, raised above, Freud, as already mentioned, was ambivalent. Religion, he believed, sustained and legitimated an unhealthy dependency, it was a substitute for something wholesome and real, it was symptomatic of obsessional neurosis, and so professionally it was his task to bring about an end to it. 'People', he insisted, 'cannot remain children forever', but 'must in the end go out into "hostile life"' (1978: 45). This development could be greatly assisted by a process that he referred to as 'education to reality'. Such education would bring about the necessary psychological change to enable people to surmount and eventually sublimate those fears and feelings of guilt and helplessness in the face of nature that were born in childhood and for which religion offered only consolations, the effects of which Freud, echoing Marx, likened to a narcotic.

On the other hand, Freud was not confident that education would be greatly successful and because of this he feared that the worst of all possible worlds might emerge: a poorly educated society that had thrown off the restraints imposed by religion and thus constituted a grave danger to civilisation. He was, therefore, reluctant to see religion disappear while a majority of people continued to act more in accordance with instinct than reason. Were education to be widespread and of good quality then society would have little to fear from the decline of religion. Freud wrote:

> Civilization has little to fear from educated people and brainworkers. In them other, secular motives would proceed unobtrusively; moreover, such people are to a large extent themselves vehicles of civilization. But it is another matter with the great mass of the uneducated and oppressed who have every reason for being enemies of civilization. So long as they do not discover that people no longer believe in God, all is well. But they will discover it, infallibly . . . And they are ready to accept the results of scientific thinking, but without the change having taken place in them which scientific thinking brings about in people. Is there not a danger here that the hostility of these masses to civilization will throw itself against the weak spot that they have found in their task mistress?
>
> (1978: 35)

We can now turn to a consideration of Jung's understanding of religion before offering a critique of his and Freud's theories in the conclusion to this chapter.

JUNG AND THE RELIGIOUS IMAGINATION

If Freud sought the renunciation and sublimation of religion through a process of 'education to reality' for the reason that it perpetuated an infantile, neurotic condition both at the level of the individual and that of the wider human community, Jung is often perceived as having sought its transformation into a universal form of wisdom. But, as previously mentioned, and as will be seen below, the opinions of Freud and Jung on religion are not always as far apart as is sometimes assumed. They were, of course, close associates for a number of years. Jung was Freud's student and colleague and this in part accounts for a certain similarity of view between them which persisted even after they had parted over differences in method and interpretation in 1913.

Jung was, of course, generally more accepting of religion than Freud and while, like the latter, his aim was to be objective and scientific he was more inclined towards relativism. He eschewed, for example, Freud's tendency to equate truth with happiness and falsehood with misery. Jung, moreover, appears to have had a less reductionist view of the nature and activity of individuals than Freud. His main concern was the pursuit of integration through the process of individuation. This process has been described by Jones:

> For Jung the fundamental psychological drive is not gratification but integration, and so the psyche struggles to become conscious of and draw upon the hidden but real dimensions (complexes) of the self.
>
> (Jones, 1991: 4)

Jung believed that traditionally it was the role of religion to guide this process of individuation.

Of course, Jung gave more than one interpretation of what he meant by religion and this makes it difficult to provide a clear account of his views on the subject. At one stage of his thinking about the phenomenon he had recourse to Rudolph Otto's concept of the *numinous* to help him formulate his own notion of what it was (Jung, 1938: 4). The numinous, Jung informs us, is:

> . . . a dynamic existence or effect not caused by an arbitrary act of will. On the contrary it seizes and controls the human subject, which is always rather its victim than its object.
>
> (1938: 4)

Religions were not to be equated with creeds; these were but codified and dogmatised forms of numinous or original religious experiences. Religion was a

> . . . peculiar attitude of the human mind which could be formu-lated in accordance with the original use of the term 'religio', that is, a careful consideration and observation of certain dynamic factors understood to be 'powers', spirits, demons, gods, laws,

ideas, ideals, or whatever name man has given to such factors as he has found in his world powerful, dangerous or helpful enough to be taken into consideration, or grand, beautiful and meaningful enough to be devoutly adored and loved.

(1938: 5)

This is a very broad, loose, vague, substantive type of definition of religion without any reference to monotheism or even to a transcendental order as such.

Religion is also understood in strongly functionalist terms and this can be seen by moving from the question of what religion is to that of being religious. This latter state for Jung was a matter of having a certain kind of temperament that enabled one to become conscious of oneself, to uncover those arbitrarily repressed *complexes* that lay hidden in the unconscious mind and invaded the consciousness with 'their weird and unassailable convictions and impulses', often reducing a person to a state of helplessness (1938: 14). Due to the difficulties to which knowledge of the unconscious might give rise many people do not wish to come to 'know' themselves. Religion, for its part, however, enables people to look at this realm and deal with these complexes. And it is more than simply a means of unearthing repressed impulses; it plays an important and indeed indispensable cognitive role by providing a more rounded interpretation of the mind than science which only treats of the conscious realm by expressing in its dogmas, symbols and rituals both the conscious and unconscious components of the psyche (1938: 59).

Jung, in seeing religion as the intermediary between the conscious and unconscious spheres and, thus, as pointing the way to individual wholeness and fulfilment, appears to present a markedly different view of it from that advanced by Freud. And this is to a large extent the case. Freud, as already indicated, never allowed for the possibility that religion might be a means of enhancing a person's grip on reality rather than simply functioning in every instance as a means of escaping from it into an illusory world. As one observer commented:

For Freud the reductive approach of tracing psychological material to its infantile origins always took precedence over the possibility that the same material might contain within it the seeds of better adaptation and thus be forward looking.

(Storr, 1973: 31)

Jung, however, was not always completely different in every respect from Freud in this. For example, he shared the idea with Freud that God was a projection from the unconscious and that the personal history of the individual was the principal arbiter of the manner and form that idea took (Jung, 1958). This, however, was just before his break with Freud in 1913. Later he was to speak of the collective unconscious, a term which, like so many others that he used, he never clearly defined, as the source of the image of God. It was, among other things, that stratum of the mind that produced myths, dreams and visions, and was common to all people regardless of their state of mind, culture or historical epoch.

But even in identifying the collective unconscious as the source of the notion of God, Jung was not moving in the completely opposite direction to Freud. The latter also wrote, as previously noted, of an unconscious mind and of how the notion of God generated in very early childhood was a product of physical continuity. Freud insisted, moreover, that the mental impulses behind the birth of the idea of God in early human history could not be completely suppressed. Indeed, he maintained that the creative sense of guilt behind this idea stemming from those times persisted to the present:

> We find it operating in an asocial manner in neurotics, and producing new moral precepts and persistent restrictions, as an atonement for the crimes that have been committed and as a precaution against new ones.
>
> (1960: 159)

Jung, however, is less clear than Freud regarding what is passed on in the collective unconscious from generation to generation. He seems to suggest – and his definition of religion already cited lends support to this opinion – that what is inherited is not so much an idea of God but a susceptibility for profound 'spiritual' experiences and a predisposition for the making of significant myths which he refers to as *archetypes*. He wrote with reference to the archetype and its content:

> Again and again I encounter the mistaken notion that an archetype is determined in regard to its content, in other words that it is a kind of unconscious idea . . . It is necessary to point out once more that archetypes are not determined as regards their content

but only as regards their form, and then only to a very limited degree. A primordial image is determined as to its content only when it becomes conscious and is therefore filled out with the material of conscious experience.

(1957: 79)

Thus, it is from the stuff of everyday experience that archetypes derive their content. Moreover, they can only be known through experience and, we may add, one, and only one, of a number of possible interpretations of an archetype is to see it as something that is experienced in an extraordinary way. It can also refer to, among other things, ideas of symbolic significance, to situations, places and persons. However, while the number of archetypes is, in theory, infinite some are clearly more important than others for an understanding of Jung's account of religion. There is, for example, the archetype of the good and bad mother which can be projected onto the real mother. And the father, although of lesser importance in Jungian than Freudian psychology, also has his positive and negative archetypes.

The positive archetype of the mother can manifest itself in a number of ways, one of these being in the form of a goddess, while the negative dimension may be expressed through the symbolism of a witch. The paternal archetype, for its part, is in its positive form symbolic of the deity that rejects pure instinctuality. In its negative form it is the devil as symbol of pure sexual desire. Other archetypes relevant to Jung's account of religion are *animus* and *anima*, personifications of the personality opposed in some sense to the conscious ego and possessing certain attributes of the opposite sex. In very general terms the former refers to the woman's image of the man and the latter the converse.

While, from this discussion of archetypes, and in particular from what was said concerning archetypes and the idea of God, it would appear that Jung was convinced that there was no way of knowing about a metaphysical God, it would also seem to be the case, nevertheless, that he held a more positive view than Freud of the role played by the image of God in the life of the individual. For example, he dismissed Freud's understanding of the origins of the image of God when, in discussing the historical process of the world's 'despiritualisation', he spoke of two 'inevitable mistakes', one being 'the materialistic error', and the other 'psychologism' which wrongly claimed that:

If God is anything he must be an illusion derived from certain motives, from fear for instance, from will to power, or from repressed sexuality.

(1938: 103)

The differences between Jung and Freud were many. Jung, unlike Freud, and like Weber, regarded religious beliefs as a valuable source of meaning. He also saw in them a source of strength enabling people to adapt and come to terms with themselves and the wider world. Moreover, by mediating between the conscious and unconscious, symbolically linking them together – God being the symbol of the union of opposites – and, thereby, facilitating the above-mentioned process of *individuation*, religion functioned as a system of healing, as a psychotherapeutic system, an idea supplied by anthropologists, among others, to the popular religions of Africa, Latin America and elsewhere. In this way religion helped to make possible the experience of *Self*, understood as the 'totality of man, the sum total of conscious and unconscious existence' (Jung, 1938: 100).

This notion of the Self as the image of God, briefly outlined here, is further clear evidence of the difference between Jung and Freud. It makes a break with the Freudian idea of God as the father-figure, and stresses the positive contribution made by religious belief to personal development, in contrast again with the Freudian view that it retards growth. The idea of the Self as the object of worship, it is also worth noting, reveals the strong influence of oriental religion on Jung. He wrote for example:

The modern mandala is an involuntary confession of a peculiar mental condition. There is no deity in the mandala, and there is no submission or reconciliation to a deity. The place of the deity seems to be taken by the wholeness of man.

(1938: 99)

Jung's views on the future of religion are also very different from Freud's, but not unlike Durkheim's. Freud, as already pointed out, believed that science should and hopefully would replace religion. Durkheim, however, saw religion being replaced by science but only in so far as its cognitive, interpretative role was concerned. Otherwise it was destined to last as long as society lasts. Jung, for his part, was convinced that people would always need myths and beliefs by which to live. Indeed, he was persuaded that individuals possessed a predisposition for believing, an archetype in the form of an innate 'psychic aptitude' for God or religion. This archetype, as already mentioned, was by no means firmly fixed in terms of its shape and content; rather it was a very flexible mould since gods come and go with the passage of time:

> That psychological fact which is the greatest power in your system is the god, since it is always the overwhelming factor which is called god. *As soon as a god ceases to be an overwhelming psychic factor, he becomes a mere name* [our emphasis]. His essence is dead and his power is gone. Why have the antique gods lost their prestige and effect on human souls? It was because the Olympic gods had served their time and a new mystery began: God became man.
>
> (1938: 98)

Man here means the Self which, as previously noted, is something total and complete. It is a new creation, of which there can be many, of the unconscious:

> If we want to know what is going to happen in a case where the idea of God is no longer projected as an autonomous entity, this is the answer of man's unconscious mind: the unconscious produces a new idea of man in loco dei, of man deified or divine, imprisoned, concealed, protected, usually dehumanised and expressed by abstract symbolism.
>
> (1938: 106)

Jung's view that religion is constant in culture is not necessarily any more acceptable to believers than Durkheim's who spoke of religion as being in some sense 'eternal' for, as already noted, it provides no basis for a metaphysical understanding of God. While Jung's view does not explicitly rule this out it suggests that it is highly improbable that there is any way of knowing God in this way.

THE LEGACY OF FREUD AND JUNG

The differences between them notwithstanding, both Jung and Freud assumed the priority of the psychodynamic factor in the origins and functions of religion: the mind of the individual was for both the independent variable, religion the dependent variable. This, of course, is one way of making it possible to carry out a 'scientific' study of religion from the psychoanalytic perspective, just as Durkheim's approach would enable a sociological approach to religion of a 'scientific' kind to be undertaken. Moreover, although Freudian theory in particular has come under heavy criticism from all quarters, including psychologists, psychoanalysts and social scientists, there are some who are prepared to salvage something from what remains of it. Among social scientists who have found it useful in varying degrees are Meyer Fortes and Robin Horton and we can briefly examine here their anthropological application of Freudian theory to religion, something that was promised both in the previous chapter and earlier in this present chapter.

In his interpretation of Meyer Fortes's classic study *Oedipus and Job in West African Religion* (1983), Horton believes that some fruitful parallels can be made between this account of religion and Freud's. For example, the notion of *yin* – which Fortes translates as 'destiny' – in Tallensi thought is, Horton believes, akin to Freud's notion of the *id* or unconscious for, like the latter, it is 'a source of impulses and purposes of which the unconscious self, unaware and afflicted by jealousy, develops an early hostility to the father' (1983: 74). Horton continues:

> Where family life is satisfactory then yin is persuaded to moderate its hostility; to accept the father; and finally to accept the society of which the father is the representative. Where family life is unsatisfactory, the yin continues its hostility and rejects both father and wider society.
>
> (1983: 74)

There are other similarities between the two concepts, for example regarding the way their effects are handled. A yin that is not controlled by the super-ego gives rise to countless problems for the individual, making life in society extremely difficult for that person. Fortes then proceeds to provide an account of the role of the ancestors among the Tallensi which closely resembles that of the Freudian super-ego or father-figure. He writes:

> In the religious system of the Tallensi the lineage ancestors have the last word . . . They are omnipotent, but not uniformly benevo-

lent or malevolent. They are just and their justice is directed to enforcing the moral and religious norms and values on which the social order rests. They do this through the power over life and death in which they are supreme. Life, which surpasses all other forms of good, and death which is the end of everything . . . are dispensed by the ancestors by what can best be described as the right of primordial parenthood. *Their powers are those of a father immeasurably magnified and sanctified* – that is, removed from the controls of cooperation and reciprocity, conscience and love, as they work in the life of the community.

(1983: 27, our emphasis)

Fortes, moreover, suggests that just as the Freudian father-figure is in time internalised through a process of socialisation to become the individual's super-ego or conscience, so likewise are the Tallensi ancestors internalised.

Thus, Fortes asserts the existence of direct parallels between Freudian theory and Tallensi religion and perhaps in this he was, as Horton suggests, mistaken. For example, the idea of the yin already mentioned is not exactly parallel to that of the id, for while the former centres on power and position the latter is organised around sexual impulses. Nevertheless, there is much that is of value in Fortes's use of Freudian theory for an understanding of traditional religion in the African setting, and perhaps of religion in general. At the very least, as Horton points out, Fortes's Freudian approach offers Westerners a framework in which African religious ideas can be discussed and a language into which these ideas can be translated for purposes of discussion (Horton, 1983: 77).

Moreover, while he would distance himself from Fortes's attempt to retain Freud's conceptual apparatus in all its detail and to make a fit between it and African religious ideas as a system, Horton, nevertheless, endorses Fortes's attempt to account for Tallensi religion as a social psychology, that is as concerned primarily with the relation of the individual to society. Indeed, Horton suggests that all traditional African religions might best be understood if interpreted in this way. This is not to suggest that they are all identical for different social systems and life-situations give rise to different kinds of problems which require different kinds of social psychologies to deal with them. Horton illustrates his theory with reference to four West African religions which, although they share a common substratum of ideas, vary in the way they handle such fundamental questions as destiny, a variation that can be accounted for in terms of the variation in social structure found among them (1983).

In advocating the use of the general concepts and framework of the Freudian system Horton is aware that he is open to the criticism of reducing religion, as did Freud, to projections. This, however, is not Horton's intention; as already indicated he seeks to avoid direct parallels between African religious notions and Freudian concepts. Moreover, it is not Freud's interpretation of religion as such that interests Horton but the framework and the language that he provides for purposes of scholarly discourse. Beyond this, Horton is keen to stress that the religious systems of Africa are best explained and understood if seen as intellectual systems in their own right, and on a par with Freudian theory. In this respect Horton is looking back to Durkheim who, as was pointed out in the previous chapter, stressed the crucial role once played by religious ideas in rendering the world intelligible. It is this understanding of African religions – as belief systems that attempt to make sense of the world and the individual's place in it – that Horton seeks to highlight and which he suggests reveals more of their character and purpose than any other way of interpreting them.

Horton's account of African religions has several advantages. For example, it avoids reducing these religions to projectionism resulting from instinctual drives. Moreover, it gives a degree of intellectual order and coherence to what otherwise would appear to be, on the surface, an extremely disparate and diverse set of religious ideas and practices. It is, nonetheless, an external, radical, reductionist account, interpreting, as it does, African religion as a 'social science' on a par with similar systems elsewhere.

Perhaps somewhat less sympathetic than anthropologists to the Freudian approach to religion are a number of contemporary psychoanalysts and psychologists who are persuaded that an 'objective' scientific approach is not possible, a view gaining ground among contemporary sociologists of religion. Such an approach is seen to reflect that linear form of understanding of development found in what is regarded as the outmoded Newtonian scientific vision, a vision clearly seen in Freud's positivist understanding of how transference actually works (Jones, 1991). Freud believed in the uninvolvement of the analyst with the patient – the former was to adopt a detached, neutral, objective stance, in line with the approach of the natural scientist. Freud's mechanistic and materialistic model of the world, it is argued, severely limited his vision of the nature of religion. He regarded religion as neurotic largely because he observed it through the lens of the 'reality principle', that is in terms of the world out there that could be objectively analysed and its real, true nature uncovered. Whatever failed to correspond with this reality was a case for treatment and religious ideas and experience fell into this category.

Those who challenge this approach do not regard analyst and patient as separate and apart with the latter projecting in linear fashion emotion after emotion onto the former. In the newer model of transference what is seen as important is the reciprocal interaction between patient and analyst, and this has important implications for the modern psychological and psychoanalytical, and even theological, understanding of religion. Moreover, there is a tendency to reject Freud's instinctually based model of transference on the grounds that it is too rigidly strapped to the past, too concerned with uncovering the childhood roots of present attitudes, behaviour and relationships, and too preoccupied with healing through making the unconscious past of the person conscious. What is suggested by way of contrast is that the human need for dependency is constant and continuity; it is not left behind or outgrown in therapy but transformed into more mature forms (Kohut, 1977). All this has a bearing on the way religion is seen. It should not be regarded in Freudian fashion, it is maintained, as a defence against the instincts, but as a way of creating and developing a cohesive sense of the self (Jones, 1991: 19).

Of course, it would be entirely incorrect to convey the impression that all contemporary psychologists and psychoanalysts believe, in opposition to Freud, that religion is beneficial where people's emotional well-being is concerned. However, what a number would claim is that it can be *ego-adaptive* as well as dysfunctional in this respect. It can serve to provide meaning and bolster identity (Erikson, 1968; Meissner, 1984).

Rather than seeing it as something static and located in a particular experience in a definite past it has become increasingly common among contemporary psychologists and psychoanalysts to regard religion as a *transitional phenomenon*, a notion derived from Winnicott (1971) and one which has been adopted to qualify the rigid Freudian dichotomy between reality and illusion. This idea of transitional phenomenon is used to postulate the existence of an intermediate area of experiencing which is the creation of interpenetrating subjective and objective worlds. God is seen to stand, as it were, at the

interface between these two worlds, as are religious belief and religious experience generally. Such experiences and beliefs are, therefore, to be understood as transitional phenomena, and, thus, neither
wholly subjective nor wholly objective but more a synthesis produced by the interaction of these two domains.

God, although a transitional phenomenon, is not any kind of
transitional phenomenon. Winnicott, whose main interest was in
child psychology and not in religion, defined such phenomena by
their use and principally the role they played in easing the passage
of the child from the maternal matrix to the wider world, and so
included in this category supports or props such as teddy bears.
Others more directly concerned than he was with religion lay much
more stress on the way beliefs in general and the idea of God in
particular function as transitional phenomena by contributing toward the development of a cohesive sense of the self (Rizzuto, 1979:
5). Rizzuto believes that the idea of God is, in fact, essential to this
development. Moreover, she maintains that unlike other transitional
phenomena, the idea of God is not outgrown but constantly re-
shaped and remoulded throughout life in accordance with a person's needs. But this may be to miss the point of what Winnicott
meant by *transitional* phenomena: it is not the phenomena in themselves that are of crucial importance but the realm of experiencing,
that area of psychological space that is created by the interaction of
the subjective and the objective, an area that can develop to accom-
modate the highest, most exalted ideas (1971: 2). This notwithstanding, there is an obvious similarity here between Rizzuto's views and
the Jungian view of the role of religion in the process of individuation
outlined earlier in this chapter.

As to how children develop their image of God, Rizzuto, among
others, maintains that this comes about by means of a process of
'mirroring' their mother's reactions: they come to see themselves in
their mother's responses to their own behaviour and generally to
their surroundings. Moreover, children have a need of God to answer the questions about existence which they pose themselves. This
implies, of course, that complete atheism is a psychological impossibility, for God is a creation of mind. But for all that God is not an
illusion for, Rizzuto stresses, the mind is a source of a reality as real
as any external object (1979: 4).

Thus, contemporary psychology, by refining its understanding of
Freud's model of transference and his interpretation of the 'reality
principle' is inclined to abandon the view of religion as an illusion

and a defence against instincts and to offer a more rational, constructive account of it, highlighting the way it assists in the development
of that core experience from which a sense of self is derived, and the
positive role it can play in the transition from childhood to maturity.

We can briefly note a further, interrelated development in recent
times in the psychological understanding of religion, and one that
also reveals connections with the ideas of both Jung and, logically
enough, Rudolph Otto whose treatise *The Idea of the Holy* has already
been mentioned. This development attempts to go a little beyond the
notion of religion as a transitional phenomenon by suggesting that it
is possible to study it starting with the sacred – indeed, that any
analysis of it should begin with a person's experience of the sacred
rather than focusing on the way a person's image of God is developed. The emphasis should be placed on how the individual's relationship to the sacred might form the basis of that person's sense of
self. This approach is very similar to the way Otto began his investigation of the phenomenon. Otto contended, as is well known, that
the experience of the holy or sacred was wholly other and while it
could be discussed it could not be precisely defined or put into neat
psychological or philosophical language, or indeed learned, but only
aroused and awakened in the mind.

However, it should be noted that contemporary psychologists and
psychoanalysts who begin their account of religion from this angle
do not accept Otto's thesis that in experiencing the sacred one is
experiencing something that is 'wholly other'. They would maintain
that the holy or god cannot be capable of being experienced and of
being beyond experience at one and the same time. Furthermore,
they would contend that because such an experience or sense of the
'holy' has the quality of an awe-inspiring and fascinating mystery
that renders it incapable of being rationalised, this does not imply
that it is this kind of thing and no other. What the sacred, or the idea
of the holy, does is to awaken in the individual what is fundamental
to that person's self experience, and it is the purpose of the psychology of religion to offer an account of that experience (Jones, 1991:
115).

Thus, although this approach moves beyond both the strict Freudian transference method of uncovering the origins of religion and
explaining its functions, and even beyond the understanding of God
as a transitional phenomenon, by allowing students to begin their
investigation of religion with the idea of God, or the 'holy', or sacred,
it does not allow for the possibility of a non-psychological explana-

tion of religion. Moreover, it is worth noting that this approach has no concern with religious beliefs and rituals as such. It places the emphasis on religion as relational, that is as grounded in the affective bonds that link the believer to the sacred or 'holy'. And it sees its purpose as the understanding of how such a relationship enacts and re-enacts the transferential patterns present throughout a person's life.

One can see numerous parallels to this psychological understanding of religion in the writings of, among others, Martin Buber who gives a pivotal role to relationships in his understanding of God. Buber discusses a special kind of relationship, an 'I–You' relationship by means of which individuals relate to others in a 'personal' way while respecting their freedom and autonomy. He also speaks of an 'I–It' or a purely instrumental kind of relationship. Both kinds of relationship are necessary in everyday life, but God as the eternal 'You' can only be related to in the first mode (1970: 160). In this way Buber not only places the locus of God in the 'I–You' relationship but also asserts that it is only in such relationships that either God, or the self, can be known. The reason why he includes the self is that he believes that it is through personal relationships that one becomes human. Human beings can lose this capacity to relate personally and in doing so lose their humanity. Only God always relates in this way and in this sense he is the *eternal you*. What this amounts to – as in the case of the psychological approach outlined immediately above – is an interpretation of a person's relationship to God rather than an account of God's nature.

CONCLUSION: A CRITIQUE OF FREUD'S AND JUNG'S THEORIES OF RELIGION

There is, then, considerable dissatisfaction among psychologists and psychoanalysts with the traditional, unrefined Freudian approach to the study and interpretation of religion. Jung also has his critics but his ideas and approach seem to be generally more acceptable and influential among psychologists of religion than Freud's. But it is not only in these circles that Freud's approach and opinions are heavily criticised. Like Durkheim's, Freud's theory of the social and psychological origins of religion has come under severe criticism. As Evans-Pritchard remarked: Freud tells us a just so story which only a genius could have ventured to compose, for no evidence was or could be, adduced in support of it (1965: 42).

From this we can turn to the criticisms of his theory of the origins of God in early childhood. One general criticism in this area concerns once again the shaky foundations on which Freud based his theory and the inferences he was prepared to make on the basis of such insubstantial evidence. His methodology is also heavily criticised. Freud did not, as is well known, base his account of religion on the behaviour of children but focused instead on certain forms of adult neuroses which he believed had their origins in childhood. He then inferred that since these neuroses resembled certain kinds of belief and practice the latter must also have had their origins in early childhood. Moreover, not only was this methodologically unsound but the range of his data was extremely limited in that he confined his investigation to a small number of people, all of whom belonged to the same religious tradition. In this way he excluded the possibility of an alternative explanation based on a broader, more representative body of evidence.

A more representative body of evidence might well have indicated to Freud that, as contemporary psychologists point out, it is often the case that people's descriptions of God contain more of their ideas concerning their mother than their father (Watt and Williams, 1988: 42). Freud's narrow interpretation of religion is also the result of his concentration on the past, something that was pointed out when we discussed his model of transference toward the beginning of this chapter. This exclusive concern with the past shuts off the possibility of seeing religious ideas and beliefs as being capable of growth and development or change in that it tends to reduce them to mere events or facts.

Reductionism is one of the most common criticisms levelled against Freud and essentialism ought perhaps to be another for, as seen more than once in this chapter, he attributed *all* religious beliefs and practices to a bundle of basic instincts.

Moreover, it is worth noting again that Freud's overall account of the relationship between religious belief and desire (an account which is at the heart of his diagnosis of illusion) is open to the same general criticisms as the similar account in Feuerbach. In Freud we have a similar general picture: of the self, through its needs and narcissistic desire for happiness, being in thrall to a hostile world. The threat thus posed is 'overcome' by its imaginary dissolution through a projected father-figure who will give the self ultimate protection and gratification. This is contrasted to a real solution of the threat, if we are intelligent and strong enough, that will come about with the application of science.

This shows that Freud can be accused of not moving beyond the notion that religion is a substitute for knowledge and control of nature (hence our reference to his 'positivism' above). It also shows that he is ignorant, just as Feuerbach is, of the ways that the self can be related to unfulfilled desire and wish that may be revealed in religion. He is thus open to the precise criticism we levelled at Feuerbach in Chapter 5. Religion, in at least some of its aspects, does not confront the problem that some of our desires are contingently unrealisable, given our ignorance, laziness or what have you. And it does not provide an alternative, wishful way of fulfilling such desires. It can be a recognition of the finitude that entails that necessarily not all desires can be fulfilled and it can teach us to cope with this fact through a *transvaluation* of our desires and our inevitable human limitations (see Chapter 5 above). This religious response to threats to the ego resists analysis in terms of illusion. It may be a response to the fact of unsatisfied desire and wish but it is not driven by them.

While Jung, as we saw, never completely abandoned all Freudian theory he nevertheless differed from him on many issues and not least on the question of the image of god as Self rather than as a tyrannical father-figure and on the question of the constructive and positive role played by religion in the process of a person's individuation or wholeness. However, while Jung might well be offering a more positive account of religion than Freud it is not necessarily any less a projectionist or reductionist account of the phenomenon.

Jung, as we have previously pointed out, was not always consistent and this makes him difficult to interpret. For example, it is possible to argue that he understood God to be a projection of the collective unconscious, and that he was unwilling, as already indicated, to discuss the possibility of a metaphysical basis for the existence of God. He certainly maintained that we can only know what we experience and the only God possible was the one reflected in our mental life (Watt and Williams, 1988: 33).

However, whether one accepts that Jung was a projectionist in matters religious will largely depend on how one understands his notion of archetype. Is it a descriptive label or did he use it as an explanatory concept? If the former then it might be said in his defence that Jung did not rule out a priori the possibility of a metaphysical basis to the existence of God but simply stressed the immanent dimension of the sacred and, therefore, is neither projectionist or reductionist in his account of religion. What Jung's account of religion shows, and this is so for many contemporary psychological accounts of religion which see it as being essentially bound up with the structures of selfhood, is that external, radical accounts can still give religious ideas positive or broadly beneficial roles to play in psychic development.

Any final assessment of psychological theories of religion must confront the questions of method aired in this study. Such theories tend to assume a determined methodological atheism (though as we have just noted, Jung may be equivocal on this point).

Any approach to the interpretation and explanation of religion from within the human sciences must assume that religion has a basis in human experience and that it connects with our psychic constitution and development. Even on the highest view of the influence of divine or sacred beings on living religion, human beings fashion religious ideas to some degree and must be psychologically predisposed to receive religious experiences. There must be some account to be given therefore of the psychological factors which predispose us to use religious notions and which enable us to have religious experiences. Description of a psychological background to the origin and development of religious consciousness need not claim to be a sufficient explanation of the origins of religion. If God is capable of being experienced our consciousness must be so structured as to reflect this fact, but this does not entail that the full reality of God is as an item of consciousness. Extra, *philosophical* assumptions are needed to yield this conclusion. Metaphysical and epistemological assumptions of the kind we saw in Feuerbach are needed to show that what can enter into human consciousness can have no existence beyond human experience.

Philosophical assumptions of this kind lie behind the Freudian, 'scientific' approach to religion. So, we believe, does a persistent dilemma which theorists of religion think they are faced with: either we explain the contents of religious consciousness on the assumption that they derive from the real influence of religious objects whose reality lies outside human experience, or we explain these contents on the assumption that such objects are unreal and wholly generated by the human imagination in some guise or other.

We have consistently argued in this study that this dilemma is a false one.

Conclusion

The purpose of this study has been to consider religion as the object of definition and explanation. This has entailed examining some of the major styles of theorising about religion. The various theories of religion considered – religious, philosophical, socio-economic, sociological and psychological – have important differences and similarities.

One of the aims of our treatment of these theories has been to bring out similarities of method and presupposition behind them. All depend on drawing a similar distinction between descriptive and explanatory knowledge in the study of religion. They are alike in supposing that the move from description to explanation in the study of religion is accomplished only by offering a large-scale theory of religion. With that move comes the inevitable attempt to give an account of the status of religion as a whole in the light of ideas about truth and rationality. As part of that attempt all such theories depend on giving an essentialist definition of religion. For they are all committed to saying something about the status and causes of an entity which is *religion* as such. None can be taken merely to be accounting for some of the forms religion has happened to take in its history.

For each of the specific theories discussed we have offered detailed criticisms, but Part One of our study has prepared the way for questioning the similar presuppositions in method found in these theories. Since these presuppositions are broadly philosophical, it can be seen that the other theories of religion depend in a manner on the philosophical. This point is most strikingly seen in the case of the socio-economic, sociological and psychological theories. In each case we have been able to point to assumptions in these theories about the nature of reason and truth which yield the diagnosis that religion is a form of illusion and therefore requires a sufficient explanation in external causes. Even the Freudian theory which endeavours to give 'illusion' a neutral, antiseptic meaning shares such assumptions, as Chapter 8 above indicates. All external theories of religion, then, appear to depend on the case implicit in the philosophical theory of religion to the effect that either reality is such that we know references to transcendent realities are delusive, or human reason is such that there is no way in which such references could be properly anchored in the manner of minimally rational beliefs. This is the inheritance of radical philosophical theorising about the metaphysics and epistemology of religious belief that all these theories appear to share. It is also an inheritance of beliefs about the human subject. For what these beliefs about reality and reason entail is a set of theses about the cognitive abilities and limitations of human beings – theses which rule out of court the notion that religion might be taken seriously as a rational institution. As our discussion of philosophical theories of religion shows, the relevant beliefs about reality and reason come down to us from the Enlightenment.

The major issue that the study of religion must face is how far it is to let its approach to the subject matter of religion be shaped by the intellectual commitments we have described. These commitments have even deeper ramifications than those into the nature of truth, reason and the human subject spelled out. For what the inheritance of the Enlightenment does is to create the sense that there this a subject called 'religion' which is the proper object of theory. The Enlightenment represents a period in our culture when it seemed necessary to make choices between 'religion' and other things: science, reason, liberty and so forth. 'Religion' means in this context traditional Christianity, particularly in its political and academic manifestations in the early modern period. Out of the debates of the Enlightenment comes the hypostasisation of an entity whose future must be decided one way or the other.

In being critical of large-scale theories of religion we are also being critical of the hypostasisation that produces the felt need for a grand theory of religion. Implicit in our approach is a rejection of the way in which the distinction between descriptive and explanatory knowledge is drawn in these debates. If we take as our model of explanation the narrative structure of the study of history we may resist the idea that to explain religion is to make a commitment to a theory.

In our view there is something to be learnt about the nature of religion. 'Religion' is, to say the least, a useful category in the human sciences and it can be given some initial definition, as Chapter 1 indicates. But our knowledge of what that nature may be is built up cumulatively. Our initial definition is not a fixing of religion's essence but a provisional, useful way of demarcating a subject of study. We shall expect cumulative knowledge to refine that means of demarcation. Here we need not suppose that there is any final understanding to be reached. General understanding guides detailed studies which lead to revised general understandings, which promote further detailed study which lead to revised understandings, and so on. Finality is not achieved not least because the phenomenon of religion keeps developing. Consider in this context the way in which 'New Religions' have revealed fresh insights into the relationship between religion and culture in our time.

The process of studying religion yields results not *a* result. These results are to be found in the description, interpretation and explanation of specific forms of religious phenomena. We need not be frightened of generalisations in such results. Generalisations about the nature of religion may be useful in guiding and stimulating areas of research. There are some generalisations to be made about the relationship between forms of religion and structures in society, history and the psyche.

In these respects the theories of religion considered in this volume should be seen as contributing to the process that is the study of religion. They have given birth to new areas of research. They have contributed to our understanding of the relationship between aspects of religion and the surrounding realities of human life. But: they should be seen as adding to features of an ever-expanding map, not as forerunners for a final theory of religion.

Bibliography

Alston, W. (1967) 'Religion', in Edwards, P. (ed.), *The Encyclopedia of Philosophy*. New York: Macmillan, Vol. 7, pp. 140–5.

Anscombe, G.E.M. (1957) *Intention*. Oxford: Blackwell.

Atkinson, R.F. (1978) *Knowledge and Explanation in History*. London: Macmillan.

Baker, T. and Hacker, P.M.S., (1984) *Language, Sense and Nonsense*. Oxford: Blackwell.

Bellah, R. (1970) *Beyond Belief*. New York: Harper & Row.

Bellah, R. (1975) *The Broken Covenant*. New York: Seabury.

Bendix, R. (1966) *Max Weber: An Intellectual Portrait*. London: Methuen.

Berger, P. (1967) *The Social Reality of Religion*. Harmondsworth: Penguin. (Also published as *The Sacred Canopy*.)

Berger, P. and Kellner, H. (1981) *Sociology Reinterpreted*. Harmondsworth: Penguin.

Berger, P. and Luckmann, T. (1966) *The Social Construction of Reality*. New York: Doubleday.

Buber, M. (1970) *I and Thou* (trans. W. Kaufmann). New York: Scribner.

Byrne, P. (1980) 'Does religion have an essence?', *Scottish Journal of Religious Studies*, Vol. 1, No. i, pp. 62–7.

Byrne, P. (1985) 'F.R. Leavis and the religious dimension in literature', *Modern Theology*, Vol. 1, No. ii, pp. 119–30.

Byrne, P. (1988) 'Religion and the Religions', in Sutherland, S.R. *et al.* (eds), *The World's Religions*. London: Routledge, pp. 3–28.

Byrne, P. (1989) *Natural Religion and the Nature of Religion*. London: Routledge.

Chadwick, O. (1975) *The Secularization of the European Mind in the Nineteenth Century*. Cambridge University Press.

Charlesworth, M.J. (1972) *Philosophy of Religion: The Historic Approaches*. New York: Herder & Herder.

Danto, A.C. (1968) *Analytical Philosophy of History*. Cambridge University Press.

Davidson, D. (1968) 'Actions, Reasons and Causes', in White, A.R. (ed.), *The Philosophy of Action*. Oxford University Press, pp. 79–94.

D'Costa, G. (1986) *John Hick's Theology of Religions*. London/Lanham, Md: University of America.

de Tocqueville, A. (1966) *The Ancien Régime and the French Revolution*, (trans. S. Gilbert). London: Fontana.

Dickson, A. (ed.) (1985) *Freud. The Origins of Religion: Totem and Taboo, Moses and Monotheism and Other Works* (trans. J. Strachey). Harmondsworth: Penguin.

Douglas, M. (1966) *Purity and Danger: An Analysis of Concepts of Pollution and Taboo*. New York: Pantheon.

Douglas, M. (1970) *Natural Symbols: Explorations in Cosmology*. New York: Pantheon.

Douglas, M. (1978) *Implicit Meanings: Essays in Anthropology*. London: Routledge & Kegan Paul.

Douglas, M. (1982a) *In the Active Voice*. London: Routledge & Kegan Paul.

Douglas, M. (1982b) 'The Effects of Modernization on Religious Change', *Daedalus*, Winter, pp. 1–19.

Durkheim, E. (1950) *The Rules of Sociological Method*. New York: The Free Press.

Durkheim, E. (1967) *The Elementary Forms of the Religious Life* (trans. J.N. Swain). London: Allen & Unwin.

Edgeley, R. (1969) *Reason in Theory and Practice*. London: Hutcheson.

Erikson, E. (1968) *Identity, Youth and Crisis*. New York: Norton.

Evans-Pritchard, E. (1937) *Witchcraft, Magic and Oracles among the Azande*. Oxford: Clarendon Press.

Evans-Pritchard, E. (1965) *Theories of Primitive Religion*. Oxford: Clarendon Press.

Feuer, L. (ed.) (1969) *Marx and Engels: Basic Writings on Politics and Philosophy*. Glasgow: Collins.

Feuerbach, L. (1957) *The Essence of Christianity* (trans. M.A. Evans). New York: Harper & Row.

Feuerbach, L. (1966) *Principles of the Philosophy of the Future* (trans. M. Vogel). Indianapolis: Bobbs-Merril.

Feuerbach, L. (1967) *Lectures on the Essence of Religion* (trans. R. Manheim). New York: Harper & Row.

Fortes, M. (1983) *Oedipus and Job in West African religion*. Cambridge University Press.

Frazer, J. (1922) *The Golden Bough* (abr. edn). London: Macmillan.

Freud, S. (1940) *An Outline of Psychoanalysis* (trans. J. Strachey). New York: Norton.

Freud, S. (1960) *Totem and Taboo*. London: Routledge & Kegan Paul.

Freud, S. (1975) *Civilization and its Discontents* (trans. J. Riviere, ed. J. Strachey). London: Hogarth Press and the Institute of Psycho-Analysis.

Freud, S. (1978) *The Future of an Illusion* (trans. W.D. Robson-Scott, ed. J. Strachey). London: Hogarth Press and the Institute of Psycho-Analysis.

Fromm, E. (1950) *Psychoanalysis and Religion*. New Haven, Conn.: Yale University Press.

Geertz, C. (1966) 'Religion as a Cultural System', in M. Banton (ed.), *Anthropological Approaches to the Study of Religion*. London: Tavistock, pp. 1–46.

Gellner, E. (1974) *The Legitimation of Belief*. Cambridge University Press.

Habermas, J. (1975) *Legitimation Crisis*. Boston: Beacon Press.

Harré, R. (1972) *The Philosophies of Science*. Oxford University Press.

Harré, R. and Madden, P. (1975) *Causal Powers*. Oxford: Blackwell.

Hart, H.L.A. (1961) *The Concept of Law*. Oxford: Clarendon Press.

Harvey, V. (1985) 'Ludwig Feuerbach and Karl Marx', in Smart, N. *et al.* (eds.), *Nineteenth Century Religious Thought in the West*. Cambridge University Press, Vol. 1, pp. 291–328.

Hegel, G.W.F. (1956) *Lectures on the Philosophy of History* (trans. J. Sibree). New York: Dover.

Hempel, C. (1970) *Aspects of Scientific Explanation*. New York: Free Press.

Hick, J. (1966) *Evil and the God of Love*. London: Collins.

Hick, J. (1973) *God and the Universe of Faiths*. London: Macmillan.

Hick, J. (1980) *God Has Many Names*. London: Macmillan.

Hick, J. (1989) *An Interpretation of Religion*. London: Macmillan.

Hollis, M. (1987) *The Cunning of Reason*. Cambridge University Press.

Horton, R. (1964) 'Ritual Man in Africa', *Africa*, Vol. XXXIV, No. 2.

Horton, R. (1970) 'African Thought and Western Science', in Wilson, B.R. (ed.), *Rationality*. Oxford: Blackwell, pp. 131–72.

Horton, R. (1983) 'Social Psychologies: African and Western Religion', in Fortes, M., *Oedipus and Job in West African Religion*. Cambridge University Press.

Hospers, J. (1967) *An Introduction to Philosophical Analysis*. London: Routledge.

Hume, D. (1976) *The Natural History of Religion and Dialogues*

210   *Religion Defined and Explained*

concerning Natural Religion (eds. A.W. Culver and J.V. Price).
Oxford: Clarendon Press.

James, W. (1902) *Varieties of Religious Experience*. Cambridge, Mass.:
Harvard University Press.

Jones, W. (1991) *Contemporary Psychoanalysis and Religion*. New
Haven, Conn.: Yale University Press.

Jung, C. (1938) *Psychology and Religion*. New Haven, Conn.: Yale
University Press.

Jung, C. (1953) 'Psychology and Alchemy', in *The Collected Works of
C.G. Jung* (trans. R. Hull, eds H. Read, M. Fordham and G. Adler).
Princeton, NJ: Princeton University Press.

Jung, C. (1958) 'Psychology of the Unconscious', in *The Collected
Works of C.G. Jung* (trans. R. Hull, eds H. Read, M. Fordham and
G. Adler). Princeton, NJ: Princeton University Press, Vol. 11.

Kamenka, E. (1970) *The Philosophy of Ludwig Feuerbach*. New York:
Praeger.

Kant, I. (1933) *Critique of Pure Reason* (trans. N.K. Smith). London:
Macmillan.

Katz, S. (1978) 'Language, Epistemology and Mysticism', in Katz,
S. (ed.), *Mysticism and Philosophical Analysis*. London: Sheldon Press,
pp. 22–74.

King, W.L. (1987) 'Religion', in Eliade, M. (ed.), *The Encyclopedia of
Religion*. New York: Macmillan, Vol. 12, pp. 282–92.

Kitigawa, J. (1967) 'Primitive, Classical and Modern Religions', in
Kitigawa, J. (ed.), *The History of Religions*. Chicago University Press.

Leuba, J. (1896) 'Studies in the Psychology of Religious Phenomena',
American Journal of Psychology, Vol. 7, pp. 309–85.

Lukács, G. (1972) 'Max Weber and German Sociology', *Economy and
Society*, Vol. 1, No. 4.

Lukes, S. (1970) 'Some Problems about Rationality', in Wilson,
B. (ed.), *Rationality*. Oxford: Blackwell.

Lukes, S. (1973) *Emile Durkheim: His Life and Work*. Harmondsworth:
Penguin.

Lukes, S. (1987) *Marxism and Morality*. Oxford University Press.

MacIntyre, A. (1969) *Marxism and Christianity*. London: Gerald
Duckworth.

MacIntyre, A. (1971) 'Rationality and the Explanation of Action', in
Against the Self-Images of the Age. London: Gerald Duckworth.

MacIntyre, A. (1988) *Whose Justice? Which Rationality?* Notre Dame,
Ind.: Notre Dame University Press.

McLellan, D. (1987) *Marxism and Religion*. London: Macmillan.

Macpherson, C. (1962) *The Political Theory of Possessive Individualism.* London: Oxford University Press.

Marx, K. and Engels, F. (1977) *K. Marx and F. Engels on Religion.* New York: Schoken Books.

Mepham, J. (1972) 'The Theory of Ideology in "Capital"', *Radical Philosophy*, Vol. 2.

Mitchell, B.G. (1973) *The Justification of Religious Belief.* London: Macmillan.

Morris, B. (1987) *Anthropological Theories of Religion.* Cambridge University Press.

Mueller, F.M. (1893) *Introduction to the Science of Religion.* London: Longman.

Otto, R. (1958) *The Idea of the Holy.* New York: Oxford University Press.

Padover, S. (1979) *The Essential Marx.* New York: Mentor.

Phillips, D.Z. (1976) *Religion without Explanation.* Oxford: Blackwell.

Pickering, W. (1984) *Durkheim's Sociology of Religion: Themes and Theories.* London: Routledge & Kegan Paul.

Plamenatz, J. (1975) *Karl Marx's Philosophy of Man.* Oxford: Clarendon Press.

Popper, K. (1957) *The Poverty of Historicism.* London: Routledge & Kegan Paul.

Reardon, B.M.G. (1977) *Hegel's Philosophy of Religion.* London: Macmillan.

Ritvo, B. (1990) *Darwin's Influence on Freud: A Tale of Two Sciences.* New Haven: Conn.: Yale University Press.

Rizzuto, A. (1979) *The Birth of the Living God.* Chicago University Press.

Scruton, R. (1980) *The Meaning of Conservatism.* Harmondsworth: Penguin.

Selsam, H. and Martels, H. (eds) (1973) *Reader in Marxist Philosophy.* New York: International Publishers.

Skorupski, J. (1976) *Symbol and Theory.* Cambridge University Press.

Smart, N. (1971) *The Religious Experience of Mankind.* Glasgow: Collins.

Smart, N. (1973) *The Science of Religion and the Sociology of Knowledge.* Princeton, NJ: Princeton University Press.

Smith, W.C. (1978) *The Meaning and End of Religion.* London: SPCK.

Smith, W.R. (1923) *Lectures on the Religion of the Semites*, 3rd edn. London: A. & C. Black.

Southwold, M. (1978) 'Buddhism and the Definition of Religion', in *Man*, New Series, Vol. 13, pp. 362–79.

212 *Religion Defined and Explained*

Spiro, M.E. (1966) 'Religion: Problems of Definition and Explanation', in Banton, M. (ed.), *Anthropological Approaches to the Study of Religion*. London: Tavistock, pp. 85–126.

Starbuck, E.D. (1899) *The Psychology of Religion: An Empirical Study of the Growth of Religious Consciousness*. New York: Scribner.

Storr, A. (1973) *Jung*. Glasgow: Collins/Fontana.

Swinburne, R.G. (1981) *Faith and Reason*. Oxford: Clarendon Press.

Tylor, E.B. (1903) *Primitive Culture*, 4th edn. London: Murray.

von Glasenapp, H. (1970) *Buddhism: A non-Theistic Religion* (trans. I. Schlögel). London: Allen & Unwin.

Ward, K. (1990) 'Truth and Diversity of Religions', in *Religious Studies*, Vol. 26, No. i, pp. 1–18.

Wartofsky, M. (1977) *Ludwig Feuerbach*. Cambridge University Press.

Watts, F. and Williams, M. (1988) *The Psychology of Religious Knowing*. Cambridge University Press.

Weber, M. (1965) *The Sociology of Religion* (trans. E. Fischoff). London: Methuen.

Weber, M. (1969) 'Major Features of World Religions', in Robertson, R. (ed.), *Sociology of Religion*. Harmondsworth: Penguin.

Weber, M. (1969) 'Gods, Magicians and Priests', in Robertson, R. (ed.), Sociology of Religions, op. cit., p. 307.

Weber, M. (1984) *The Protestant Ethic and the Spirit of Capitalism* (trans. T. Parsons with an introduction by A. Giddens). London: Unwin.

Wiebe, D. (1981) *Religion and Truth*. The Hague: Mouton.

Williams, B. (1973) *Morality*. Harmondsworth: Penguin.

Wilson, B.R. (1990) *The Social Dimensions of Sectarianism*. Oxford: Clarendon Press.

Winch, P. (1958) *The Idea of a Social Science*. London: Routledge.

Winch, P. (1970) 'Understanding a Primitive Society', in Wilson, B. (ed.), *Rationality*. Oxford: Blackwell, pp. 78–111.

Wittgenstein, L. (1958) *Philosophical Investigations*. Oxford: Blackwell.

Yinger, J.M. (1970) *The Scientific Study of Religion*. New York: Macmillan.

Index